++

Globe, Northam
6 April 1991

EDITH SITWELL
Selected Letters

1919-1964

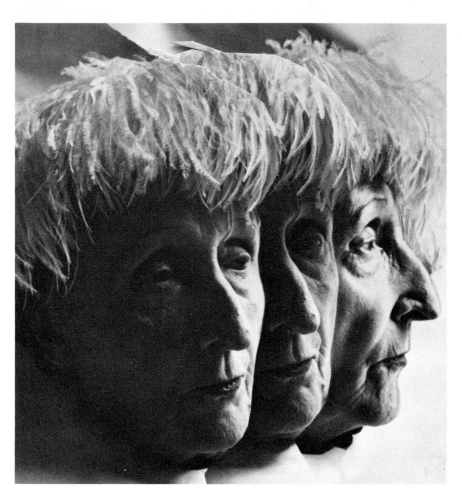

EDITH SITWELL
From a photograph by Cecil Beaton

EDITH SITWELL

Selected Letters

1919-1964

Edited by

JOHN LEHMANN

and

DEREK PARKER

THE VANGUARD PRESS, INC.

NEW YORK

CONTENTS

LIST OF ILLUSTRATIONS

INTRODUCTION

This selection of the letters of the late Dame Edith Sitwell has been prepared under certain limitations, some inherent in the letters themselves, some external.

First of all, we were asked not to include any family letters, that is, letters to her mother and father, or letters to her two brothers. As her relations with these brothers were extremely close, in artistic ventures as in everything else, obviously an important element has been lost by this restriction.

Second, though we wrote to as many of Dame Edith's close friends and associates as we could find addresses for, and though we advertised our intention of preparing this book in the press, some of her friends did not answer and some expressed their unwillingness to allow her letters to them to be published while they were still alive.

Third, the large number of letters she wrote to the artist Pavel Tchelitchew are locked away at Yale University, and now that she herself is dead no permission can be obtained to study or reproduce them until the year 2000.

So much for the external limitations. In the letters we actually received, we had to face two problems. To the end of her life, Edith Sitwell was a most copious, uninhibited and energetic letter-writer. There was clearly never any idea in her mind, as there often is in the case of more self-conscious correspondents, that she was writing for posterity. All her thoughts and feelings tumbled out as they came to her in the moment of writing, enthusiastic or tart critical judgements, affection, prejudice and ridicule. This has meant, first, that in certain cases large portions of her letters have had to be eliminated because we did not wish to cause offence to living persons (she may have changed, and indeed often did change, her opinion of them twenty-four hours later), or run the risk of libel proceedings in the more extreme cases.

Second, we have had to deal with the propensity she had for describing the latest dramatic turn in her life, or the latest grotesque stories she had heard, in several letters to various correspondents at roughly the same time. In these cases, we have tried to choose either those letters which gave the best account, or those which were more interesting as a whole.

We regret that letters from the earliest period of her literary life are so scarce. The letters to Wilfred Owen's mother are a find indeed; but that we have been able to trace so few other letters of the same period is rather our misfortune than our fault. Her best, most characteristic, most informative, most entertaining and most illuminating letters were written in the middle years of her life. During the closing years, she had been too weakened by illness and exhausted by incessant effort too exacting for her physique, too hypersensitive to criticism, for her letters to represent in general her great gifts of mind and spirit. Our selection is therefore by choice as thin in the last period as it is by necessity in the earliest period.

We are aware that many of Edith Sitwell's letters have been quoted in other publications. We have chosen, on the whole, to ignore this fact, because we feel that a selection such as we have brought together should stand entirely by itself. We may have made some mistakes of transliteration; but Edith Sitwell wrote at such a speed that her hand sometimes defies exact scholarship.

ACKNOWLEDGEMENTS

Thanks are due to Mr Francis Sitwell for the use of the letters included in this volume, and for his constant interest and assistance. Letter 36 to Dylan Thomas follows the text printed by E.S. in *Taken Care Of*. Letters 31, 38, 39, 98 to the Editor of *The Times Literary Supplement* are reprinted from that journal. We are indebted to Mr Benjamin Britten for Letter 76 to Colin Hampton; Mrs Mary Campbell for Letter 157 to Roy Campbell; Mrs T. S. Eliot for Letters 34, 95, 97, 100, 114, 139, 140, 158, 159 to T. S. Eliot; Mr Alberto de Lacerda for Letter 168 to Jean Cocteau; Mr Harold Owen for Letters 1, 3, 4, 5, 6, 7, 8, 9, 10, 11 to Susan Owen; and Mrs C. J. Purnell for Letter 129 to C. J. Purnell. We should also like to thank Messrs David Higham Associates (formerly Pearn, Pollinger and Higham) for Letter 43 to David Higham and Letters 61 and 65 to Ann Pearn; and Messrs Macmillan for Letter 33 to themselves, Letter 52 to Daniel Macmillan and Letter 126 to Rache Lovat Dickson. We are grateful to the following institutions for making available letters in their possession: The British Museum (and Lady Aberconway) for Letters 30, 35 and 56 to Christabel, Lady Aberconway and Letters 70, 79, 83, 84, 85, 86, 87, 88, 89, 96, 105, 116, 119, 122, 123, 125, 127, 128, 130, 132, 133, 146, 147 to John Lehmann; The University of Iowa for Letter 143 to Lady Bantock, Letter 109 to Maurice Carpenter, Letters 42 and 110 to Raymond Marriott, and Letter 2 to Robert Nichols; King's College, Cambridge, for Letter 74 to Lord Keynes; The Henry W. and Albert A. Berg Collection, New York Public Library, Astor, Lenox and Tilden Foundations for Letter 27 to Terence Fytton Armstrong, Letter 54 to Sir Edward Marsh, Letters 71, 75, 77, 78, 81, 91, 94, 99, 111, 163 to Stephen Spender, and Letters 17 and 25 to Virginia Woolf; The Academic Center Library, The University of Texas for Letters 32, 45, 107 to Ronald Bottrall, Letters 120, 136, 166 to Jack Lindsay, Letter

57 to Dr Dorothea Walpole, Letters 48 and 53 to Sir Hugh Walpole, and Letters 64, 66, 67, 68, 80 to Denton Welch; The Beinecke Rare Book and Manuscript Library, Yale University Library, for Letters 12 and 13 to Arnold Bennett, and Letters 162, 164, 173, 176, 189 to James Purdy.

All the other letters are in the possession of their recipients, to whom we tender our thanks.

THE LETTERS

1. *To Susan Owen*

22, Pembridge Mansions, Moscow Road, W.2
March 14, 1919

Dear Mrs Owen,

My brother[1] has asked me to write to you for him, and acknowledge the safe arrival of your son's very beautiful poems.[2] Before I go any further I must tell you how very sorry we are that owing to a misunderstanding between us, we did not tell you of their safety before this. My brother was ill when he handed them to me; he is still ill and has had to go to the south of France to recover; and unfortunately, he thought I had written to you, and I thought he had written. As soon as he returns to England (in three weeks' time) he is going to see what can be done about publication. For my part, I am *most* anxious, if you will allow me, to publish some in the next number of *Wheels* (the anthology I edit). I will write to you about this in a week's time. I am particularly anxious to have the honour of producing some of the war poems; if you do not mind my saying so, I consider them among the very finest poems of the war. Believe me, yours sincerely, Edith Sitwell.

The poems are safely in my hands; I will take the greatest care of them.

[1] Osbert Sitwell.
[2] Wilfred Owen was born in 1893, and killed in action on 4 November 1918.

2. *To Robert Nichols*

[March 1919]   Pembridge Mansions

Dear Robert,

I was so delighted to get your letter, which arrived a couple of days ago, after an interminable Odyssey. I shall always like the Americans now, because they have taken you to their hearts . . . but then I knew you would take them by storm, for with all their faults, they do recognise real vitality when they see it. You have probably done more to them than either you or they can guess yet, and this will bear fruit presently. . . . Why, in heaven's name why, haven't they got a poetry of their own? Of the poets you mention (those among them whose work I know at any rate) Lindsay and Eliot seem to me to be the only live writers. Perhaps you will galvanise the others; if any man could, it would be you. As for the kind of women you mention—they should have been allowed to remain an organism with as much life as a sea-anemone. The trouble is, that these creatures realise that it is fashionable to be smeared with brain, and in consequence they lose their one point of usefulness. I have written a poem about this . . . vaguely about it, which I send you together with two more. I have destroyed all the poems I have written in the last three months except these three, as they were the product of anaemia. The horror of Scarborough has, however, acted like electricity upon me. What a strange place—partly a clownish bright coloured tragic hell,—partly a flatness where streets crawl sluggishly, and one drop of rain (no more) drops on one's face halfway down the street, and there are no inhabitants, or so it seems, but boys so indistinguishable in their worm-white faces that they have to wear coloured caps with initials that one may be known from another. Osbert didn't 'get in'.[1] I suppose they found out he is a poet.

Talking of poets, I went to a depressing evening where all the guests were female poets. Miss Klemantaski, who is a very

[1] Osbert Sitwell stood as a Liberal candidate at Scarborough in the General Election of 1918, but failed to be elected.

nice girl, got this up so that I might meet Charlotte Mew. What a grey tragic woman—about sixty in point of age, and sucked dry of blood (though not of spirit) by poverty and an arachnoid mother. I tried to get her to come and see me; but she is a hermit, inhabited by a terrible bitterness, and though she was very nice to me, she wouldn't come. Besides her, I met an appalling woman called Madeleine Caron Rock, extremely fat and exuding a glutinous hysteria from every pore. I sat beside her on the sofa, and became (much against both our wills) embedded in her exuberance like a very sharp battle-axe.

Whenever anyone mentioned living, dying, eating, sleeping, or any other of the occurrences which beset us, Miss Rock would allow a gelatinous cube-like tear, still warm from her humanity, to fall upon my person, and would then leave the room in a marked manner. A moment afterwards, the flat would be shaken by a canine species of howling, and after an interval, Miss Rock would return and beg all our pardon with great insistency. . . . She is rather a good poet, all the same.

Osbert may be going on a lecturing tour to America in the autumn, taking Sachie[1] as secretary, and he says will I *beg* you to drop a few hints to the Americans. I don't know what he means exactly, but no doubt you will.

I have sent you the new *Wheels* and *Art and Letters*. *Wheels* is very bad this year, for the reason that as most of us have had books, all our better work was exhausted.

Thank goodness you are coming back at the end of April, though it is some time off still. We have all missed you most dreadfully, and are longing for you to come back.

[The end of the letter is missing.]

3. *To Susan Owen*

June 21, 1919   Pembridge Mansions

Dear Mrs Owen,

Thank you so much for your letter. I am so very sorry for the delay in writing, which was caused partly by illness, and then

[1] Sacheverell Sitwell.

by the fact that the poems are (without exaggeration) so magnificent that it has been almost impossible to choose. But I have at length, after infinite thought and care, decided to ask you if *Wheels* may have the great privilege and the sacred honour of producing 'The Show', 'Terre à terre',[1] 'Strange Meeting', 'The Sentry', 'Disabled', 'The Dead-Beat', 'The Chances'. These poems should overwhelm anybody who cares really for poetry. . . . I am telling everyone I know about these wonderful and terrible poems. You will, I hope, forgive us if we seem a little long about the rest of the poems, because, as you know, there are in so many cases more than one version of the poems. And it needs such care. Your son's poems did not, I am sorry to say, appear in *Art and Letters* so far, because my brother was taken so ill that he had to go abroad to recuperate, and the other editor[2] had to get on as best he could, with no material. I have nothing whatever to do with *Art and Letters*, or those poems should have gone in.

The moment the new *Wheels* with your son's poems appears (in the autumn some time) a copy shall be sent to you. But how *can* you suggest that I should allow your son's mother to pay for a volume in which he shall be a most reverenced contributor? It is out of the question.

There is a tribute that it is my hope to pay to your son, if you will allow me. It has not quite taken shape; but as soon as it has, I will write. I want to do the utmost to show in what honour I hold him. I can't tell you what it has been like—copying out these poems of his for *Wheels*. They get home so hard that one finds oneself crying. . . . It has been sometimes impossible to go on.

I told the editor of a new quarterly called *The Coterie* about the poems; he wanted me to ask you if you would allow him to produce one? I have said I will ask you. . . . Ralph Hodgson is one of his contributors, T. S. Eliot, and myself. I also told Hendersons the publishers (The Bomb Shop, Charing Cross Road) about them. Young Mr Henderson asked if he might see them (I suppose with a view to publishing them). I said I would

---

[1] This poem was in fact given the title of *A Terre*.
[2] Frank Rutter.

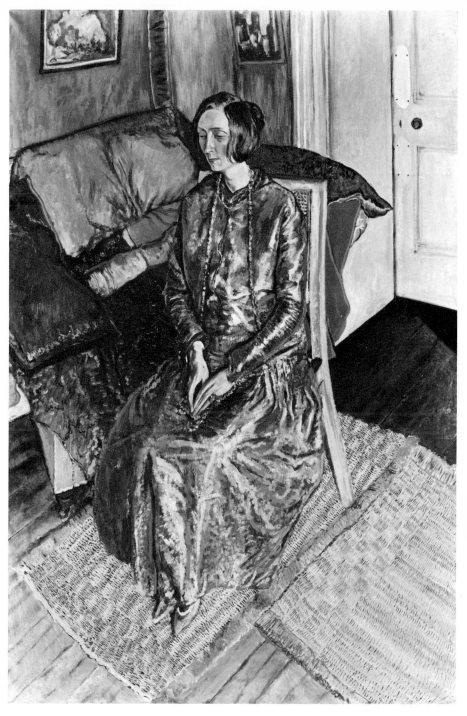

EDITH SITWELL
From a portrait by Alvaro de Guevara in the Tate Gallery

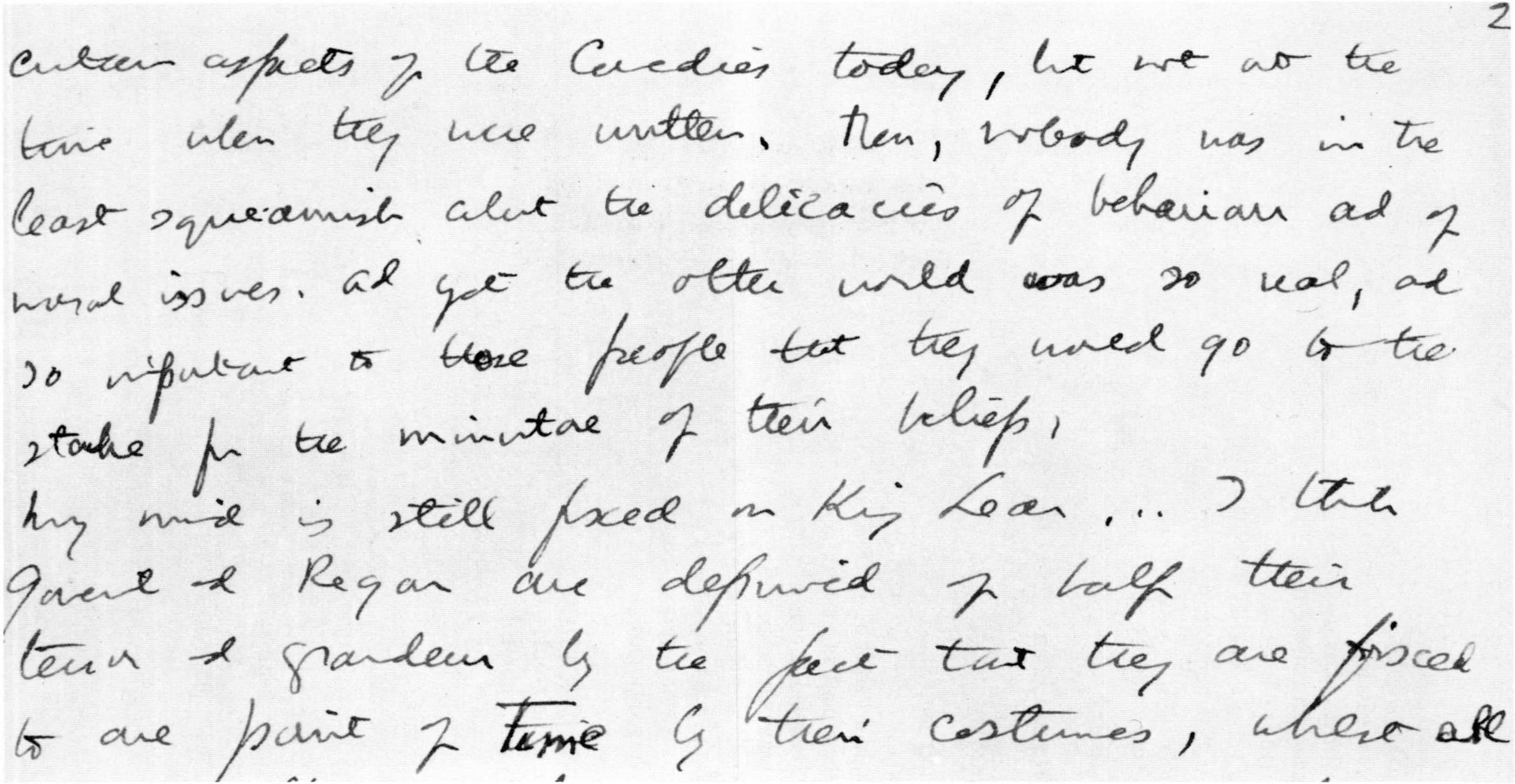
2

certain aspects of the Comedies today, but not at the time when they were written. Then, nobody was in the least squeamish about the delicacies of behaviour and of moral issues. And yet the other world was so real, and so important to those people that they would go to the stake for the minutiae of their beliefs.

My mind is still fixed on King Lear ... I think Goneril and Regan are deprived of half their terror and grandeur by the fact that they are forced to one point of time by their costumes, whereas all

EXTRACT FROM LETTER 106 TO JOHN GIELGUD

ask you. He is a good publisher, but if the poems went to him, it would be necessary to get a man (say Siegfried Sassoon) to see to the business ... as he (Henderson) needs a firm hand.

Is it likely that you would be in London soon? I should feel it such a privilege to see you; one *cannot* convey in a letter the kind of reverence one feels for this poetry and for this personality. This letter conveys nothing of what I feel.

Believe me, my dear Mrs Owen, with my deepest sympathy, Yours very sincerely, Edith Sitwell.

4. *To Susan Owen*

30 July 1919   Renishaw Hall, Derbyshire

Dear Mrs Owen,

I send you the proofs of your son's poems which are to appear in *Wheels*, and I shall be awfully grateful if you will please let me have them back as soon as possible. They look magnificent in print; I copied them out faithfully exactly as they were written—punctuation and all.

If you will allow me, I should like to dedicate this year's *Wheels* to the memory of your son—as a tribute. Will you really send me a photograph of him? I should value it as one of my most valued possessions. Thank you, dear Mrs Owen, so much.

I shall be at the above address for some time, so will you please return the proofs to me here? Believe me, with gratitude, yours very sincerely, Edith Sitwell.

5. *To Susan Owen*

Wednesday [August 1919]   Renishaw Hall

Dear Mrs Owen,

I feel I cannot thank you enough for having sent me your son's photograph. I assure you I shall value it. What a wonderful face he has—the noble head and eyes of a visionary; one

would know that face for a poet's anywhere. His face is so
extraordinarily like his work; it radiates goodness. How proud
you must be to be the mother of such a son.

I know what it must have meant to you to correct his proofs
... I hesitated before I sent them to you, and then I thought the
pride you must necessarily feel at his magnificent work, would
help you to bear it.

The reason why 'Deranged' has not gone in is that I thought
it better not to put it with this selection,—the mass of misery
would have been too overpowering. As it is, the heroism and
the restraint will make a most powerful impression. Thank you
too, for sending me the official notice of how your son won the
Military Cross. What a fine character he must be. I should love
to hear anything about him that you feel you can bear to tell
me.—I do not know if it will be possible, but if it is possible, I
should like to write an essay about his work ... but I must find
out first what paper would take it. It is rather difficult to get
critical essays into papers unless one is on the staff—Siegfried
Sassoon stays a lot with my brothers at Swan Walk; the last
time I saw him, he was ill with sciatica,—looking a perfect
wreck.

He felt it terribly about your son. We have talked about it.
Believe me, dear Mrs Owen, with most grateful thanks, yours
very sincerely, Edith Sitwell.

6. *To Susan Owen*

9 September 1919   Pembridge Mansions

Dear Mrs Owen,
I returned to London yesterday, and tomorrow afternoon my
brother Sachie and I are going to spend (and I shall spend
many, many more, though Sachie is going to Italy) in arranging
and copying out your son's poems. Tomorrow morning I shall
take the proofs of his poems in *Wheels* to Hendersons in the
Charing Cross Road, also to Poetry Bookshop, so as to prepare them for the manuscripts in full. It will not be long now

before the manuscripts are ready. Meanwhile, those in *Wheels*, which ought to appear in about a month's time, will awaken all those who care for poetry to the fact that he is by far our greatest war poet. I have never seen Sachie so affected as he is by these poems; he told me he little dreamt that when he shook hands with your son he was shaking hands with the greatest poet of our time.... You cannot *think* what it means to me that you should allow me to see to his book; I think it is the greatest and most sacred honour. I have to copy out the poems one by one and slowly, as frankly they upset me so terribly I often have to stop. I don't think my letters can ever give you any impression of what your son's poems appear to me—simply as the greatest poetry of our time. Though shorter than Dante's *Inferno*, they rank with that poem.

When they are copied out, you shall have the sorted copies before I take them to the publisher. But there are so many different versions of each poem it will take some time. As we must not, we *must not* make any mistakes.

The manuscripts ought to be ready in about a month from now. I shall put all other work aside, and devote myself entirely and exclusively to this.

I hope you are very well. Each time I write to you, I write with the kind of reverence and humility with which I should have written to Dante's mother. You have given the world the greatest poet of our time. Believe me, yours very sincerely, Edith Sitwell.

'Aliens (Mental Cases)' is safe in my care. It was among his other poems.

7. *To Mrs Owen*

3 October 1919   Pembridge Mansions

Dear Mrs Owen,

I have delayed writing this very important letter for fear it should never reach you owing to the strike; but there seems no hope of a settlement for the moment, and I can delay it no longer.

Thank you so much for your letter; it was so very kind. I am so distressed to hear you are in ill health. I know. It is just then that those terrible longings creep in and tear you, when you have no defence. There is nothing to say to a woman who has lost what you have lost. But oh, what reason you have to be proud. And the day will come, dear Mrs Owen, when you will hear your boy spoken of as the greatest poet this war has produced.

I have now entirely disentangled your son's war poems, with the exception of two; the end of one was very much deleted and written over; the other had several versions and I did not know which was correct. I wrote to Captain Sassoon, to ask him if he could help me about them. He came to see me; and told me it would have been your son's wish that he (Captain Sassoon) should see to the publication of the poems, because they were such friends. In those circumstances I could do nothing but offer to hand them over to him; though it has cost me more to relinquish them than I can tell you. ... I feel doing so more than I can express. I have only one comfort; at least some of his most wonderful work is coming out in *Wheels*; and I *have* worked heart and soul at getting his work ready for publication. I hope there will not be much delay before a book appears. You cannot imagine what joy it will give me, and how I shall think of the pride you must feel.—

I think it must have been so wonderful for your son to have such a mother. Your sympathy with his work must have meant so much.

I have showed your son's work to Robert Nichols, himself a poet of genius. ... He was absolutely *overwhelmed*. He says your son knocks everyone else completely out. I have never seen him so excited.

I showed the proofs to Hendersons, who were extremely excited, and who asked for the 'first refusal' of the book; which means that they would take it almost for a certainty. But Robert Nichols says it would be stupid to let them have it, as *any* big publisher would take it.—Captain Sassoon will see to all that.

It is dreadful about 'Deranged'. I will do my utmost to trace it. I have never seen it.

Sachie is my younger brother; he is a really wonderful poet, —not at all of your son's school, but like the Italian Futurists. That makes his appreciation count, as it shows that *all* the schools will regard your son as a supreme master. I have never known Sachie so overcome; he can think of nothing else; and he has always been entirely out of sympathy with 'war poems'. He says these are the greatest poems of the kind that he has ever seen, and that their beauty and poignancy are absolutely overwhelming. I agree with him.

I assure you, that London will be 'on fire' when *Wheels* comes out—at least *all* London that cares about poetry, and a great many people who have never read poetry before.

Please, when the strike is over, and it is safe, send his other poems to *me*. I'll promise Captain Sassoon shall get them, only I do so want to see them, and it will be my only chance (until the book comes out), if you send them to me. I do hope that our correspondence will not cease, even though Captain Sassoon is seeing to the publication. May I write to you? You can have no idea what a pleasure it is to me. And however many thousands of people come to reverence your son's name—not one of them can ever do so more than I do. Will you let me have a little line just to tell me of the safe arrival of this letter— if it is not giving you too much trouble. Believe me, yours very sincerely, Edith Sitwell.

When the strike ceases, I want to send you a little book of my own.

8. *To Susan Owen*

3 November 1919   Pembridge Mansions

My dear Mrs Owen,
All my thoughts are with you today, and will be tomorrow,

unceasingly.[1] If only one could express what one feels, ever. My heart aches for you. I am dumb when I think what—not only you, his mother, but we all, have lost. I shall keep the 4th of November always, as long as I live, as a day of mourning.

I know you are broken-hearted; but oh, you are just the mother for such a son.

Tomorrow, his first poems in book form will be with you,— the immortality of his great soul. What a wonderful moment it will be for you, though an agony, too.

I cannot write more, because words are so little: before the face of your loss and your grief. They sound too cold.

I shall write in a few days' time. God bless you.

All my reverence and all my thoughts, Yours ever, Edith Sitwell.

9. *To Susan Owen*

Monday [early December 1919]   Pembridge Mansions

My dear Mrs Owen,

I am *so* happy; it is too wonderful .Your son's genius has been adequately realised by the *Athenaeum*,—recognised enough to satisfy even me—and you know what I think of his work.— You will find it all under 'The Present Condition of Poetry'.[2] Please read through *all* the article, even about the Georgians, because it refers to him. No, really, I am so frightfully excited, I can hardly write.

Dear Mrs Owen, how I wish I could see you whilst you are reading this. How proud you have reason to be. I met several critics and publishers' readers at Mr Edmund Gosse's house, at dinner, and they all rushed up to me, and said 'I hear there is a wonderful new poet.' I said to them 'He is the one genius the war has produced.' Soon, all London will be ringing with it.

[1] 4 November 1919 was the anniversary of Wilfred Owen's death. The number of *Wheels* containing Owen's poems was published on 2 November.
[2] A review by Middleton Murry of *Wheels* and *Georgian Poetry* in the *Athenaeum* of 5 December.

I know how mingled your emotions will be. Don't think I am not thinking of the other side of it too. I am. I shall be with you with my whole heart while you are reading this. Some time ago, I gave the Editor of the *Saturday Westminster* a poem of your son's; she thinks it *too* wonderful. I never saw it in the paper, because for some reason my newsagent chose not to send me that number; but I now hear it was in. I have ordered the back number in which it appeared, and enclose it. It was really too bad of the newsagent. They invariably, almost, do the same when my work appears, and they are also rather erratic at the *Westminster* office. *The Coterie* will be out in a few days, containing that wonderful poem 'Mental Cases'. You shall have it at once. I do hope your anxiety about your son who was so ill is at an end. It must have been terrible for you.

I am really too excited to write a sensible letter. Forgive this scrawl, and believe me, Always yours, Edith Sitwell.

I send you a little book of mine, inscribed to you.

10. *To Susan Owen*

Monday [late January 1920]   Pembridge Mansions

My dear Mrs Owen,
Do forgive my delay in writing; I know you'll forgive me when you know the cause. Captain Sassoon has suddenly gone off to America, leaving all you son's manuscripts with me to get ready for the printers by February 1st. Captain Sassoon has done *nothing* in the way of preparing them.

All he has done in the matter is to arrange with Chatto and Windus to publish them. This is a very good thing; and in a few days' time I shall take the manuscripts to them, Captain Sassoon thinks, and I agree with him, that we must aim at supreme quality, rather than quantity, in this book. We are therefore putting in all his finest work, but (and do not let this distress you) *not* his earlier work, as it would tend to diminish his reputation. The book will appear in the autumn; Captain

Sassoon (who has great experience) says this is not [at] all too late. People are already expectant. I have had a most *lovely* letter from Mr Middleton Murry, the editor of the *Athenaeum*, about the beauty of 'Strange Meeting'. I have unfortunately mislaid the letter for the moment; but this is what he said. I had written to him (though I do not know him personally) to thank him for his beautiful notice of your son's work. He replied: 'It is rather for me to thank you. Reading "Strange Meeting" was a memorable experience; *I have read no modern poem which moved me more profoundly.*' He has put your son's beautiful *Insensibility* in the *Athenaeum*.[1] He is an *exceedingly* powerful man, both as critic and as editor. 'Mental Cases' is in the *Coterie*. I send you both the *Coterie* and the *Athenaeum*.

The editor of the *Saturday Westminster Gazette* has sent me the guinea for your son's poem (as she did not know your address). I will forward it to you as soon as I have a moment to go and get it changed.

I can't help feeling a little vexed with Captain Sassoon—not because it entails extra work to me, because I think I need not tell you that *no* work could be too great for me to do with the greatest joy and the greatest pride, that will help to make your son's glorious work known; but simply that here I have been hanging about waiting to hear, when I might have been working at them. Still, they will be done in time. Trust me for that.

If this letter seems a little vague, I know you will forgive it, as I am so hard pressed. I will write and tell you *all*, as soon as I have handed the manuscript to the printers.

Believe me, with all my thoughts, yours very sincerely, Edith Sitwell.

I dined with Mr and Mrs Arnold Bennett a few nights ago; Mr Bennett spoke with admiration—great admiration—of your son's work.

Thursday P.S. I have just sent off your son's manuscripts to Mr Swinnerton of Chatto and Windus. Here is a list of what will be printed. I will return the originals to you in a few days.

[1] Of 16 January 1920.

'Preface'; 'Strange Meeting'; 'Greater Love'; 'Apologia pro Poema Mea'; 'The Show'; 'Mental Cases'; 'Parable of the Old Men and the Young'; 'Arms and the Boy'; 'Anthem for Doomed Youth'; 'The Send Off'; 'Insensibility'; 'Dulce et Decorum est'; 'The Sentry'; 'The Dead-Beat'; 'Exposure'; 'Spring Offensive'; 'The Chances'; 'S.I.W.'; 'Futility'; 'Smile, Smile, Smile'; 'Conscious'; 'Disabled'; 'A Terre'; 'Wild with all Regrets'; 'The End'; 'The Next War'.

11. *To Susan Owen*

Thursday [end of February 1921]   Pembridge Mansions

My dear Mrs Owen,
I should have written ages and ages ago, but I have been so ill that the doctor wanted me to go to bed for two months. Of course it was impossible, but for some weeks I could not write any letters, or even read, because my breakdown was complete. Now I am nearly better. I am so very distressed to hear you have been so ill; it is really dreadful; I do hope you are a little better.—I can understand too, that the reception of the poems must have almost overwhelmed you. Isn't it *wonderful*? I should think no poet ever leapt into such great fame so quickly. And it is absolutely deserved. That is the wonderful part of it. How proud you must be, and how deservedly proud—Have you seen Mr Middleton Murry's article in the *Nation* of last week?[1] It is the *finest* notice he has had. It is a wonderful piece of writing; someone said to me 'If one can give anything such high praise, it is almost worthy of the great poems he is praising.' I shall send you the manuscripts back tomorrow. I know how you must be longing for them. You should have had them before, but I did not dare to send them back before I could see to them myself. They are far too precious. I sympathise with your great pride. It is the greatest pride of *my* life that I was privileged to arrange the greatest poetry of the generation for publication. I am going to lecture about his poetry (in the course of a lecture about modern poetry) on the

[1] A review of the book in the *Nation* of 19 February 1921.

17th of March, and again on the 26th of May,—at the last-named lecture Captain Sassoon is going to be my chairman. I wish you could be there. It is to be delivered to the Tomorrow Club, but I am allowed to take guests; so that if there is any chance of your being there, *please* let me know. Believe me, my dear Mrs Owen, with all my sympathy, Yours always, Edith Sitwell.

12. *To Arnold Bennett*

1 May 1922   Pembridge Mansions

Dear Mr Arnold Bennett,
You cannot think what pleasure and pride you have given me by your mention of me in the *Outlook*.[1] It has compensated me for all the neglect and the rudeness I get from people who don't count. I can't thank you enough for your kindness; but I wish I could tell you how much praise from you has helped me to go on with my work, at moments when I have been most discouraged. I am very grateful. Yours very sincerely, Edith Sitwell.

13. *To Arnold Bennett*

14 November 1922   Pembridge Mansions

Dear Mr Bennett,
I am about to send up a new collection of poems to any publisher who will be idiot enough to publish them. The collection consists of a good many new poems, as well as the whole of *Façade*, and all my poems which appeared in the 1920 and 1921 *Wheels*. I wonder whether you would do me the great honour of allowing me to dedicate this book to you? It would give me

[1] In the *Outlook* of 29 April 1922 Bennett wrote in an article on James Joyce's *Ulysses*: 'Valery Larbaud . . . once amazed and delighted me by stating, quite on his own, that the most accomplished of all the younger British poets was Edith Sitwell: a true saying, though I had said it before him.'

such great pleasure that I feel you will. I want to do it as an act of homage to your work, and in proof of my gratitude for your great kindness and encouragement.[1] Please do let me.

Helen[2] and I both send our love. Yours very sincerely, Edith Sitwell.

14. *To Harold Acton*

Wednesday [May 1923]   Pembridge Mansions

Dear Mr Acton,

I was meaning to write to you for ages and thank you so much for your book,[3] and the charming inscription written in it, and also for the new *Oxford Broom*. The reason I haven't is not neglect, but A. my battle with Alfred Noyes, B. the preparations for the performance of *Façade*,[4] and C. the fact that I have been very unwell for a long time now.

I am so glad my review gave you pleasure; 'Contrasts' is very well done indeed, and I am glad Mr Stephens agrees with me that it is the best poem in the book. You know, it is a very good thing if a young poet *can* do that kind of work, and it should certainly be encouraged. You are infinitely better at that kind of work than you are at the kind of work I do, for instance. You see, my work is (apart from its technique, which is the result of many things, including terribly hard work) very much the result of my particular personality, and it is therefore not a suitable medium for other people.

Every poet must find out *what is his own personality*, and then act upon it. I do not mean that he must cultivate that particular style. Your personality finds its best outlet in poems like 'Contrasts'. Persevere in that style, and you will find in it your best development.

---

[1] E.S. dedicated *Bucolic Comedies* to Bennett in much the same terms as she uses here.

[2] Helen Rootham became E.S.'s governess and companion in 1903, and remained a close friend until her death.

[3] *Aquarium*, a book of poems, which E.S. reviewed in the *Weekly Westminster Gazette* on 12 May 1923.

[4] The first public performance of *Façade* took place on 12 June 1923 at the Aeolian Hall.

You must not be depressed: one always is, when a book has appeared, but do not be. Let me tell you that when *my* first book appeared, I had, it is true, a fine notice from Mr de la Mare in *The Times Literary Supplement*, but, apart from that, a few lines in the *Daily Mail*, and a few lines in some obscure Scotch paper!! nothing else. I liked your poems in the *Oxford Broom*, though I wish you had given it another title. I thought your editorial *most admirable*. But one word of warning; do be careful of your quotation marks. I speak from personal experience. When 'The King of China's Daughter' appeared, some idiot thought I was copying an old nursery rhyme without making acknowledgements. Whereas I thought the original was so universally known, that no acknowledgement was needed. You have got my image about the 'round blue pebbles of the rain' without quotation marks, and if you aren't careful, somebody will be after you about it. The poem you sent me the other day is quite *obviously* sincere; the suffering in it is absolutely genuine and the poem is on nice big lines. That is what I like to see you do, write in the grand manner. The more you do it, the better you'll be. You persevere!

With any luck, I am going to start a reign of terror in the *Westminster*. That makes praise from me, as when I praised your 'Contrasts', all the more valuable—

Oh, I'm working so hard for *Façade*. Is there any chance of your being in London for it? How are you getting on, and how do you like Oxford? Yours very sincerely, Edith Sitwell.

Come and see me when you come to London; I do hope you will.

15. *To Harold Acton*

Tuesday [1923]   Pembridge Mansions

Dear Harold,

You are expecting me to lecture on the 10th, aren't you—at 4 o'clock or so. I haven't heard from the Graves family yet, but if they *can't* have me, I will come down all the same, and return to London the same night ... (I presume there is a train). I'll let you know later what time I arrive. It will be such fun, and I'm looking forward to it immensely.

Has Willie Walton written to you about doing *Façade* at Oxford? He was going to. We thought we would come to Oxford some time in October (unless you think *this* term would be better)—providing enough seats are guaranteed to cover our expenses, which would be £40 (that, of course, covers the band). Will you help us sell tickets? We thought of having so many slips printed, each representing a ticket (of varying prices). People would take these, and when it was nearer the time, we would send them the tickets. What do you think about all this?

Or would *this* term be better. Do, if you can spare time, write and tell me your opinion about the whole thing. I enjoyed seeing you so much when you were in London, and am looking forward very much to lecturing.

Good luck to you! Yours ever Edith Sitwell.

16. *To Harold Acton*

Friday [1923]   Pembridge Mansions

Dear Harold,
Thank you so much for your letter. I am looking forward immensely to lecturing on the 10th, and afterwards shall go on to spend the weekend with the Graves family.

I am feeling miserably disappointed. I've seen Osbert, who tells me it is impossible for me to do *Façade* at Oxford. He says in the first place, they have decided to go abroad, which will mean Willie Walton will not be here,—and I cannot manage the music side of it,—also he says that after *London Calling*[1] I cannot risk it, as probably little Coward's supporters (being far in excess of intelligent people in number) would flock to the

[1] A revue written by Noël Coward and Ronald Jeans in which a sketch based on the first production of *Façade* was included (Duke of York's Theatre, 4 September 1923).

performance to insult me, and that it would be too undignified to expose oneself to it.

I am most frightfully sorry and angry and disappointed, and I do *hope* you have not taken a lot of trouble already. If you have, we will think of a good excuse,—one can say that my health is not good enough, or something. Meanwhile, I'm looking forward enormously to the lecture, and *please* forgive me about *Façade. I want* to do it, but if I did it, and anything went wrong, you can understand things would be impossible.

I will come by the train you mention.

Thanks awfully, Harold, for being such a loyal friend and supporter. I'll never forget it. Yours ever, Edith Sitwell.

17. *To Virginia Woolf*

Wednesday [1924]   Pembridge Mansions

Dear Virginia,

I am so disappointed you can't come tomorrow. Of course I shall love to come to tea with you. May it be one day the week *after* next? It sounds ages off,—but next week will be a dispiriting one, devoted to a bad but persistent sculptor, a niece of a friend of my mother's, and a reading at the Poetry Bookshop. Any day the week after would suit me beautifully.

I'm having such trouble with the lady who will write me letters about her chef. However, I've written her pages—with quotations,—about the destructive qualities of the Wombat;—one of the species has, apparently, prevented Melbourne from getting a drop of water for six weeks, and has also caused a landslide,—by persisting in burrowing.—I have said that will she let me have *at once* any information she may possess about the Wombat, and will she tell me also if an *ordinary* bat could or would do such a thing. Yours ever, Edith Sitwell.

18. *To Harold Acton*

Chez Madame Wiel, 129, rue Saint-Dominique, Paris VII
Sunday [Late 1924]

Dear Harold,

I have been very quiet here, all this time, and have seen practically nobody, as I am in hiding, doing my writing. But Valéry
Larbaud has been to tea with me,—last week,—and I shall be
seeing him again in a day or two. He is dedicating a prose poem
to me, in *Les Feuilles Libres*, but I haven't seen it yet. And this
afternoon, I am going to tea with Gertrude Stein. I shall be
back in England, presumably, about the end of March. I don't
know when my own new book, *Troy Park*, is appearing, but
soon, I hope.[1] The proofs have gone back to the publishers. Of
course you shall have a copy when it does appear. And now I
am in the middle of working out a joint production—a book of
poems by Osbert, Sacheverell and me, with illustrations by
Albert Rothenstein.[2] This ought to appear in the summer.

I have received, from a doctor at Ipswych (I can't spell) the
photograph of fourteen children (presumably his) who have
been brought up on my poetry. They are dressed in Highland
costume, and above them is printed *Scots wha hae*. Imagine my
unbounded horror and disgust.

All affectionate good wishes, my dear Harold, and best
thanks, Edith Sitwell.

19. *To Noël Coward*

6 December 1926   Pembridge Mansions

Dear Mr Coward,
I accept your apology. Yours sincerely, Edith Sitwell.

[1] *Troy Park* was published on 12 March 1925.
[2] *Poor Young People*, published in October 1925. Albert Rothenstein had
by then changed his name to Rutherston.

20. *To Tom Driberg*

January 17, 1927   Pembridge Mansions

... I'm glad you liked the article in the *Weekly Dispatch*.[1] Do,
I beg of you, write to the editor, and I implore you to try and
work up people in Oxford to write. The editor-in-chief has
just returned from the South of France, in a vile temper. He
won't have anybody under 80 mentioned, unless I say what
they look like. Also, it is a case of England for the English. I
mustn't mention Matisse, or Picasso, or Stravinsky, because the
readers of the *W.D.* have never heard of them!—I may mention John, Wilson Steer, Sickert, George Moore, Hardy.—He
wants to know if I never chat with them!—*I* want to be
allowed to write about the art of the present and the future.
There never was such a chance for the real modernist out to
capture the multitude, as this chance of my being allowed to
write every week in the *Weekly Dispatch*. But what is the use if
I'm not allowed a free hand? As it is, my article for this week
has been thrown out. That is why I shall be so grateful if
people will write up to the *Weekly Dispatch* about this new
feature. Also there is the fear of my being thrown off the paper
altogether because I like the young and living as much as the
old and dead. ...

21. *To Allanah Harper*[2]

Whit Monday [9 May 1927]   Pembridge Mansions

Dearest Allanah,
Pavlik's[3] vernissage is on Tuesday the 2nd, at the Galerie
Vignon. And he has asked me to 'receive' the people, as
Choura[4] is too shy. So I am going over there on Saturday.

[1] The first of E.S.'s 'causeries on the three arts' was printed in the *Weekly Dispatch* on 9 January 1927.
[2] Allanah Harper (Mrs Robert Statlender) edited the review *Échanges* in Paris.
[3] The Russian-born artist, Pavel Tchelitchew.
[4] Tchelitchew's sister.

He has asked me to absolutely *beg* you to go over there *as soon as possible*, and either to send him lists of people to whom to send cards,—or, better still, to send them yourself. And I do *beg* you to do so, too, as I want the exhibition to be a huge success. Pavlik says he is sure you will do this for him, as he says you have been so extraordinarily kind to him, and have helped him so enormously. *I* shall need your help, as well as Pavlik, on the day of the vernissage; in fact, if it is possible, I simply must have you there.

I was wondering, too, whether you would feel like giving a joint party with me, in honour of Pavlik, on the night of the vernissage? I feel it might be a great help to him if people knew you were so interested. We would give it together.

I do feel this exhibition is very important. Could you come to tea either tomorrow (Tuesday) or else Wednesday, to talk about this. And I shall hope to have cards to send out by then. Please *do* make people come. Best love, Your affectionate Edith.

Let us have a real campaign.

22. *To Allanah Harper*

[*c.* 1928]   Pembridge Mansions

Dear Allanah,

Thank you so much for your letter. I shall love to come to tea with you tomorrow.—I don't think you have any idea how much heart you put into me, and how much you help me. I am profoundly grateful to you.—You know, I write for a small—a very small—audience. Perhaps you don't know how important it is to a poet to have just a few friends with the kind of intelligence and sensitiveness you possess to such a rare degree.

I'll send Monsieur de Leval some poems with the greatest

pleasure, and when I see you tomorrow, we'll discuss what. Some of the things I send may have to be old ones,—as I haven't much new work available,—but we'll see. How grateful I am to you for what you've done for me in Belgium. You are doing that most important work for poetry,—perhaps you scarcely realise how important your work is.

I'm in the middle of writing a lecture, and thought perhaps these notes from it might interest you.—This is what I've said:

'A great many of the poems by the most advanced school,— those poems which appear strangest to us,—deal with the growth of consciousness,—or with consciousness awakening from sleep.—Almost all my own poems are about this,—or a great many, at any rate.—Sometimes you find a consciousness that has been like that of a blind person, becoming aware,— intensely aware,—of the nature of a tree, or of a flower, or of the way in which rain hangs or falls from certain objects,—for the first time, and, through that nature, guessing that there is a reason, a design, somewhere outside this present state of consciousness. This is what I've written about in the "Aubade". —Sometimes you find a terrible groping animal consciousness, —a consciousness which knows only the flowering and urge of its own hot blood and desire, and, through this, its relationship to other material aspects of the world. You find this in a poem called "Dark Song" (*Bucolic Comedies*), where the dissonances which end the lines in the place of rhymes give the discontent of the subject,—the groping for something without finding it.—Sometimes again you get the animal consciousness knowing its own utter segregation and loneliness, cut off from the outer world by the lack of that higher consciousness which alone can bring us to those correspondences, as Swedenborg has said, whereby man may speak with angels. You find this in "The Bear" (*Troy Park*).—This heavy lumbering rhythm, this queer half amusing outline and design and the laughable nature of the images, are full of purpose. The animal appears to man, not as a struggling half-awakened nature like his own, but as a blot of thick black darkness, as something whose queer antics raise his laughter, and at the same time, fear.'

I've been having a lot of trouble with silly little Bloomsburys lately. They all think that it matters to me if they, and people like Desmond MacCarthy, like my poetry. It doesn't. I don't expect them to. They've civilised all their instincts away. They don't any longer know the difference between one object and another,—or one emotion and another. They've civilised their senses away, too. People who are purely 'intellectual' are an awful pest to artists. Gertrude Stein was telling me about Picasso, when he was a boy, nearly screaming with rage when the French version of the Bloomsburys were 'superior' to him. 'Yes, yes,' he said, 'your taste and intellect is so wonderful. *But who does the work?* Stupid, tasteless people like me!'

How irritating it is, though. In the 1890s, 'superior' people discovered that ugliness is beauty. But the modern intellectual is a bigger fool than that. He has discovered that everything is ugly,—including beauty. Till tomorrow, love from Edith.

23. *To Allanah Harper*

[16 January 1929]   Pembridge Mansions

My dear Allanah,

I was so delighted to get your letter yesterday. I was so disappointed you didn't come to tea that day, but thought you had probably gone to Paris.—I'll *try* and do another poem for the Review,—try my very hardest. At the moment I have nothing. I can't tell you how grateful I am to you for what you are doing for my poetry on the continent. You have worked *so* hard for me, and with such sensitive understanding of what I am doing, and why. It is almost impossible for me to tell you with what gratitude I regard your work for me, and for poetry in general. I think I have never known anyone excepting the few poets who *are* poets, who has such an extraordinary love for and understanding of poetry as yourself. It is, really, quite extraordinary,—not only very unusual, but extraordinary.—I am

sending you a *proper* copy of my *Gold Coast Customs next week*,
when the book appears. Meanwhile, I am sending you the
proofs (which have been put into this awful cover by Siegfried
Sassoon)—in case they are any use to you in the essay you are
writing.

In the *Gold Coast Customs* poem itself, there are all sorts of
queer technical devices that I have tried to get (though I do not
need to point them out to *you*, I can't resist discussing them
with you). For instance, on page 9, the $1\frac{1}{4}$ syllabled words
'rear' and 'tier' make you feel that the houses are toppling over.
Then, on the same page, there is the difference between the
deadness of the 'n' sound in 'grin' and 'skin' and the acerbity of
the word 'strings' (of nerves)

> '. . . only the grin
> Is left, strings of nerves, and the drum-taut skin.'

Of course, there are double rhymes over and over again, giving
extra emphasis. On page 11 with the 'black gaps' and the 'ape'
there is an empty separation between the 'black' and the 'gaps'
owing to the assonance, and the 'ape' tightens the thing into a
higher key because of the 'a' sound,—hurriedly followed by
the fresh lightening in 'chasing'[1] and on page 16 there is the
complicated pattern of

>   'dead
> Grass creaks like a carrion-bird's voice, *rattles*,
> *Squeaks* like a wooden *shuttle*, *battles*'

the shuttle battle performance makes it tuneless, as I had meant
it should be.

And on page 20 the last verse has got a sort of worm-like
turning movement because of the assonances.

[1] 'On all fours now come
The parties' sick ghosts, each hunting himself—
Black gaps beneath an ape's thick pelt,
Chasing a rat.'

'The *calico* dummies
Flap and meet:
<u>Calculate</u>: "*Sally go*
Pick up a sailor".'

and occasionally the lines lengthen themselves out, rear up, and
come down with a crash on one's head, as in the first two verses
on page 27, where the rhythm gets imperceptibly slower and
more forceful. The whole thing has been awfully interesting to
do.

Oh how I laughed about what you have done to Richard
Aldington. Serve him right. But it *is* difficult to know what to
do about Davies. I am afraid it may hurt his feelings to send the
poem back.—

Goodness, I had such a time yesterday. There has been a
vulgar sordid murder of a man called Messiter, of whom I have
never heard in my life. But the *Daily Express* had a huge front-
page double-column with headlines 'MYSTERY SOLVED.
RELATED TO SITWELL FAMILY OF POETS.' They had routed
out the fact that my *fourth cousin* (whom I have seen twice in
my life), married as his second wife a woman who is sister to
the murdered man's wife,—from whom he had been separated
for twenty years!

!   !   !

They dragged out the whole of our family history. . . . Really, I
do think it is an outrage.—Reporters were on my doorstep all
day, from the *Daily Express* (which has had orders from its
proprietor *never* to mention us as artists, because, of course, we
are not artists, we only write poetry to gain publicity!) I gave
the reporter absolute hell! I said 'How *dare* you come here and
interrupt my work to ask me about this cock-and-bull story.
You behave as though we were trapeze artists, not serious
artists. Go and ask Yeats, or Shaw, or Davies, or Wells, or
Bennett, the sort of artists we are. But you won't do that. All
you want to know is, if I've seen the victim of some squalid

murder. They said: 'Have you got a photograph of Mr Messiter, Miss Sitwell?' I enquired: 'Has your editor got a photograph of *Cain?*' The reporter said: 'I don't quite understand.' 'Don't you?' I asked. 'Then you shall! I am the same relation to Mr Messiter as your editor is to Cain, from whom I understand he is descended, unless the Bible is wrong, and Darwin right, in which case he is descended from a monkey!' *That* shut them up, then I said: 'You have come here to ask me about something ugly; but I will show you something beautiful' (and I showed them Pavlik Tchelitchew's pictures). I said to the *Express* representative: 'You have dragged me into this ugly scandal. In return, you shall please me by photographing these beautiful pictures, and speaking respectfully of the great artist who painted them, in your paper.' And they have sent round a photographer, so I am hoping they will do what I ask.

Much love, dear Allanah (and the proper edition of *Gold Coast Customs* will come in a few days). And so much gratitude from Edith.

24. *To Allanah Harper*

16 January 1930   Pembridge Mansions

Dearest Allanah,

What *can* you think of me for not writing to you before, both to thank you for your letter, and to express my delight over the first number[1] (I enclose a cheque for my subscription, and I am longing for the second number to appear.) I hope you will forgive me for my silence when I tell you that I have been nearly worked to death with *A* correcting the Proofs of *Pope*,[2] and *B*, collecting my poems (altering them extensively in places) for the collected edition. So *please* forgive me.

[1] The first number of *Échanges* appeared in December 1929 and included two poems by E.S., 'The Ghost Whose Lips Were Warm' and 'The Peach Tree' with translations into French. *Échanges* ran for five quarterly numbers. No. 3 contained an article by E.S. on 'Modernist Poets' and No. 5 a reproduction of a portrait of her by Tchelitchew.

[2] *Alexander Pope* by E.S. was published on 7 March 1930.

I think the first number is splendid. To my mind, the finest thing in it is the poem by Rainer Maria Rilke, which is really superb. A *beautiful* poem. Do tell me something about him? I once saw a translation of another lovely poem by him in that awful paper *Transition*. Arthur Waley, to my great distress, tells me he is dead, which is a real grief to me, because I feel and believe that he must have been a great poet. I can't tell you how excited I was when I read that poem, and how proud I was that *you* had found it. The first number is a tremendous credit; it really is, and it should teach the French a lot about English literature. I don't see how you could have bettered it, really I don't. It is the first 'alive' magazine I have seen. What a splendid thing it is that you are doing this great work for literature. It is a really great thing that this is in your hands, for you have the most *real* feeling for poetry that I have come across. It is a thing in which one cannot be deceived. I admired the article on the Brontës very much, and liked Virginia's story.[1] I long to know what will appear in the second number.

I nearly cried with laughter when I saw to what you had reduced Mademoiselle Camille on the title-page! How funny; and what a good thing you were so properly firm.

Pope will be out next month, some time, and of course you shall have one of the first copies,—needless to say. The *Collected Poems* (which of course I shall send you too, as soon as it is out) will appear in March. Several of the poems are altered.

My dear. I absolutely hate to bother you: but would it be possible, somehow, for me to have the two Paston books on Pope in which you so very kindly looked out references, returned to me? Because the London Library is *howling* for them, and I ought to return them at once.

Allanah dear, do come back to London soon. You don't know how much I miss you. You are one of the few people I really love talking to. You always make me feel everything is so worth while,—work, and life. Best love and best congratulations and pride in the first number, which is first rate. Yours Edith.

[1] A translation by Georgette Camille of 'Slater's Pins have no Points'.

25. *To Virginia Woolf*

11 July 1930   Pembridge Mansions

My dear Virginia,

I cannot tell you how much I appreciated your writing to me, and how much pleasure your letter gave me. You know that you are one of the only living writers whom I can read with joy and perpetual astonishment and satisfaction, and the fact that you like my poems makes me proud and happy. Not only are you one of the only living writers whom I can read with delight, but you are one of the only people whom I *really* enjoy talking to. I wish I saw you more often,—but I am afraid to suggest coming to see you, or your coming to see me, because of your work.

Now if only I lived nearer to you, I should not be so afraid of disturbing you,—though that is quite illogical.

I should have written this letter days and days ago, but have been ill, on and off, for weeks with all my glands poisoned. A horrible disease, believe me.

Thank you so much again for having written me a letter which gave me so much happiness. Yours ever, Edith Sitwell.

26. *To Anthony Powell*

[23 September 1930]   Rue Saint-Dominique

My dear Tony,

Thank you *ever* so much for sending me that daisy Wyndham Lewis's pamphlet;[1] and also for your letter and the enclosed photograph. Will you please beg the printers to realise that I have *not* got a black nose? It is long, but it is not black. Otherwise, I think it isn't as gloomy as some.—I have christened the young man 'Tip Toe Through the Tulips', and he never stops a

[1] *Satire and Fiction*, published September 1930.

feeble-minded giggling for two minutes,—however, you will
be the sufferer.

I am writing, very uncomfortably, in a hotel room, trying to
balance the writing paper on my knee. That is why my writing
is even more curious than ever.

Before I forget, will you please be most awfully kind and
keep a copy of Cecil Beaton's book for me?[1] I forgot to say that
before.

Everything here is very gloomy, and one is absolutely
gnawed to the bone by gnats. I am longing for the anthology to
come out.[2] Ever so many thanks again, Yours ever, Edith Sitwell.

27. To Terence Fytton Armstrong[3]

27 August 1931   L'Auberge Blanche, Le Trayas, Var, France

My dear Fytton,
Thank you so much for your letter, which reached me this
morning. I feel a beast for not having answered your other
letter before, and your postcard; but I've been having an awful
time with that wretched book about Bath,—working six hours
a day (which is a lot) at constructing it, and writing it. I just
hate writing it,—it bores me, but I must, because of money.—
I've been terribly overworked now, for three months or so,
otherwise I should have written to you fully about your poems.
I *will* on my return. Mr Balston[4] told me I must hurry with
finishing the 3rd volume of my anthology, *The Pleasures of
Poetry*, or it wouldn't be in time for Christmas. As soon as I
had hurried it, he said he couldn't print it till the New Year! and
I've got 90,000 words to write about Bath,[5] when *I* want to
write poetry, which is my work.

---

[1] *The Book of Beauty* (sketches of various contemporary women), just
published by Duckworth, where Mr Powell was then working, included a
photograph and description of E.S.

[2] E.S.'s anthology, *The Pleasures of Poetry* (1st Series), was published in
November 1930.

[3] Poet and editor, who took the name of John Gawsworth.

[4] Tom Balston, working at the time for Messrs Duckworth (director 1924),
author and artist as well as publisher.

[5] *Bath* by E.S. (1932).

I'm delighted with your idea of publishing this pamphlet about cruelty to animals, and shall be more proud than I can say to appear at the same time as Sir Ronald Ross. I'll look the speech out as soon as I return: I must have it somewhere. Meanwhile, I've got another short essay I did on stag-hunting, which I'll mix up with the other, because it is rather good, and I can quote a great deal from Pope's superb essay on cruelty to animals. It is about time people were told the truth about themselves, when they do these foul things. The *Daily Mail* has just refused my 'stag-hunting' essay, on the score that one must not 'offend public susceptibilities'!!!! Good God! One of the reasons for which I was made was to give 'public susceptibilities' a good shaking, and, if possible, get them on their feet instead of on their heads.

If you like, I'll ask Mr Tchelitchew, when I see him, if we may reproduce a perfectly superb drawing which he has just given me,—(it is, really, a series of notes) of lions and tigers in a circus, being driven out of their cages, etc. I cannot tell you the tragedy, the beaten look, of those poor beautiful creatures. That drawing nearly makes me die of rage and despair.

I'll willingly give you the essay for nothing. We'd probably have to pay Mr Tchelitchew a fee, but I don't suppose it would be much, as I'm a friend of his.

I go to Le Trayas on Saturday,—or rather start on that day for Paris, arriving on Monday. I shall be back in London, I expect, the 2nd or 3rd week in October. Did you have a lovely holiday? I do hope so. Yours affectionately, Edith.

28. *To Veronica Gilliat*

Thursday [December 1932]   Rue Saint-Dominique

My dearest Veronica,
This is to wish you and Frank and the Monument[1] the very happiest of Christmases. My dears, I do miss you most terribly. You are, literally, the only people in London whom I *do* miss.

[1] The Gilliats' young son David.

Christmas cards from here are not possible, for they consist entirely of pictures of rather disreputable-looking fat women with false yellow curls, dressed up as angels. And anyhow, I'd rather write to you any day. . . .

My dear, it is so good of you to ask if I am coming over to London soon, and to ask me to stay. I shall, I need not say, simply love to come to stay with you. Do you think I might propose myself for about the 20th of February? The Boyar[1] is having a show at Tooth's then (on the 23rd) and I had promised him to come over and help him. And as he is longing to see as much of you and Frank as possible, it will give *him* a lovely opportunity of worrying you night and day, as well as giving *me* a lovely opportunity of doing ditto. And if you can't have me then, my dear thing, please do tell me and let me come some other time, when it suits you. The Boyar will probably kiss Frank when he sees him. I do think it would be so lovely if I were staying with you for his show. I took Osbert to see his new work the other day, and even he (who has always been very sceptical, because the B. is my friend) was left breathless, and says there can scarcely be a doubt that he is far the greatest living painter—indeed as great a painter as El Greco.

What news have I?? I am *longing* for my exile to be over. I work about seven hours a day at this confounded book on Eccentrics:[2] I've just been offered a big contract for a book on Classicism and Revolt in Modern Poetry, with an advance of £200 for England only. I see nobody, excepting the Boyar and his family. And when I feel cross, which is often, I tease Wyndham Lewis. Osbert and I tease him without stopping. You will remember what he looks like—his dirt, his black patch over the eye, his cloak, and his hat. Well, who does the enclosed remind you of? Osbert found a photograph of these two 1890 actors at Renishaw, and promptly had it converted into postcards. (Even the way of sitting and the look of mystery is like Lewis.) *Every day* that man gets one of these postcards either from London, or from the country in England, or from Paris.—Once I pricked my big toe and planted the

[1] Pavel Tchelitchew.
[2] *The English Eccentrics* (1933).

mark on the p.c. and wrote '*Rache*' on it. We also send him
raving mad telegrams. I got one sent to him from Calais to his
address in Percy Street, which ran thus—(the German is a
reference to his book on Hitler):

Percy Wyndham Lewis, 21 Percy Street, etc. Achtung.
Nicht hinauslehnen. Uniformed commissar man due. Stop.
Better wireless help. Last night too late. Love. Ein Freund.
Signed. Lewis Wyndham, 21 Percy Street.

And two days ago he got a telegram saying 'Achtung. Nicht
hinauslehnen. The Bear dances.' Meanwhile, Osbert's secretary
lost one of her teeth, which snapped off, and Osbert sent it to
Lewis with Sir Gerald du Maurier's card, which he happened
to have. Also, L. hates being thought to be a Jew, and Osbert's
secretary, finding out that a man called Sieff is organising an
exhibition of Jewish artists, has written in the unfortunate
Sieff's name to Lewis, asking him to exhibit, with the result that
Lewis and Sieff are having a fearful row, and all the Jewish
artists are vowing vengeance on Lewis for insulting their
race.

And now we come to the greatest discovery ever for the
Female Face. My dear, there is an old lady who is an illegitimate Hesse, and a clairvoyant, who determined suddenly to
discover the stuff which Ninon de Lenclos used on her face.
All I can say is, that though it looks more repellent when put on
the face than anything you can conceive,—it is made partly of
the blood of the lamb, and one looks like a cannibal—one
comes out looking *at least* fifteen years younger. I have easily
never seen anything to touch the effect. You write to

> Madame Stephanie,
> Huttensteig 10
> Zürich 7.

and send her *6 Swiss francs*, and ask her for Rösan.

Tell her you are my cousin (as we are in perpetual correspondence). It is *no* trouble. You spread the thing all over your
face and neck (when they are damp after washing) leave it on
for three minutes, then sponge it off and wash it with cold
water. One looks like the young dawn. *Don't* let Frank see you

with it on. Because I should think any man would have a fit.

In a few days I hope to send you a poem. I *hope*, I say. Do write to me, please, my dear thing. Very best of all possible love and Christmas wishes, Your ever loving, Edith. And of course my best love to Frank and the Monument. Has the latter found out yet what Life Is? You might tell him this poem:

> There was a young man of Cadiz
> Who inferred that Life is what it is!
>   For he early had learnt
>   If it were what it weren't
> It could not be that which it is!

29. *To Geoffrey Gorer*

Sunday [November-December 1933]   Rue Saint-Dominique

My dear Geoffrey,

I am *furious* with Fabers for returning your book,[1] and think they ought to be ashamed of themselves. I do hope it will be published soon, and if Lane doesn't take it (though I firmly expect they will) why not try Duckworth? In that case, you can use me as much as you like. The fact that Professor Haldane admires the book so much ought to help, enormously. Tell me if there is anything I can do to help? How very odd of de la Mare to say that is 'not the aspect that interests the public'. I am not sure that I am not rather shocked.

Your remarks about 'Romance' brought me real happiness in the midst of absolutely unparalleled gloom. Nobody could conceive what my life is like here. I can't go into details in a letter, but what between the misery of seeing poor Helen so desperately weak and ill, and the fact that I am supposed to be slightly insane (I am treated as though I were) it is a little depressing. I *know* I look wild and odd when I've just been writing; but they'd look wild and odd too if they wrote my

[1] *The Revolutionary Ideas of the Marquis de Sade* (1934).

poetry. This is, of course, between ourselves. Then, too, Osbert and Sachie have definitely been cut out of Father's will, and the dear old Baronet has left, attached to his will, a long list of all our misdeeds.

In addition to this, I am very worried about Pavlik. I am afraid his money affairs are *very* bad again. I hardly ever see him now, though, as he is too occupied with that creature who wrote the immortal book we know. He is always making excuses not to see me: first the *chauffage* went wrong, then Choura had influenza, then he had a cold. He then wrote and told me that it was so sad our both being in the same town and only seeing each other once a week—and I found out that in spite of all the disasters I have mentioned, the genius had spent his whole time there, every day!! I am not unnaturally a little hurt. I am also cross at being supposed to be a fool. I am trying to write some poetry, but it doesn't come off at the moment. But I dare say that is natural after 'Romance', which I only finished this summer, after having been 'at it' for eighteen months. *Scrutiny* is still affording me some innocent joy. It is all that mincing about which pleases me so much, together with the camel-like bobbing about rhythmically with which Fr. Leavis endows Milton. He makes Milton's lines move just like a fleet of camels. I was mad with the *Referee* for not printing your admirable, and very funny letter.

Mary Beaufort has asked me to help her get up a pageant at Badminton for the summer. I do think it will be fun. I'll try and turn out some sort of Ben Jonson-like masque. It's an incredibly lovely and romantic house and park, and just the date I happen to know something about, so we ought to have great fun. But I do hope they won't want me to write 'parts' for the hounds.

Well, this is all my news. Did I tell you, though, that the 24th of January is the date when I am going to be given my medal by Sir Henry Newbolt. With my love, dear Geoffrey, Yours ever, Edith.

Enclosed is the 10s. with which you rescued me at the station.

30. *To Christabel, Lady Aberconway*

As from Hotel Excelsior, Levanto, Spezia, Italy
[January 1935]

Dear Christabel,

Your letter made me so happy and delighted. I am so very glad you like the book,[1] and that the first chapter made you laugh. I must say—(there is nothing like laughing at one's own jokes) —I laughed till I nearly cried as I was writing it.

I thought it might amuse you to hear of some of the repercussions. Lewis is absolutely *howling* with rage. He has taken refuge with the old ladies of *Time and Tide*, and from the shelter of their skirts, and amidst the atmosphere of lavender and old lace, is yelling defiance at me. What has infuriated him especially is my reference to the fact that he was 'formed to be loved',—to his sentimentality, and to his age! (He is revoltingly sentimental. That is the trouble.)

A Mr Stonier—(heaven knows who *he* is) has rushed to the defence of Dr Leavis in the *New Statesman*, and has accused me of plagiarising Dr Leavis by making the same quotations from Yeats, and from other sources ... (if one writes about Yeats at all, one *must* quote those particular passages from *Autobiographies* and *Essays*), and he accuses me, too, of plagiarising from Grigson by quoting a passage from Yeats's *Packet for Ezra Pound*. So I have written the Editor the following little billet-doux. (As they want a fight, they shall have it.)

'Sir, with regard to Mr Stonier's review of my book *Aspects of Modern Poetry*, may I reply that had I known that Dr Leavis was the author of Andrew Lang's sonnet *The Odyssey* (and I think him capable of it) I should have acknowledged my debt to him. Had I known that he was the author of Mr Arthur Symons's book *The French Symbolists*, of Villiers de l'Isle Adam's *Axel*, of Mr Yeats's *Autobiographies* and *Essays* and of *The Oxford Book of English Verse*, I should have acknowledged my debt. But this is the first I have heard of it. Before we know

[1] *Aspects of Modern Poetry* by E.S.

where we are, we shall find that Dr Leavis is the Dark Lady of the Sonnets! Again, Mr Stonier says that, whilst attacking Mr Grigson, I "appropriate, without acknowledging" (sic) "an exceedingly apt quotation from Yeats's *Packet for Ezra Pound*, which Mr Grigson used in a review in *New Verse.*"

'I had not read Mr Grigson's review. Mr Yeats, with great kindness, sent me the *Packet for Ezra Pound*, when it first appeared, with most interesting notations in his own hand-writing, and the book is one of my most prized possessions. I was unaware that I had to thank Mr Grigson for this. I thought my debt was to Mr Yeats, who sent me the book.

'It is right and natural that Mr Stonier should prefer Dr Leavis's criticism to mine. It reminds me of Miss Nellie Wallace's appeal to her slightly denuded feather boa: "For God's sake, hold together, boys!"

'Yours faithfully, etc.'

I send you this, because I don't suppose the *New Statesman* will have the decency to print the letter, so I want you to see it. I think always with so much happiness of the perfect days I spent with you at Bodnant, of how happy I was, of the peaceful and lovely atmosphere, of our talks, of you with the children. It is, I think, the only time that I have ever seen a perfect home with children. . . .

31. *To the Editor of The Times Literary Supplement*

3 January 1935

Sir,

Mr Grigson accuses your reviewer (for no reason whatever) of being 'superficial, ill-informed and prejudiced'.[1] The attack seems to have been made solely because he refuses to be a bore, and this naturally surprises Mr Grigson. Your reviewer did not think it worth while to dwell upon what must be obvious to every reader—the fact that, owing to hasty proof-correcting

[1] In a letter in the issue of 20 December 1934, Mr Geoffrey Grigson had accused E.S. of misquotation and carelessness, and of plagiarising from Herbert Read's *Form in Modern Poetry*, in her book *Aspects of Modern Poetry*.

(since my book was late for the press), there are a great many lamentable printer's errors. As for the 'plagiarisms' from Professor Read, I have said elsewhere, and I repeat again, wearily, that I see no reason why, because Professor Read says that Sprung Rhythm is *not* an innovation, I should say that it *is*. I repeat again, that because Mr Grigson, apparently, was unaware until he read Professor Read's admirable *Form in Poetry* that Sprung Rhythm is the rhythm of Piers Ploughman and of Skelton, he should not therefore deduce that I was in the same state of ignorance. Thirdly, when I referred to Hopkins's 'acute and strange visual sense' I explained how, to my mind, he produced those acute visual impressions that help to make his poetry so remarkable. In this I have taken nothing from Professor Read. Fourthly, Coleridge is not, as Mr Grigson seems to think, an unknown writer!; and I have been in the habit of quoting the particular extract from Coleridge to which he refers over and over again in my lectures for the last ten years—and in much the same connexion. Fifthly, 'the principle of modern poetry' and 'the need for inherent form' mean two completely different things. I only wish to heaven that inherent form *was* a principle of the latest poetry.

As for Mr Grigson's accusations about my 'queer debt' to Dr Leavis, your reviewer has proved, and I have explained, over and over again, what must be obvious to any fair-minded reader. That is, that I am unable—and any critic would be unable—when writing of either Mr Yeats or Mr Eliot, to avoid referring to certain facts which are common knowledge. I am unable to see why the fact that Dr Leavis has read Mr Yeats's *Autobiographies* and *Essays* should have made it incumbent upon me not to. And to take two passages from *The Waste Land*, I did not need Dr Leavis's book to tell me that the title of this poem was taken from Miss Weston's *From Ritual to Romance*, or to tell me that a passage in *The Burial of the Dead* refers to the Tarot Pack. Mr Eliot's notes to the poem establish both these facts. Were I to begin mentioning the names of every critic who has referred to these matters of common knowledge I should never have finished. . . .

I am, Sir, yours faithfully, Edith Sitwell.

32. *To Ronald Bottrall*

16 March 1935   Rue Saint-Dominique

Your very kind and charming letter has only just reached me,
for the reason that I was in Italy, staying a few days here, a few
days there, and so for some time my letters were not forwarded
to me for fear they should be lost.

I was particularly glad to get your letter, for I was intending
to write to you when I returned to Paris. I think I cannot have
made my meaning plain enough with regard to what I feel
about your poetry, in my *Aspects of Modern Poetry*. I had
hoped my meaning was clear, but perhaps it was open to
misconstruction, and I am very sorry.

I think your poetry has deeply moving qualities, and it most
certainly is a living thing; of that there cannot be any possible
doubt. The line, for instance, 'Is it worth while to make lips
smile again' is a really beautiful and most moving first line. The
lines

> '. . . recant
> Our late betrayal and plant
> Within the shadow of the rock
> Our bloodless bodies . . .'

are equally beautiful and moving.

When I spoke about 'a lesser gift for bareness of statement',
I expect it sounded much harsher than I meant it to be. When
one has a great deal that is really valuable to say, as you have, it
is difficult to eliminate. And elimination in poetry is both the
devil and all (as I know only too well), and absolutely necessary.
I do feel at moments that there are phrases, lines in your poetry,
which would be superb in prose, but which are not in their
place in poetry. And I'm not trying to put forth a plea for
poetry that is a hysterical outburst, nor am I asking poets to
write unreal bosh like 'I did not know the Dead could have
such hair.'[1] (I've always wondered why on earth they shouldn't.

[1] Stephen Phillips: *Paolo and Francesca.*

What *can* Mr Phillips have thought he meant?) But there are certain facts of our daily life which are deeply significant in novels, but which I firmly believe are not *quite* right in plays, and are certainly not right in poetry. But a great deal of your poetry has moved me deeply, and I find the rhythms invariably beautiful, significant, moving, and born from the subject. In some, I find a changing of the scale, though, from something great, pregnant, significant, to something temporary and smaller. (I'm always flying at my brother Sacheverell for doing that, too.)

Now I'm reading *Festivals of Fire*, which I had sent for before I got your letter; it was most charming of you to offer to send it to me, and I think it remarkable, and it is obvious that you are a real poet. As I said before, the rhythmical quality of *The Loosening*, its fluidity and perfect control, was most remarkable, and I never doubted that you have a most remarkable mind; all I wanted was more sifting of the material. When I know *Festivals of Fire* properly. I shall write to you again. And I shall ask the Editor of the *London Mercury* if he'll allow me to review your next book, so as to correct any false impression about my true outlook on your poetry which my *Aspects* may have given.[1]

I am scarcely author of the book: the *printers* are. I could not have believed, I would not have credited, such a state of affairs. If they didn't like a word—or a whole line—they simply deleted it. They actually rewrote quite a lot of Hopkins; they left out a line in Milton, the stressing in the same passage is *their* stressing, *not* what I wrote (and corrected, over and over again). They took matters into their own hands from the very beginning, and broke my nerve, very effectively, by changing Mr Yeats's lines (page 86) to

> 'She that has been wild
> and barren as a *broken nose*'!

and a phrase at the end of the essay on Mr Pound, to 'a living evocation of the modern *hall*.' But Heaven protected me, and I was able to remove these errors.

[1] E.S. reviewed *Festivals of Fire* in the *London Mercury* for February 1936.

I think, speaking of Mr Pound, that your essay on him in
Scrutiny is by the far the finest that I've seen. I was overwhelmed with admiration—Thank you very much for pointing
out the mistake I made about Stephens. And, to revert to your
letter once more, what you say about the 'ordinary' throws a
new light. It was incredibly stupid of me, though, not to have
realised it. I'm so very glad you agree with me about Messrs
Grigson and Read. The latter seems to me not to have the
remotest gift for poetry, and his ideas about it seem all wrong.
The former is simply a noisy nuisance. He was *furious* about
the first chapter in my book, and so was Wyndham Lewis, and
the pair of them howled themselves hoarse. I'm shortly going
for them again in a pamphlet, which is to be called *The May
Queen*, and my theme songs are two. The first is that Mr Lewis
resembles that other starry-eyed adolescent, the heroine of
Lord Tennyson's poem *The May Queen*, inasmuch as both of
them are always just *going* to be crowned Queen of the May, or
were crowned Queen of the May a year or two ago, but neither
of them are ever Queen of the May at the moment. And both
want the whole wide world to be there, so as to witness their
little triumph. The second theme-song is that for years Mr
Lewis has been howling that if only we'll pay him sufficient
attention, he'll produce a rabbit from under his hat,—that,
until now, nothing has been produced but an absolute cloud of
bats from the belfry,—but that now suddenly he *does* produce a
genuine, if very small rabbit, in the shape of Mr Grigson!
There, I think, we have the matter in a nutshell. . . .

33. *To Messrs Macmillan*

5 June 1935   Rue Saint-Dominique

Dear sirs,
I have read today in the *London Mercury* that Mr Yeats will
celebrate his seventieth birthday on the 13th of this month.
Most unfortunately and stupidly I have mislaid his address in

Ireland. I would be most deeply grateful if you would have the kindness to send it to me, so that I may send him some flowers.

It must be every poet's wish to do homage to Mr Yeats; but in addition to this feeling towards our greatest living poet, there is, in my case, the memory of great personal kindness.

I hope, therefore, that you will most courteously and kindly waive what I know is the rule of all publishers, and send me Mr Yeats's address—for which I enclose an addressed and stamped envelope, for I should be most unhappy if his seventieth birthday should pass, and I should not have the happiness and privilege of welcoming it. I am, Yours faithfully, Edith Sitwell.

34. *To T. S. Eliot*

26 June 1935   Rue Saint-Dominique

Dear Tom,
I am coming to England on the 8th of July, and am so sorry that you will be out of England all the summer, and that so I shall miss seeing you. It is a great disappointment.

I have just read the unpublished poems of a young man called Thomas Driberg. They seem to me to show really remarkable promise, and, at moments, achievement. He is very greatly under your influence (though not in form; he needs more shaping). But then, who is not? Yours ever, Edith Sitwell.

35. *To Christabel, Lady Aberconway*

18 December 1935   San Feliu de Guixols, Cataluña, Spain

Darling Christabel,
I have wanted to write this letter such a long time ago,—and then I waited till I had finished writing about that old bore Queen Victoria,[1] so as to have a fresh mind, and be able to write a less tiresome letter. . . .

[1] *Victoria of England* (1936)

It is so lovely here, with orange trees, and flowering shrubs whose names you would know, but which are mysteries to me. The only drawback is that the gentleman next door has chosen this moment to put a bathroom into his house, and that the hammering in consequence is something which must be heard to be believed. It sounds as if houses were being plucked up by the roots, and then hurled down, whole, from enormous heights on to the stone pavements. Beyond that, there are few trials, excepting a few debilitated mosquitoes the size of mayflies, very old and with long weeping whiskers, who tickle one with the whiskers in question, and then nibble one in a feeble manner.

I am, however, rather bored; having finished Victoria, and being, at the moment, too tired to begin anything fresh. So bored that I have been reduced to reading *Wolf Solent*,[1] which was lent me by kind Mr Eddie Marsh. There is a great big primitive experience! I suppose that the Messrs Powys were the first writers who experimented in deliberately boring their readers, and if so, I must admit this particular brother is wholly successful. Also, there is a curious film of dirtiness over the whole book, which one can't explain. I am sure as a boy he never washed his hands, but drank ink and kept mice in his pockets.

How brilliant the chapter from Osbert's new novel, that has come out in *Life and Letters*, is.[2] And how it does show up everything else in that paper, excepting Dylan Thomas's poem. It isn't one of that young man's best poems, but I do think he stands a chance of becoming a great poet, if only he gets rid of his complexes. He is only twenty-one. . . .

[1] By John Cowper Powys.
[2] 'The Villa Angelica', eventually published in *Those Were the Days*.

36. *To Dylan Thomas*

[January 1936]

Dear Mr Thomas,

Though we have never met, I am unable to resist writing to you to tell you, however inadequately, with what deep admiration and delight I have read your very beautiful poem which begins with the line

'A Grief ago'

and the beautiful and strange poem in this quarter's *Life and Letters*. It is no exaggeration to say that I do not remember when I have been so moved, profoundly so excited, by the work of any poet of the younger generation, or when I have felt such a deep certainty that here is a poet with all the capabilities and potentialities of greatness. I am completely overcome with this certainty and this admiration. Only a young man who is going to be a great poet could have written the lovely, true, and poignant poem in the programme—(the first one also, has a fine quality)—I cannot recover from it. I think I am learning it by heart.—And as for the poem in *Life and Letters* only a poet with real greatness could have written those extraordinary second and third lines of the passage which begins:

'What is the metre of the dictionary?
The size of genesis? The short spark's gender?
Shade without shape? The shape of Pharaoh's echo.'

Or the wonderful two lines which begin the poem,—or the line

'Death is all metaphors, shape in one history'

I have just finished writing about 'A Grief ago' for the *London Mercury*.[1]—My friend Mr Herring writes me that a new book of yours will be appearing soon. I have already told my agent that I wish to review it, but I would be most deeply grateful if you could tell me who is publishing it, and when it will appear so

[1] 'Four New Poets', *London Mercury*, February 1936.

that I may make certain to have the delight and honour of writing about it.—I have a great admiration, too, for many of your 18 poems, but your two latest have excited and delighted me beyond measure.—I must confess that the first poem I read of yours I did not like, technically—and felt it my duty to say so though without mentioning your name, taking the former only as an example. I know now, without any possibility of doubting it, that in you we have a poet from whom real greatness may be expected.

This is a very inadequate letter. I hope we may meet one day. There are innumerable questions I want to ask you. Your work has, I can assure you, no more true admirer than Yours sincerely, Edith Sitwell.

37. *To R. G. Howarth*

24 February 1937   Rue Saint-Dominique

Dear Mr Howarth,

I am shocked and distressed to think how discourteous and ungrateful you must believe me to be, inasmuch as I have not written before to thank you for your very brilliant and penetrative and helpful—(helpful both to author and reader) essay on my poetry.[1] But my failure to do so is due to no fault of mine, but to an odd and unfortunate accident! A boy at my publisher's office, in a state of abstraction which in any other country would have got him certified, forwarded the pamphlet and several letters to my house in Catalonia, which I had left five days before the civil war broke out! He had seen me time after time in the office since then, but I suppose he thought—(if he thought at all)—that I was a ghost. Catalonia was no place for letters, still less for pamphlets at that time, and the pamphlet was sentenced to be pondered over by all the communist

---

[1] Published in *Some Recent Developments in English Literature* (Sydney, 1935), and reviewed in *The Times Literary Supplement* on 20 February 1937.

authorities in the province, and then to be buried in my deserted house. Now, at last, I am glad to say, it has found its way back to me, together with some, but not all, of my luggage. Such is the history of its odyssey!

Your essay has given me the greatest possible pleasure, and has helped me—(and this is a quality which the author needs more than any other in the critic) to resolve certain difficulties of my own. It has shown me certain obscurities of which I was entirely unaware. I am indeed most grateful to you, both for your chivalrous attitude towards my work, and for your profound understanding of its intentions.

There are many parts which I would like to discuss with you, and I hope it will not weary you if I do. To take these as they occur in the essay: you are, without exception, the only critic who has understood why I wrote 'The stars were like prunes'. It isn't a successful line; I prefer the star-fruit imagery in 'The Sleeping Beauty'; but that *was* what I meant, and, to quote a phrase of yours on page 21, it *was* 'disconcerting to be asked what it was all about'. Partly for the reason that in many cases I could not express the exact shades of my meaning in any other words, in any other way. For instance, in 'Madam Mouse Trots', 'Furred is the light', referred to misty moonlight,—but to misty moonlight of a particular greyish kind; and how inadequate it would have been if I had put the latter phrase into the rhythm of the verse! The most trying attitude of all that the public has adopted is that of accusing me of trying to '*épater le bourgeois*'—(such bad manners. One assumes intelligence in one's audience) and of doing this in order to get publicity. . . . That is the reason why I live here, now, instead of in London; for it is no use people trying to get at me and behave as the crowds behave to the wretched lions and tigers at the Zoo. I can work undisturbed here.

I was particularly impressed and delighted with your explanation of the reasons for making one sense do the work of another, and the reasons for light being 'spoken of as sound'. You have done an incredible, enlightening, pioneer work in criticism, not only for my poetry, but for all modern poetry in your essay, and the paragraph of which I speak is a very fine example.—The word 'light' means to me many things. It is, of course, the light of day, but it is also the light as it is used in the Bible. Sometimes it takes on the form of the physical world, an animal aspect; the 'ventriloquist sound of light' (a phrase that you think a private counter, but there, for once, I disagree) meant to me the unreal light, the priest's light, the false prophet's light, the light that has removed itself from us and that sounds now, hysterical, high unnatural, deformed, twisted, from the lips of the false prophets, the light that is imitating the murdered light, the light that appears very clear, very bright, white as bone, pretending to be alive.

The phrase 'Aubade', defined by the dictionary as 'a musical announcement of dawn', made me laugh very much. How unkind! But it creaked on purpose, as I don't need to tell you. The poem was written like this: it was about a year after I had emerged from a longish period of poverty in London—(I am the poor member of a rich family). . . . I wanted rain in it, but rain in London is ugly, and dull, and anyhow, what do I know about London? I am a country woman. So I must fuse my experience with somebody else's.

You have shown me that I have made a great mistake. The rain in the poem wasn't falling, it was swinging from, and trembling on, the boughs. To me, this is always most beautiful. But I should have made it clear. Actually, the whole experience was mine *and* the servant's, but seen through my mind.— Incidentally, of course you are right in saying that one wouldn't expect 'such a rustic creature to know anything about stalactites or solid geometry'. I don't, either. But we have—both the servant and I—seen shapes that were called by those names.

I have asked my publishers to send you my Selected Poems, because the book contains a long essay I've written, trying to explain what I mean or what I've tried to do in certain poems.

Incidentally, I've just started a very friendly battle, a jousting match, or fencing match, with you in *The Times Literary Supplement*, apropos of what you say about my criticism. Are you sure, *are you sure*, Mr Howarth, that you are right in what you say? I've never pretended that a poet sets out primarily for sound, *of course* he doesn't 'pick vowels and consonants up and fit them into a mosaic'! What happens is that he is born with an instinctive genius for fitting the manner to the theme. Or rather, in him the two are indivisible.

One more word. My temper is NOT spoilt. I am absolutely non-homicidal. Nor do I ever attack unless I have been attacked first, and then Heaven have mercy upon the attacker, because I don't! I just sharpen my wits on a wooden head as a cat sharpens its claws on the wooden legs of a table. That is all.

I am therefore all the more grateful for insight and learning in a critic. Believe me, I am most grateful to you for your very brilliant and learned essay, which must have done more to help towards an understanding of my poetry than almost any essay that has been written. I hope very much that we shall meet one day. If you come to Europe, do please let me know, so that if it is possible we can arrange to meet. It would give me such very great pleasure to discuss all these matters face to face. Believe me very sincerely and gratefully yours, Edith Sitwell.

38. *To the Editor of The Times Literary Supplement*

[27 February 1937]

Sir,

I was much interested by the essay on modern Australian criticism which appeared in your issue of February 20. May I, in no querulous spirit, but because I *am* interested, break a friendly lance with Mr Howarth, one of the critics in question, *apropos* of certain remarks he has made about my own criticism?

I have never—as he infers—suggested that poets should 'pick vowels and consonants up and fit them into a palpable mosaic'. That would, indeed, be an absurdity. I have, however, suggested—and I hold—that an acute sensitiveness to sound and the relationships between sound and meaning, and a genius for producing that relation in poetry—these gifts are a part, and a large part, of the poet's equipment.

Mr Howarth says that my 'perception must be divination—water divining'. It is, the simile is very apt. That is, again, part of the poet's equipment. And is Mr Howarth quite certain that I am talking nonsense when I hear and sense a connexion between sound and meaning that is not immediately apparent to him? He should re-read Wordsworth on the subject of the poet and the reader. What, at first sight, seems to the reader to be 'private language' and 'really offensive to the reader's intelligence and honest willingness to understand,' will be public language to-morrow. When I published my *Bucolic Comedies* in 1923, there was a great outcry against me because I wrote about the 'creaking light' of dawn; the 'braying light' of midday—about 'shrill grass', &c. These phrases were used then for the first time; now they are, or phrases resembling them are, part of the language. I do not think that Mr Howarth can be sure that 'to nobody but' myself 'would the alliteration of quelled and quenched suggest moisture.' 'Qu's' *placed in certain arrangements, do* give a feeling of moisture, whether Mr Howarth likes it or not. And has he ever paid any thoughtful and observant attention to an aspen? The leaves appear to an observer like myself (who is not a scientific observer, but who is accustomed to thinking about what she sees) to be always wet, owing to the continually changing light on the shivering leaves, which gives a glitter like that on water.

As for the quotation from Bottom, that is easily answered. The arrangement of the 'qu's' is different, they have not the same neighbours in the line which he quotes,[1] and the two lines immediately preceding it run thus:

'O Fates, come, come,
Cut thread and thrum'.

Not a very dewy sound *that*, I think!

Finally, why should Hopkins be forced to *say* that the leaves were dew-laden. Poems are not inventories. People will

[1] 'Quaile, crush, conclude, and quell' (*Midsummer Night's Dream*, v i 294).

complain next that he did not say that the leaves were green—
and pale green at that!

I write all this in the friendliest spirit. I enjoyed Mr Howarth's
essay, as I enjoyed that of your reviewer, very greatly, appreciated them both, and am grateful. I am, Sir, yours faithfully.
Edith Sitwell.

39. *To the Editor of The Times Literary Supplement*

13 March 1937

Sir,
In answer to Mr D. S. MacColl's letter[1]—in 1892, when he says
that he published an article in the *Spectator*, from which he
declares that I have taken certain phrases, I was exactly five
years old, and though I could read with ease between the age of
three and four, the *Spectator* was neither then nor at any other
time my chosen literature.

Has Mr MacColl published his essays in book form? Otherwise, it would scarcely have been possible for me to have seen
the phrases in question—and even if he has, I have not had the
pleasure of reading the book.

As far as I know, I have never read anything by Mr MacColl,
and if I had, I am unable to believe that I should have forgotten
it, as the paragraph he quotes is both memorable and beautiful.

I imagine that Mr MacColl, like myself, was much influenced
by Rimbaud, and that we have found a common source of
inspiration for imagery in his work. I am, yours faithfully,
Edith Sitwell.

[1] In a letter of 6 March, Mr MacColl had suggested that E.S.'s phrase 'the
chattering lights of noon' derived from an article on Wilson Steer's painting
Boulogne Sands, which he had written in the *Spectator* in 1892.

40. *To Ree Gorer*

5 May 1937   Hotel Excelsior, Levanto

Thank you ever so much for your letter, which I was so
delighted to get. And how extraordinarily kind of you to send
me *The Road to Wigan Pier*, which arrived the day before
yesterday, and which seems to me, as it does to you and
Geoffrey, a most remarkable book.

I really was so happy to get your letter. One feels so cut off
from one's friends when one is away for so many, many
months. I *do* look forward to seeing you in a couple of months'
time.

You must be longing for the moment when Geoffrey returns.
I wonder whether, when he has explored the last remaining
corner of the earth, he will stop at home, or will discover some
means of getting to Mars! I feel that is the next contingency
with which we shall all be faced. I've never known anything to
touch it.

My novel[1] is getting on very well. It is the only prose book
(excepting for criticism) that I've ever been pleased with. (I
mean, *naturally*, the only prose book of *mine*!!!) What an odd
sentence that looked, without explanation. But I must say I'm
nearly dead with fatigue. My usual time for starting work is
5.30 a.m. I'm never later than 6. It is the only time when I can
be sure of being quiet.

To return to Orwell. The horror of the beginning of *The
Road to Wigan Pier* is unsurpassable. He seems to me to be
doing for the modern world what Engels did for the world of
1840–50. But with this difference. That Orwell is a real born
writer, whereas Engels, fiery and splendid spirit though he was,
simply wasn't a writer. One had to reconstruct the world
from his pages for oneself.

Do you think he was *meaning* to be funny when, after
writing about an episode in connection with those dreadful
lodgings, in the first pages—(an episode which made me feel

[1] *I Live Under a Black Sun.*

that I couldn't ever face food again)—he explained that he gave notice because 'the place was beginning to depress me'? . . .

This hotel has changed sadly. The food is worse, the noise awful, and it is infested with gibberingly appalling people. I shall probably talk about being 'pukka sahib' on my return. Well, perhaps not! Orwell may keep me straight!

41. *To Anthony Powell*

[11 February 1939]   Rue Saint-Dominique

My dear Tony,
I had begun this letter days ago—(or rather another letter, which I've now torn up as being demodée)—when the man who is producing a play of mine for the B.B.C. suddenly turned up and said I had to alter the script in dozens of places!!¹ And at once. That is why this letter is so late. But I hope my wire arrived.

I really can't tell you what a delight the book² is to me—I am enraptured by it,—nor how delighted and proud I am of the dedication. All my most grateful thanks.

I've been looking forward to the book for months, but it has really exceeded my hopes. It is absolutely wildly funny, from the opening on. There isn't a touch that doesn't come off. The description of the seance at the beginning made me cry with laughter. (George Eliot's longing to be called Mimi is a particularly happy thought.)

As for Hugh! I think he is one of the best characters you have ever produced. I must not be misunderstood, of course, when I say I feel I have known him well, have often visited him at his office, and clattered down the chess-board to his dinner-parties. Also I feel I know those sudden bursts of temper and argumentativeness, the laugh, and the feeling of a blackboard as spiritual background.—The rows in the office are fine, also the very gradual working-up to religious mania. (I am much attached to Mrs Gulliver-Lawson's letter, incidentally).—The

¹ 'Romeo Coates', based on *The English Eccentrics*, broadcast 23 February 1939.
² *What's Become of Waring?*

climax at the second seance is really magnificent.—Oh, and I
think your choice of publications for the firm is admirable,—an
attack on theosophy, Welsh proverbs with lino-cuts, and *Lot's
Hometown*. (I'd have liked to have known more about the
chapters in that masterpiece where Irving and Wayne listen to
the whip-poor-will.)

Until the very moment when Eustace gave Hudson a book
belonging to Robinson, I had thought Eustace was Waring,
and it was a blow to me, at first, when I found he was not,
because Eustace had fired my fancy, from the opening scene.

I do really think this is one of your very best books. It just
is, as I said before, magnificent from beginning to end. I do
hope it will have all the success it so richly deserves.

I don't think I have any news. I'm hard at work on an
enormous anthology,[1] but feel it hard to keep at work because
of the inroads made on my time by persons suffering from
mental afflictions. The other day, a young man was brought to
lunch here; I had only seen him once before, I may add. He
began to cry as soon as we sat down to lunch (rather before one)
and continued to cry until a quarter to six; at one moment he
asked if he could lie down. I was then told, by the man who
brought him, that he was on the verge of nervous breakdown,
and was asked if I could take him over to London, in an aero-
plane, and see him safely home!

Most grateful and delighted thanks, once again. My love to
you and Violet. Yours ever, Edith.

42. *To Raymond Marriott*[2]

26 February 1939   Rue Saint-Dominique

Dear Mr Marriott,
Thank you so much for your very kind letter. I was so glad to
get it, and to recover your address, which is now safely written
down.

---

[1] *Edith Sitwell's Anthology*, published 29 January 1940.
[2] A young journalist, see Letter 46, page 69.

How very dreadful, how anguishing for you, about **Mr** Roberts. At twenty-eight! The sense of waste, as well as the terrible sense of your personal loss! What a dreadful, dreadful thing. *Of course* you couldn't possibly have begun to recover from it yet,—the grief, and the shock, and the feeling of emptiness. It is terrible that this should have come to you when you are young. It is all wrong that one should be unhappy in youth.

My poor friend I couldn't wish back.[1] She suffered six months of unspeakable torture, and as she was nursed in this tiny six-room flat, both her sister and I were worn out. What *I* am suffering from, is delayed shock.

One gets over that. Only I ought not to have done any work for a time, and was told not to, by Lord Dawson. But I *had* to, and so did.

And I expect the same happened with you. In time, I hope and believe the anguish with you will be—covered over. That is the only way to express it. It is like new skin covering a wound. That doesn't mean that one forgets the people who have gone away.

I do hope you will like my *I Live Under a Black Sun*. It is an allegory, in a sense, as you will see. The reason I put Swift into modern clothes is because the spirit of the modern world is power gone mad. And Swift was power gone mad.

I have tried to show the futility and barrenness of hatred. It is a terrible book, I think.—I felt as if I had been through an earthquake, after I had written it.

I shall be very much interested to hear what you feel about it, when you've read it. I am so happy that you like my work.

I look forward very much to seeing you in July. Yours very sincerely, Edith Sitwell.

Yes, wasn't it perfect about my lady Duchess.

[1] Helen Rootham died in 1938.

43 *To David Higham*

8 March 1939   Rue Saint-Dominique

Dear Mr Higham,

Thank you *ever* so much for taking all this trouble, and being so generally kind about my American tour. Very many thanks for your letter and the contract. There are one or two points to be discussed.

First, I am sorry, but I cannot *possibly* lecture *excepting from manuscript*. They say I must not lecture from manuscript, but if they won't let me, then I can't go. I have no memory at all, and my lectures are highly complicated, and, in the case of those on poetry, very highly technical. One slip would be fatal.

Couldn't it be pointed out to them that I am an extremely experienced lecturer, that I delivered two of the Northcliffe Lectures at London University in 1937 (to audiences of 3,000 each) that I have lectured at Oxford, Cambridge, Edinburgh, and all over the rest of England, but that I have never yet been asked to lecture excepting from manuscript.

They must think I'm not an artist but a trick cyclist. Next they'll want me to deliver my lecture cycling round and round the platform balanced on my nose with my feet in the air, and declaiming at the same time on the effect of texture on the caesura! So if they won't let me lecture from manuscript, then I cannot go to America. If they *will* let me, I'll give them what I think will be very good lectures.

The other point is, they don't say in the contract how many lectures I am expected to give a week. And that I *must* know. I really am sorry to give you all this trouble. You have been more than kind, and I am so very grateful. Yours very sincerely, Edith Sitwell.

44. *To Ree Gorer*

Saturday [March 1939]   Rue Saint-Dominique

Dear Ree,
We've all (by all I mean Moby Dick, the maid and myself) been
down with influenza, or I should have written ages ago to say
how enormously I am looking forward to our trip to America
next January. *What* fun we will have, and how very happy I am
that I shall be going with you. I simply couldn't face it if I
were not.

At the moment I am having a protracted argument with the
agent, Mr Colston Leigh, on the subject of whether I am, or
alternatively am not, a trick cyclist. As far as I can make out, he
would like me to bicycle round and round the platform on the
tip of my nose, with my feet in the air, intoning at the same
time on the effect that texture has on the caesura. In other words,
he is making everything as difficult for me as possible by
insisting that I must not *read* my lecture. I have no memory, and
as the lectures on poetry are highly technical, and any slip
would be fatal, I have said that I am *going* to read them. . . .

I'm getting on grandly with my anthology, which will be
finished fairly soon, and with which I am really satisfied. (But it
isn't improving my handwriting, as you can see. I have such an
enormous amount of copying to do). Of course that infernal
influenza put everything back. Poor Moby Dick had it worse
than me, and succeeded in producing the phenomenon of, at
the same time, trumpeting like an elephant and spouting like a
whale. Poor old soul, her appearance, her *cosmetic* system, are
getting more and more peculiar, so that she no longer looks as
if I had gone in for a lucky dip in the most louche quarter of
Port Said, and had brought out something very special, but as if
she were Lamia before she changed into a lady:

> 'She was a gordian shape of dazzling hue,
> Vermilion-spotted, golden, green, and blue;
>
> Striped like a zebra, freckled like a pard,
> Eyed like a peacock, and all crimson-barr'd; . . .

She seem'd at once, some penanced lady elf,
Some demon's mistress, or the demon's self.'

She has taken a great fancy, too, to the works of Dr Cronin,
which makes everything still more difficult.

45. *To Ronald Bottrall*

August 29, 1939   Renishaw Hall

... I am enjoying *The Turning Path* more and more, and am
busy reviewing it for *Life and Letters*. This would have been
done ages ago, but Mr Gollancz said I *had* to let him have my
anthology by the middle of August. The long critical essay was
a terrifically hard piece of work, sometimes I had to work at it
for seven hours a day, and writing about, say, the Elizabethans
puts one's hearing out for writing about modern verse, and
vice versa. One can't hear either properly. And Pope and
Dryden bring the state of affairs about still more.

I hope you will like the review when you see it.—The book
gives the reviewer every kind of opportunity, because the
quotations one can make (this is leaving everything else aside)
give one such a shock of surprise and delight, such a feeling of
life.

Isn't it curious how one has only to open a book of verse to
realise immediately that it was written by a very fine poet, or
else that it was written by someone who is not a poet at all. In
the case of the former, the lines, the images, though they are
inherent in each other, leap up and give one this shock of
delight. In the case of the latter, they lie flat on the page, never
having lived.

46. *To Tom Driberg*

24 September 1939   Renishaw Hall

My dear Tom,

I am just passing through London, on my way to Renishaw, and have been telephoning to you madly since Friday on the chance of seeing you. Twice I got on to the *Daily Express*, but was cut off promptly without the *D.E.* finding out who I was or what I wanted, or who I wanted to speak to. But I hope to be up in London again in about a month.

I am now going to pester you, and I hope you won't curse me. There is a young man called R. B. Marriott, who is in absolutely *desperate* straits. He was a journalist on the *Era*, and now, owing to the war, has lost his job. He is very experienced, but, poor young man, has absolutely no money.

I am writing to ask if you can and will help him get a job on the *Daily Express* or the *Sunday Express*.

I was told privately, yesterday, that it is possible, and indeed probable, that the *Sunday Express* is in need of someone to do *film* criticisms. You really would be an angel if you could do something for him.

You must get hundreds of requests of this kind, and indeed I would not bother you if Mr Marriott was not in such a desperate state. He looks dreadfully poor anyhow, poor boy. If you would ask him to come and see you, it would be extraordinarily kind. He *must* find something soon, or I don't know what will happen to him. His address is

R. B. Marriott
25 Fairfax Road,
N.W.6.

Do forgive me for plaguing you. I shall hope to see you when I get back. Yours ever, Edith.

47. *To Geoffrey Gorer*

29 December 1939   Renishaw Hall

My dear Geoffrey,

Our letters must have crossed—I mean that we wrote each other soon after this hideous infamy of a war broke out. I hope you will have as decent a new year as is possible for anyone under these terrible circumstances. I miss you *very* much, and long to see you and have a talk.

I saw your mother and Richard about a fortnight ago, and had news of you from her.

I hope you got my cable at Christmas. When you have time (I know you are extremely busy) do write and tell me how you are feeling, and what, exactly, your work consists of. I know *roughly*, of course, but I would like to know all kinds of details. I hope you are able to lose yourself in it, so that you are not too much alone with the misery I know you (with all thinking and feeling people) must be enduring.

I am writing poetry again. I had meant to send you two poems, but I've only just enough paper to finish this letter. But I *will* send them. (Also, I can't think what I am doing at the moment, as Mr Sandy Macpherson is making that horrible cow-like noise on the B.B.C. organ). . . .

Bobby Helpmann stayed here for two days over Christmas, and gave me a spirited description and imitation of the trouble Arnold Haskell has been having with Aldous's aunt, the old girl who pursued you because of your 'dog-like eyes'. It seems that she inveigled poor Mr H. to dine with her alone, and then, sitting down beside him on the sofa, put her arm along the back of the sofa and said, languorously, 'Tell me!—do you enjoy *kissing?*' . . .

48. *To Sir Hugh Walpole*

February 1940   Renishaw Hall

Dear Sir Hugh,
It was extremely kind of you to send me such a charming message, and it has given me the greatest possible pleasure to know that you like the anthology. I am very delighted, too, that you sent me the message, because it has given me the opportunity of saying that my temper has always been a bigger source of worry to me than it could possibly be to anyone else, and that I shall now see more clearly than ever how stupid it is for me to let it carry me away.

The anthology, I may say, has been nearly as much of a worry to me as my temper, and the proof-reading was enough to drive me quite demented.—I am now thinking of doing an anthology of modern poetry.

Very many thanks again, I am, Yours sincerely, Edith Sitwell.

49. *To Robert Herring*

20 August 1940   Renishaw Hall

Dear Robert,
It is only now that I have heard from David about your poor mother. What you must have suffered. Poor Robert. You see, I know only too well what it is like. When the end comes, though one's grief is unchanged, one can only be thankful that for them, all the dreadful suffering is over. I know that is what I felt when poor Helen died. But one is utterly exhausted by one's misery and by the horror of having to know that they suffered so. It is a dreadful martyrdom for them. But it is for us, too. I look back with horror on what one went through.

I do *hope* you are taking proper care of yourself, because there is such a danger of one becoming really ill, not at once,

but sometimes months afterwards. So I hope you are not
working too hard, and that you are making yourself eat, however disinclined you may feel.

I had not liked to write to you before, because I thought it
might be worrying you in the last moments. And, as I say, I did
not know that it was all over until David told me, when I was
enquiring after you. I do feel for you more than I can ever say.
I know how dreadful your sadness must be, and how lonely you
must feel without her, and how more than terrible those last
months must have been. For her and for you. It is a nightmare,
as I know only too well, and there is nothing one can say to
show how much one understands, and how deeply one
sympathises and feels for your grief. At first one feels, I know,
as if nothing could ever, ever dull the grief and the gnawing
wretchedness. But at last that does happen,—though it takes
very long. Please take care of yourself.

With all my thoughts and sympathy, Edith.

50. *To Ree Gorer*

2 October 1940   Renishaw Hall

Darling Ree,

. . . I am so *thankful* you are in America. It is one of the only
things I have to be thankful for, at the moment. How more than
wise the boys were, to insist on your going. I do hope that you
are as happy where you are as it would be possible for you to be
at this time. I miss you terribly, and miss the thought of you
being here; but I am thankful that you are not. . . .

There is, of course, very little news excepting that which
everyone knows. I am afraid we are all a dreadful disappointment to the dear sweet-minded Germans, and have not given
them quite the welcome they expected. But there you are. My
God, I hope we continue to give them the thrashing they
deserve.

I have still no news whatever of Evelyn Wiel. It is really very
terrible, poor old soul, and I am horribly worried about her.

The Board of Trade were very kind and allowed me to send her a small sum in three deposits, but I do not know if it has ever reached her. Her brother, of course, who is a solicitor, just exists beautifully and leaves me to do all the work about making enquiries, seeing to sending money, etc.

My Papa, you will be relieved to hear, is safe, and has sent a message through to say that 'Sir George is completely undisturbed'!! That is so typical. I suppose he thinks that this is just a slight international misunderstanding, which will soon blow over. If he had been in the Mont Peléer earthquake, he would simply have taken his pulse, and put himself to bed on a milk diet 'to rest the heart'. He is always 'resting the heart', though he has never given that organ any work to do whatsoever, from any point of view. . . .

51. *To Geoffrey Gorer*

28 October 1940   Renishaw Hall

My dear Geoffrey,
I have thought, and do think, of you so much, and I only have not written for some time because I have been muffled in a kind of grey horror, a sort of nightmare in which I have found it difficult to move. I write poetry, because that is my natural function, and I spin it out of myself as a spider spins threads out of itself,—but that is all. When one writes letters to one's friends, one has to have a *different* kind of reality, and, at the moment, I am not real, in ordinary life.

I am thankful, more than I can say, that you persuaded your dear mother to join you. It was one of the most sensible and far-sighted things that you have ever done. I think she would have been heart-broken if she had remained here. I miss her, and you, terribly, though. When shall we all sit together quietly, again, talking. Or when, if ever, shall we have any happiness? Who could have thought such causeless wickedness and misery could have come upon us. . . .

I have no news of the wretched Evelyn, and am horribly

worried about her; I cannot *bear* to think that perhaps she may be in want. I have done everything I can. My maddening old father is in Italy; and has sent through a message to say that if we cannot send money through to him by December, he will be starving. What an end and climax to a life in which one has been a constant nuisance to one's offspring! Of course Osbert is asking the authorities here what he can do, and what they advise . . . but still!—

I hear that Willie M[augham] (I do not know if this is true) found himself being reconciled—(One of those air-raid-shelter reconciliations)—with his ex-wife, at a hotel in London the other day. That great woman, who was about to leave for America, said, in an effort to enlist his sympathy: 'Oh Willie, I *know* I shall be torpedoed!' 'Then', said Willie, true to type as ever, 'I have only one piece of advice to offer you. Keep your mouth open, and you will drown the sooner.' Mrs M. began to cry.

I haven't any personal news, excepting that I am going to try to write a play for Alec Guinness, with whom I have been making great friends. His young wife, incidentally, is a cousin of mine, and is a most sweet young creature. As I have no news—largely because we never move from here, and hardly ever see anyone—I send you two poems, instead. It seems to be my only form of showing I am alive. . . .

52. *To Daniel Macmillan*

13 February 1941　　　　　　　　　　　　　　Renishaw Hall

Dear Mr Macmillan,

This letter would have been written days ago, but I've been so unwell, as the result of the strain we've been through.[1] Osbert, Sacheverell and I can never, *never* be grateful enough to you for your great kindness in coming to witness for us. Your help was

---

[1] In 1940 Edith, Osbert and Sacheverell Sitwell were libelled in *Reynolds News*, and brought a successful action.

absolutely *invaluable* to us. And everyone there must have been most strongly impressed.

The papers, with their usual low cunning and meanness, have left out, in their reports, everything inconvenient to themselves. Nobody reading most of the reports would have any idea of the sternness of the judge's summing-up, for instance.

The Buffalo,[1] in his final speech, threw out a few hints, during about five minutes, about blackmail. Apparently, only the fact that we are not entirely destitute saves us from the charge of being blackmailers. So that, you see, only rich plaintiffs dare bring an action to protect themselves. Such a luxury is not for the poor!

They really are a revolting lot, the defendants. And during most of the time I was in the witness box, they were making faces at me. As though their natural ones weren't bad enough! It was *so good* of you to give up your time, in this odious case, and we are indeed so grateful that we can never express our gratitude. I do feel that we have all struck a blow for the arts. Believe me, Yours sincerely, Edith Sitwell.

53. *To Sir Hugh Walpole*

Saturday [February 1941]   Renishaw Hall

Dear Hugh,

Osbert, Sachie and I can *never* thank you enough for your extraordinary kindness and chivalry to us throughout this wretched business of the *Reynolds News* case.—Your letter to the *Daily Telegraph* is invaluable: it will prove to people that the action was not a petty personal one, but an action that had to be fought for everybody's sake.[2]

We can never be sufficiently grateful.

I would have liked you to see the defendants, and their librarian, in Court.—Mr Wilson, of Bumpus, told a woman I

---

[1] G.D. Roberts, K.C.

[2] Walpole's letter in the *Daily Telegraph* of 14 February said that all writers should be grateful to the Sitwells for their action.

know that he thought he was used to tough people, but that he
had easily never come across anyone to touch them.—Nor were
they pleasing to the view; one was a furtive grey and black
rodent type, one was a thick bat-woolled young man like an
Australian bushman, and the third, Mr Hamilton Fyfe, was like
some sort of insect. They sneered at us throughout the hearing.

The papers, with about two exceptions, gave no real idea of
the case at all,—they left out everything which threw a bad
light on their charming confrères.—Nobody could have
gathered, from the papers, the impression made by the terror
of the Defendants at the idea of the witness box, nor could it be
realised how extremely severe was the Judge's summing up.

It was a very mean, and a very dirty, defence. Yours ever,
Edith Sitwell.

54. *To Sir Edward Marsh*

22 March 1941   Renishaw Hall

Dear Sir Edward,
(Or don't you think we might really by now call each other
Eddie and Edith?)—you cannot know with what delight and
excitement I have been reading your and Horace's beautiful
poems.[1] The exquisite order, grace, shape, restraint, and jewel-
fire of the colours give one a strange feeling of permanence and
of mental comfort. And when there is sorrow, there is no
horror attached.—After all, I suppose that all ugliness passes,
and beauty endures, excepting of the skin.

I have been reading the book now ever since Friday afternoon, when it arrived, at all times of the day and very late at
night, and it comes with a fresh shock of delight, always. At
present, I feel Nos. XXX, XVII and IV of the First Book, Nos.
XIX and V of Book II, and No. XVIII of Book III are perhaps the
most beautiful of all.

What a lovely work to have accomplished.

I do feel that everyone who cares for poetry ought to be

[1] Marsh's translation, *The Odes of Horace*, 1941.

grateful to you: both scholars and those unfortunates (now less unfortunate, because of this) who can't read Latin,—like myself.

I do thank you, most gratefully, for having translated the book, and for your great kindness in sending it to me. Yours ever, Edith Sitwell.

55. *To Alec Guinness*

Saturday [Spring 1941]   Renishaw Hall

... Will you please ask Merula, with my love, to send me that pattern of a pull-over she was talking about in her letter? Because then I shall begin one for you.

The two gramophone records are *most beautiful*, the 'Serenade: Any Man to Any Woman' just as beautifully shaped by you as the 'Lullaby'. I cannot tell you how happy I am to have them. They are very greatly appreciated by all who hear them. You give them a fabulously elegant shape and movement, and it sounds at once very strange and very beautiful to have such terror with such elegance: in short, they are exactly what the poet would most dream of them being,—and I cannot express my gratitude in any adequate terms. It is the first time I have heard you recite the 'Serenade', and it is a very great experience for the poem's author. The movement you have got in it is truly most beautiful.—In the 'Lullaby' you have got an appalling mechanism of movement which is terribly impressive.

Osbert played them last, last night when we were in the middle of a raid. A man who did not know the poems was staying here, and said the performance was more terrifying than the raid!

Osbert and Sachie and I felt very melancholy because it was impossible to get hold of you when you paid a visit to our Case. You vanished before anything could be done. The whole thing was blue hell, and Mr Roberts was a great blundering buffalo of a man.—We had a lot of trouble with the Pip-

squeakery afterwards, but in the middle of it all, dear Mr
Bernard Shaw came down on them like a flash of lightning
and a clap of thunder, with the enclosed letter.

I've been reading some most wonderful very early poems.
Do you know the religious poems of Richard Rolle, who was a
hermit born in 1300, who eventually died of the plague? I think
this enclosed poem is one of the most moving religious poems I
have ever read. I cannot get it out of my head, with its sad
gentleness.—I've also been reading a lot more Skelton and a lot
of John Gower,—who, (if you don't happen to know him, and
I believe he is very little known) is, at his best, what William
Morris ought to have been, and sometimes, but not often, was.

I will, from time to time, copy out some poetry for you,
when it is otherwise unobtainable. Tell me what Dickens you
would like, and I will send you some. . . .

Enclosed:

My Truest Treasure. . . .
Richard Rolle.

My truest treasure so traitorly was taken
So bitterly bounded with biting bands;
How soon of thy servants wast thou forsaken,
And loathly for my love, hurled from their hands.

My well of my weal, so wrongfully wreathed,
So pulled out of prison to Pilate, at prime,
Their dules and their dints, full drearly thou dreed
When they shot in thy sight both slaver and slime.

My hope of my heal, so hied to be hanged,
So charged with thy cross, and coroned with thorn;
Full sore to thy heart thy steps they stranged,
Methinks thy back burd break, it bends for-born.

My salve of my sore, so sorrowful in sight;
So naked and nailed; thy rig on the rood
Full hideously hanging, they heaved thee on high,
Let thee stab in the stane all stecked that there stood.

My dearworthy darling, so dolefully dight,
So straitly up-right strained on thy rood;
For thy mickle meekness, thy mercy , thy might,
Thou bete all my bales with bote of thy blood.

My fender gainst my foes, so fond in the field,
So lovely alighting at the evensong tide;
Thy moder and her menghe unlaced thy shield.
All wept that were there, thy wounds were so wide.

My peerless prince so pure, I thee pray
By mind of this mirror thou let me nought miss,
But wind up my will to wone with thee ay
Be buried in my breast, and bring me to bliss.

Amen.[1]

56. *To Christabel, Lady Aberconway*

2 April 1941   Renishaw Hall

... How are you bearing everything? The—if anything—
increasing savagery, and horrible sense of waiting for an
attack? The constant anxiety, and feeling of stultification and
personal and general misery?
   ... Nothing seems to have happened, personally, just lately.
I mean, not since the case. I have learnt one lesson from that,—
never to commit a murder (which I have often longed to do).
Entering the witness box with nothing on one's conscience
except having written some poems, is quite bad enough. What
can it be like if one has something to hide? Mr Roberts is a
great blundering bison of a man. Arthur Waley was wonderful
with him, in true toreador form. He got badly gored once or
twice.—I gave what I consider a really beautiful performance
of a sweet, sunny-natured old lady, stinking of lavender and
looped with old lace, in whose mouth butter, even in the palmy
days when it could be procured, would not have melted.—

[1] E.S. has modernised the text of this poem, the original of which can be
found in her anthology, *The Atlantic Book of British and American Poetry*
(Boston, 1958; London, 1959).

This baffled Mr R. who could cheerfully have killed me. Osbert was marvellous, and kept his head to a degree one couldn't believe. All acquitted themselves (and were acquitted) with distinction, including dear Mr Wilson, of Bumpus.—The defendants were a deflated, noiseless Comus-rout. . . .

57. *To Dr Dorothea Walpole*

1 July 1941   Renishaw Hall

Dear Dr Walpole,

I did not write at first, because I knew you would be overwhelmed with letters, but I have felt for you so very deeply in your great sorrow and terrible loss.[1]

How much we all shall miss him!—My brother Osbert and I talk of this every day. We are only three—(my two brothers and myself)—of the many, many people to whom he has shown endless kindness, practical sympathy and help,—and such a wide and generous understanding of motives, of aims, pioneer work, of everything that came under his eyes.—There can never have been a more generous-minded man, or a man with a broader outlook, and all this in addition to his own fine work. —How did he ever find time to do *that* work, and all those kindnesses?—Osbert showed me your letter; I can understand what a brother he must have been, knowing the *person* he was.

I remember so well the time, many years ago, when Hugh and I were both on the committee that was going to choose a present for Thomas Hardy on his 80th birthday,—all the givers and signatories had to be under a certain age,—I forget now what age. But Hugh said, suddenly: 'We must ask May Sinclair.' 'Oh,' said somebody, 'she is *much* over the age limit.' 'I don't care,' said Hugh. 'She must be asked. It will hurt her dreadfully from every point of view if she is not.'

Only a small thing, perhaps, but so typical of that delicate feeling for others, that warm kindliness.

We have been more angry,—are more angry—than you can

[1] Sir Hugh Walpole died on 1 June 1941.

know, over the mean, petty, *envious* notice in *The Times*, and that letter from the man Pollock. He is disgraced for ever by having written such a letter. We feel terribly about this pain having been added to what you are bearing in grief, and the dreadful suddenness of that grief.

In what contrast is that mean, petty, cheative envy to Hugh's generous warm recognition of qualities in every writer of worth.

And in what contrast is that meanness to the noble tributes of T. S. Eliot, Sir Kenneth Clark, and J. B. Priestley. Those will remain. The others will go where all dirty things go.

You must not dream, please, of answering this letter.—I just had to try and express how much I feel for you and for Hugh's brother in your grief,—and to tell you how much we shall miss him.

Believe me, the deepest sympathy, Yours sincerely, Edith Sitwell.

58. *To Merula Guinness*

7 August 1941   Renishaw Hall

My dear Merula,

I did not write for some days, because I suspect that you are very like me and cannot *bear* to be touched when one is un-happy,—at first, I mean.—I think it is terrible not being allowed one's privacy, at first,—and I know how utterly wretched you must have been, and are.

These last few days must have been beyond any words, before Alec's ship went. My dear, I have thought of you both *so much*. I presume his ship *did* go, didn't it?—I mean, the last I heard was, that it was about to leave, and I am writing this to you on that assumption.

Oh how I hope and pray this frightful war will soon be ended, and Alec at home with you again, and working again.—How sad I was, and Osbert was, that it wasn't possible to see him before he went. It was those infernal household rows,—

and they had been promised a week's absolute time to themselves, partly to rest and go to bed early, partly to do the rest of
their confounded spring cleaning!—It *would* happen, just at
that moment.

I saw Charles Morgan some time ago,—(his visit, bringing,
as it were, a trail with him, was one of the reasons the household
had to go, subsequently, into purdah!)—and we talked of
Alec. He said that Alec is far the finest young actor of our
time, and in short, the only *romantic* one.—I can never remember if C.M. is, or is not, still dramatic critic of *The Times.*—
You and Alec must meet him, some time. I know you don't
know him, because I asked him.

Osbert is off to stay with Queen Mary *again* next week! It is
becoming a habit.

I have finished,—as far as knitting is concerned—your son's
and my cousin's white woolly suit. It must now be ironed by
Barbara, and I will then send it.—This will be in a day or two,
for she has a shattering cold in her head, and I do not wish her
to sneeze over it.—When it does come, will you please tell me
if it does, or doesn't, fit him? A jury of matrons sat on it, and
seemed to think it would.

Dear Merula, how much you must have felt leaving your
house, even though it meant your going home to your parents.
—One's own surroundings mean so much to one, when one is
feeling miserable.

I do hope I shall see you very soon. I tell you who I hope
to see next week: Miss Martita Hunt and Mr Gielgud, for they
will be appearing at Sheffield. (Mr Gielgud I have not met,
yet.)—Again I shall be in purdah,—this time Kitty and Susan
will be going away for a holiday, and I shall be left with a
housemaid and kitchenmaid, living on kippers, but I shall ask
them to come to tea.

I think of you so much. Bless you. Much love from Edith.

59. *To Merula Guinness*

Wednesday [Summer 1941]   Renishaw Hall

My dear Merula,

... I went to stay with Sachie, and got back here just in time
for the bores.—Sachie is writing the greatest book he has written
yet, but is the prey of every kind of chattering magpie and
busybody.[1] When I was there, I glowered at them through my
spectacles, and frightened them, but I expect the effect has
worn off by now.—I seem to have the effect on some people of
terrifying them, but cannot make out *why*. I should have thought
that never was there a milder woman ...

I've been trying to work, but the infestment made it impossible, and has so debilitated me that I have gone flabby, and
can't, for the moment. Why *cannot* those sort of people go and
consort together. Why come here?—Do you hate a fashionable
voice?—I remember, once, asking a now deceased cousin of
mine for a description of some woman. He replied: 'Oh, an
empty sardine tin on a sandy shore!' It fits this person, too.

I am waiting for proofs of what I *pretend* is an anthology for
children.[2] But of course it isn't. When the book appears, I'll
send it to you. I don't know when it will be out. It contains a
good deal of your beloved Herrick.

Osbert is going *again* to stay with Queen Mary next month.
She has started 'giving lifts' to the forces, and the other day,
when out driving with the Princess Royal and Osbert,—seeing
a youth in Air Force uniform, trudging along, she stopped the
motor, and the youth was propelled into it. It wasn't until he
got in that the awful truth of the company he found himself in,
dawned upon him. First, he looked at the Princess Royal, and
thought: It can't be true. Then he looked at H.M. and saw that
it *was*. Osbert says the poor boy threw a fit, and was too
frightened to say where he wanted to go, so found himself in

---

[1] *Splendours and Miseries*, published in 1943.
[2] *Look, the Sun!* published on 29 September 1941.

Bath when he probably wanted to go in exactly the opposite direction.

Much love to you, dear, Yours affectionately, Edith.

60. *To Alec Guinness*

7 September 1941   Renishaw Hall

My dear Alec,

I received your letter just over a fortnight ago,—between that and three weeks. And I should have written to you long, long ago—(your letter took a great time in coming, anyhow)—but two days after I received it, a really terrifying telegram reached me, about my old friend in Paris, via unoccupied France, and I have been in such truly dreadful grief and distress, and have been, too, so busy trying to do something to help that the days have passed without my writing any other letters.

The telegram was worded, to my Bank; 'Tell Edith Sitwell send money urgent', then, in French, 'situation désespérée'. As you know, 'désespérée' is about 100 per cent worse in French than 'desperate' in English.—The friend in question is an Englishwoman married to, and deserted by, a Norwegian, the sister of my governess who brought me up and was like a mother to me. She—(Madame Wiel) was my secretary and looked after the flat in Paris, where my darling little cat who has been my constant companion for fourteen years, and whom I love most dearly, is.—I have been sending her money *every* month,—and there has been some mistake. *Not* mine. She must just think I deserted her. And I *suppose* my poor little cat must have had to be put to sleep. She, Madame Wiel, must have starved. The whole thing has been a nightmare.

Well that, my dear Alec, is why I haven't written before.— The officials responsible have been most kind,—and are doing everything they can to help. It seems some clerk just forgot to include her name on a list. But forgetfulness of that kind costs the victims rather dear. God knows just what that forgetfulness *has* done. It cannot be traced, yet, who has been responsible for this ghastly thing happening—but that is what is supposed to have happened. . . .

I had, some time ago, to read a life of Mrs Siddons for those confounded Women I had to write about.[1]—Even reading a thoroughly bad book, one feels her greatness. She must have been like a tidal wave, or like some other gigantic force of nature. The description someone gave of her 'taking the earth' (as Constance) 'not for a shelter, not for a grave, or for a resting-place, but for a throne.' The description of her 'walk which affects you like seeing a whole procession'—all gives you the impression of mental and physical genius.

Beyond that—before that dreadful telegram came, I was hard at work writing poetry, and am going, I trust, to have a small book in the autumn, which of course I shall send you; and was also reading up for an enormous book I am going to do about Elizabeth. It ought to give me great scope, because of the enormous contrasts,—the contrasts between the splendour and the amazing fantastic clothes, and the horrible squalor of the beggars and underworld, the contrast between the vast genius and the actual enlightenment, apart from genius of Shakespeare, and the vile and monstrous, black cruelties of the time.—Also, I was getting on with my book on poetry.

I had a letter from Pavlik Tchelitchew, that great painter of whom you have heard me speak, in which he said that Auden has had 'a terribly offerly Flop'. Such a good expression. By 'offerly' he means awfully. His letters—he usually writes to me once a week—are perfection. Once, crossing the Atlantic, he wrote: 'Oh, yesterday was so terribly offerly. Oh yesterday was so offerly terribly. Oh the sea she go up and she go down. Oh the ship she go down she go up. All ways at once, and for no reason—choos' (in other words 'just') 'like our Revolution.' Such a good description, both of the sea and the Russian revolution, I think! . . .

[1] *English Women*, Britain in Pictures Series (1942).

61. *To Ann Pearn*

21 September 1941   Renishaw Hall

Dearest Ann,

Thank you for your letter. I would be obliged if you will be so kind as to send this letter to Rache Lovat Dickson for me.

I am very anxious to be published by Messrs Macmillan, for whom I have a great respect, based on the reports that reach me from their authors of their kindness and ability.

I will, therefore, accept the 10 per cent royalty on this book of poems, though I consider it a very low royalty, and must point out that I am a poet of such established reputation and of such fame, that the publication of a new book of poems by me, after a lapse of years, should, if properly handled, attract the greatest attention and obtain a most favourable sale.—Whilst I will accept this 10 per cent royalty for this book of poems, at the same time, as I am sure you will be the first to agree, I cannot possibly accept a contract which saves up the money earned by one book, to be paid as an advance on the next, which is what the offer I have received would seem to suggest. But I think there *must* be a mistake about this detail in the offer.

I cannot make out how the sum it is suggested I should be paid in advance on *Eliȝabeth*, can be regarded as an advance also on the poems, when they will by that time have been out for fully a year. But I renounce all idea of an advance for this book of poems, though I consider that the sums earned for it should be paid on agreed dates.

I agree to the *terms* for *Eliȝabeth*, though I fear I cannot agree to the manner in which it is suggested that the advance should be paid. I must earnestly ask Messrs Macmillan to reconsider this. My financial position is about as bad as it could be,—indeed, most urgent, as I have lost all my possessions and most of my income. I *cannot* go on being supported by Osbert: it simply is not fair on him, and it is most painful for me. I *must* earn money: I must pay my way. I do not wish to speak about my financial affairs, but if you like, I will tell you

the actual sum that I now have a year, and you will understand
that it is a matter of the utmost urgency that I should earn
money.

Leaving that aside, in any case a life of *Elizabeth* written by
me is a first-class proposition. I would therefore ask Messrs
Macmillan to pay me £*100 now* on account of *Elizabeth*, and
£100 in a year's time.

I am sure that Messrs Macmillan will see the justice of what
I say, and that some arrangement can be made which will
please both the parties concerned. Much love, Yours affectionately Edith.

62. *To Ree Gorer*

10 January 1942   Renishaw Hall

... How awful it all is, and how insanely futile and wicked.
Anything one can say would be just stupid; there isn't anything
to be said. Excepting that one hopes, now the Russians seem
to be giving the Germans what they have asked for, that
perhaps the whole frightful thing will soon be over. Do you
suppose those infernal Japs would give over, if the war col-
lapsed in Europe?

... Here I have stayed, for a whole year, with the exception
of one week spent at Sachie's—without moving—for what is
there to move for? ... one tends to go on with one's daily life,
and regard the whole time,—excepting for the unspeakable
horror and disaster of it,—as a railway journey which has to be
undertaken. But when one thinks of the thousands of millions
of wrecked lives, it is a little difficult to think of any life as
continuing at all.

... I try and work—writing poetry and reading up for and
planning out my book on Elizabeth Tudor. I have never known
anything to touch the whopping lies Froude tells about Henry
the 8th. Indeed, nobody writing at that time,—Protestant or
Catholic—seems able to speak the truth for two consecutive
minutes. Foxe's *Book of Martyrs*, which I am being obliged to

read, annoys me *very* much. I have, naturally, the greatest reverence for the extraordinary bravery of the martyrs, but I should like to wring Foxe's neck. Nasty, smug, self-complacent creature. And not one word about the treatment of the Catholics!

Christmas this year was particularly trying. I was driven to tea with a neighbour who had, staying with him, a lady who had been 'upset', by the war. The village motor, which drove me there, disappeared into thin air the moment it had delivered me, and I was left there for two hours,—listening to the following sort of conversation:

'Oh, Miss Sitwell, what a *beautiful* name yours is! I think S is such a beautiful letter. It always makes me feel I am getting underneath something, when I hear it! Don't you sometimes feel you would like to get underneath something? I always want to get underneath anything!'—Since the time when Sachie, as a boy of nineteen, was asked by a lady if he ever pressed his ear to the ground and listened to the dawn, I don't think I have come across anything comparable. Now, I should have enjoyed it if I could have undergone the experience in your and Geoffrey's company. But as it was, I simply blasphemed.

Beryl[1] has become such a *midwife*! She is always delivering unwanted babies into other people's houses. She has just sent us someone whom Osbert can't stand and I haven't seen for 15 years, to try and get in here. She has an invariable flair for the people one least wants to see. The last thing she tried to do was to land us for the duration with a couple of Italianate brothers (English by nationality, of course) who walk, or seem to walk, when seen from the rear, like demented metronomes from the waist downwards. . . .

63. *To Ree Gorer*

9 March 1942   Renishaw Hall

. . . *Street Songs* is having really terrific reviews. Of course the

---

[1] Beryl de Zoete.

Undertakers Gazette and the *East Anglian Advertiser* speak about 'these pleasant pages' and tell me where I get off, and a Mr Austin Clarke in some Irish paper says that though it is obvious that I feel things, my technique is so bad that I can't express it,—or words to that effect. But on the other hand, *The Times Literary Supplement*, which I can't help feeling is slightly more important, has fairly let itself go, about 'this majestic assurance', 'noble and unassailable simplicity', 'the true greatness of her poetic art'. And Stephen Spender, who never, I think, cared much for my poetry before, now says the poems are extremely beautiful.

... I am working away hard at Elizabeth. I find the divorce trouble about Mary Queen of Scots and Bothwell started with their playing golf together! I now think that woman is one of the greatest murderesses and most evil liars in the whole of history. The book will be a very sinister one, I think. But I have only just started it.

... A certain eminent author has returned to England, having been absent for some years. I am told it has had a serious effect on the wine shortage. The other day he went to lunch with a friend of mine who is sorry for him. She heard a loud commotion in the hall, and going out, found his extremely large frame being supported by her very small elderly maid. 'Just one more step, Sir', said the maid, patting his arm—'and you will be there!' 'Oh, I am so giddy, Oh I *am* so upset!!' he groaned. 'Poor gentleman', the maid whispered to my friend, 'nearly blind, isn't he?'

We have news, occasionally, from, or rather of, Father. He was very ill, but seems to be recovering. He is also very dictatorial with the nurses and doctors, and, we hear, was extremely rude to the matron when she wished him a happy Christmas.—When that happens, he usually shuts his eyes irritably, moves his head from side to side, and says '*I know!!*' So amiable!

Forgive this dull boring letter, but I am living a kind of odd muffled existence, mentally. Only not muffled when I am feeling horrible sadness (and it is true that is most of the time) or writing poetry.

64. *To Denton Welch*

14 September 1942   Renishaw Hall

Dear Mr Welch,

It is the greatest pleasure to me to sign my *Street Songs* for you, and I have done so. I have only just received your letter and the book.

I cannot tell you how much my brother Osbert, with whom I am staying, and I, enjoyed your alarming experience with Mr Sickert.[1] We laughed till we cried—though really in some ways it was no laughing matter. But one thing came out very clearly, and that is, that you are a *born writer*!

Nothing could have been more admirable, for instance, than your description of the stringy man who was about to lose his hair.—There was always a person of that description at his parties in the past, and one never found out why they were there, or what was the link.

We knew Mr Sickert very well, and my brothers have often undergone that dancing and singing experience. But the boots are new to us.

We never found out why he behaved like that. He could be kindness itself. I can't tell you how kind he was to me when I was seventeen, and trembled with shyness when spoken to!— Sometimes he would pretend to be ninety. At other moments he would give recitations from *Hamlet*. I think his one aim was to observe reactions! As I say, we were full of admiration for the *writing* of your adventure. And my brother Osbert was going to write to Mr Connolly to tell him how very greatly we admired it.

Our one sadness is that Mr P. Wyndham Lewis is absent from England. We are determined that when he returns, you *must* be asked to write a reminiscence of a meeting with him. What are you writing now?

I do hope you have recovered completely from your terrible accident, and that you are able to paint.

[1] Denton Welch's essay 'A Visit to Sickert at St Peter's' was published in Cyril Connolly's periodical *Horizon*, September 1942.

And I hope, very much, that we shall meet one day. I'll promise not to sing, or to dance! Believe me, Yours sincerely, Edith Sitwell.

P.S. I think the page in my book that is meant to be signed must be of blotting paper. It is like that in all the copies of the 1st edition!

65. *To Ann Pearn*

16 September 1942   Renishaw Hall

Dearest Ann,

Thank you so much for your letter. I think it is extremely good of Rache not to expect me to do actual slave labour for him, unpaid.

He seems not to realise that I am an *expert* on the subject of *poetry*. Nor, apparently, does he realise that I left Faber's very largely because they were so impertinent as to offer me £50 in advance for a book on poetry,[1] and that was *before* I had had the very great success I have had with *Street Songs*. Although Rache is my publisher, he seems to have no idea whatever of the position I now have.

Mr Gollancz gave me £500 for my anthology, and £100 for my *Look, the Sun!*

If you think £50 (and the sum accrued up to two months after the publication) *is* fair, I will, of course, take it. I will be guided absolutely by you. But in any case, I must have the *advance now*. I cannot go on living as I am. My poverty is really dreadful, and I am eaten alive by demands for money. If they give me £100,—then I would take £50 *now*, and £50 and the rest of the sum earned by sales up to two months after publication, *then*.

The scale of my royalties seems to me quite fair. As I say, I will be guided *absolutely* by you in all this, only I *do* want the advance now. Christmas is coming on, and all my tips to servants, etc., and I have had to pay for typing, which in this case was very expensive.

[1] *A Poet's Notebook*, published by Macmillan 30 April 1943.

Oh yes, one thing more. They have forgotten to put in any clause about paying for copyright of those passages I have quoted. I probably will have to pay Arthur Symons, etc. Would it not be best for them to say they will pay *up* to a certain sum, without paying the sum to me, and then I would let them know as the demands come in.

It is *extremely* generous of Mr Gollancz to let me have those quotations. I have always liked him extremely as a person, and this confirms my feeling.

Rache seems to have no idea, either from his offer, or from his letters to me, that this is an extremely important book. He knows nothing about poetry. But unless I am mistaken, he is going to have a very big shock.

By the way, when is some more money coming from Macmillans for *Street Songs?* There have been, I think, two fresh editions since I had their first account. Do those come under slave labour too?

If this book is on the short side, I can easily give him some more. Will you please tell him that?

I would very much like to do a play for Mr Gielgud, and I'll think up an Eccentric.

Ann, dear, you are an angel to be so sympathetic about poor Evelyn. I just am broken down by this horror. Best love, all gratitude. Take care of yourself. I hope you have got my letter about your high blood pressure. Yours affectionately, Edith.

Of course I know I can rely on your invariable tact to put all this to Rache.

66. *To Denton Welch*

21 September 1942   Renishaw Hall

Dear Mr Welch,

I was delighted to get your charming letter. And I cannot tell you [how] deeply touched and pleased I am that you should think of dedicating your book to me.[1] It has indeed pleased me

---

[1] *Maiden Voyage* (1943), to which E.S. contributed a foreword.

far more than you know, and of course I accept with the greatest pleasure. Thank you.

I look forward to seeing it with eagerness. I wish the Sickert tea party was going to be included; but if this new book is half as good as the description of that tea party, it will be admirable. There were so many facets of admirableness, too. Your partial self-portrait (the portrait of the shyness in you), your portrait of the friend you took with you,—the stringy man, of course, and also, in some odd way, you succeeded in getting the actual *movements* of Sickert dancing.

I didn't quite explain what I meant when I said he wanted to 'observe reactions'. He was not treating one like a mouse. But he wanted to know what one would do.

My brothers were present when Mr Sickert got Wyndham Lewis so entangled that he had to invent, on the spur of the moment, a character in his book *Tarr* who had not figured in that work. The trap laid was, I am told, of a really marvellous ingenuity.

Lady Oxford *would* have been right, *in certain cases*. But in that particular case—perhaps the only case I know, it added greatly to the general sense of danger, and the power to disconcert.

My brother Osbert is away at present. He will be very glad to know I have heard from you. He takes in *Horizon*, so it was he who saw the tea party first—and, as I say, was full of admiration.

Oh, I am very distressed to hear your health is so precarious. I do hope that you do not suffer pain. I know nothing about what happened, excepting what I saw in the tea party record. I hope so much that you will recover from it, even if it takes a very long time. But it obviously is not true that you 'are not much use to anybody else' as you said in your letter.

I shall send you my notes on poetry when they come out— sometime in the new year, I think.

I hope we shall meet very soon. Of course it is singularly difficult in war-time. Still, we *will* meet, and, I hope, very soon. With all best wishes, and *so many* thanks for the dedication, so very pleased and touched thanks. I am yours very sincerely, Edith Sitwell.

67. *To Denton Welch*

25 October 1942   Renishaw Hall

Dear Mr Welch,

I am so truly sorry not to have written before, but I have been
rather ill, so you must please forgive me.

I cannot tell you how *delighted* I am to hear your news. It is
splendid that the book has been taken, and I do hope it will
have an enormous success. I am looking forward tremendously
to reading it. If it is anywhere near as good as your adventure
with Mr Sickert, it will be very, very good indeed.

Yes, Mr Read is a most delightful, kind, and charming being.
He was a shy and charming youth, and was part of the happy
life of my youth, when I lived in London. We used to have
large tea-parties on Saturdays, and Herbert Read and two
others, sometimes four others, of our very intimate friends used
to stop on afterwards, and help cook the supper.

Herbert Read was a constant and delightful companion, and
we always felt happy with him.

When will the book appear?—I hope very soon.—I have to
pull myself together, and get my notes on poetry ready for the
publishers. It is a terrific job, because some are rather abstruse
—or would be to persons who do not habitually read poetry.
They seem to me clear as daylight, but the publishers always
want one to explain the unexplainable.

You must, I think and hope, be feeling extremely happy that
your book is coming out.—It is a wonderful event in one's life,
when one's first book comes out.—My first book was one of
five pages; it had dark brown paper covers, and I paid £5. 10s,
—a vast sum to me at that time, to have it published. It came
out at 6d—its name was *The Mother*, and it is now worth
anything up to £10 a copy!! Isn't that strange?

This is a very dull letter, but I still feel very odd.—I will
write when I feel better and more alive. But I did first want to
write you a note to tell you how delighted—truly delighted—I
am to hear your news, and to send you all my very best wishes.
Believe me, Yours very sincerely, Edith Sitwell.

68. *To Denton Welch*

11 November 1942   Renishaw Hall

Dear Mr Welch,
I am really *delighted* with the book, indeed the more I read it, the better I am pleased with it.

It is obvious—as I've said so often that it is redundant to repeat it, and yet I must repeat it—that you are a real writer. Nobody but a real writer would get such exact descriptions,— the 'dog's lips' of the schoolmaster, for instance,—that description could not be bettered by anyone. For some reason, as well as being an accurate physical description, it gives one the life and mentality of the man. All the people are very alive, and, as I said in my former letter, one moves and lives inside their minds.

I am particularly struck, amongst other things, by your evocation of that appalling corpse surrounded by flies. It is a really wonderful piece of spiritual and mental horror,—and by your evocation of that horrible hotel in which you were stranded for a night.—You have got, among other gifts, a real gift for that particular kind of writing, and I advise you to write a dramatic, packed, short story with those sorts of atmosphere in it.

But apart from everything else, I find it an extremely *moving* book. I am, myself, very much moved by it. It has a touching and beautiful quality of youth and innocence about it, which has none of the silliness of youth,—only a longing for experience, and a moving longing for warmth, as well as a sad loneliness.

The end is dreadfully sad, and Vesta is so real that I long to know what has become of her.—I find the writing about that last scene really *extraordinary* . . . those lips that were 'pale as I had seen them sometimes on cold days'—is, I think, a wonderful phrase. It is quite horribly moving, and gives me a feeling of despair, that nothing will ever be quite right again.

I don't really *know* the book yet, and shall be writing again

later, but I feel really impelled to tell you what I feel, even at
this early stage. (Though the book has been with me, now, for
a while, the fact that it is manuscript needs more careful reading
than with print. By that, I mean the *shape* of a sentence needs
more examination. For in print, the shape immediately hits one
in the eye.—This is so with *all* manuscripts.)

Yes, I feel the contract is all right for a first book. I may say
at this point, that no publishers at this moment give large
advances. Some try not to give any. Next book, I think it
might be as well if you go to our agents. But we can think
about that later.

This is just a forerunner of another letter. But *I am excited*
about the book, and wanted to tell you so again.

All of my best and warmest wishes for the book and for
yourself, Yours very sincerely, Edith Sitwell.

69. *To Alec Guinness*

Monday [1943]   Renishaw Hall

... How *maddening* it was that I missed you, on Saturday. I
left the Club at 9 in the morning, and had one ceaseless rush all
day.—Then, I had to leave to go to stay with Mrs Gordon
Woodhouse, the harpsichordist, at Stroud,—to see her, and
also because I am hoping to be given,—yes *given*,—a house in
Bath. ...

It is very like a Tchekhov play, the idea of the house in Bath.
Either one will go on talking about it for ever, and not buy it,
—or will buy it, and not have the money to live in it! However
the thought of it is fun. I *may* buy (all this is between ourselves)
Mrs Thrale's house in Gay Street. It has a very bleak, ornate,
Beardsley 19th-century facade looking on the street,—two
huge rooms with enormous bay windows looking out on a long
paved garden at the back, which, again, looks on a park, and it
is at present inhabited by an old lady of 96, who is going to be
moved from the house next month, because a nurse cannot be

found for her.—Doctor Johnson frequently comes and tries to browbeat her by glaring at her,—but I shan't mind that, for I have a theory that we shall get on well together. I am a born listener, and have a sense of respect. So I don't expect to be 'tossed'. Nor will *you* be.

It was delightful staying with Violet Woodhouse, who is a very old friend, and not only a *very* fine artist, but a most remarkable and enchanting woman,—very beautiful, too. One has no idea what Mendelssohn's music for the *Midsummer Night's Dream* is really like,—its wonder,—until one has heard Violet play it on the virginals. It is then shown as having been woven by one of Shakespeare's own fairies out of cobwebs.—She played me Henry VIII's own setting of *O Western Wind, when wilt thou blow*. Have you heard it? That man simply had genius as a composer—(whilst being a very bad and boring poet)—What a strange character. I can believe anything of him. That particular song is exactly like the sound of a dark soft south wind blowing among flowering trees . . .

70. *To John Lehmann*

May 28, 1943   Renishaw Hall

Dear Mr Lehmann,

Your letter delighted me. I am *very* happy that you like my *Notebook*,[1]—it has given me the greatest pleasure to think that you do. And it has given me so much pleasure that you have asked me to write for *New Writing and Daylight*. I shall love to.

Now the series of literary reminiscences or sketches for a poet's autobiography would be rather difficult for me—for this reason, that Osbert is writing his autobiography, and that if I were to write of other poets personally—much of our material would clash. But of course if you were meaning a series of notes about what had formed the trend of one's mind, that would be easier.—Or what about further notes on Shakespeare?

[1] *A Poet's Notebook*, published on 30 April.

I am intending to write a large book on the old gentleman. The Shakespeare notes would be the most enjoyable to do. I hope the idea pleases you.

I am very grateful to you for sending me the *Penguin New Writing*. It seems to me one of the most admirable numbers you have produced. It is really packed full of interest. I am astonished that one book by so many varieties of writers *could* have this great vitality, which makes it into an entity. Mr Capetanakis's poem seems to me really astounding. It has a force and concentration of tragedy, and a real fire and passion which must prove to anyone that he has the life of the poet before him.—I am going to write to him about the poem, which has moved me greatly.

Until I saw these new poems of his in *New Writing* I had never cared for Mr MacNeice's poems. But I am most deeply impressed by these. 'Brother Fire' and 'Whit Monday' seem to me *superb*, and I shall probably feel the same about the others when I know them as well as I, by now, know those two.

My admiration is great for this whole number.

In September, I shall be coming to London again—to lecture to schoolmasters on poetry,—and look forward to seeing you then very much indeed. Believe me, Yours sincerely Edith Sitwell.

—— —— says *you* won't have her poems. No. No more will Messrs Macmillan. *Or* Messrs Faber. Now she is going to send the whole lot to me, and will I tell her where to send them.

Have you a feud with any particular Publishing Firm? If so, let me know, and I'll avenge you.—She is getting up a Poets' Reading at Tunbridge Wells.—It is all very ageing, and if one didn't have to run so fast, to get away, I know that one would, by now, be positively crippled as the result of all the strokes and heart attacks, etc., brought on by every fresh development. I'm *worn out*.

71. *To Stephen Spender*

20 June 1943   Renishaw Hall

Dear Stephen,
Thank you a thousand times for sending me the Lorca.[1] What a
wonderful poet, and what a wonderful thing for him that he had
such a poet as translator.

I cannot bear to think that he is dead. It seems one of the
most terrible things that has happened to us. How I hate the
hate that killed him.

His poems have such an intoxication that when reading
them, and for many, many hours after, days after, one feels like
a bumble-bee that has been for a whole afternoon in the heart
of a tiger-lily flower. (We once had a lily here that bore *108*
flowers on one stalk: it was photographed naturally for all the
gardening papers. The bees came from miles and miles, and
there were the most disgraceful Bacchanalian scenes: bees
hardly able to find their way home. That is what I feel like
about Lorca: excepting that one does *not* fall asleep, but
becomes, on the contrary, extremely awake.)

The poems have an incredible beauty. How wonderful is the
girl gathering lilies

> 'with the grey arm of the wind
> encircling her waist'

—that poem has haunted my mind ever since you first translated it.

I am so happy to have this book, given me by you.—Again,
this book contradicts what Shelley said about translation. This
has all the honey left to it, and all the heady flower scents, and
all the human blood, too. What a terrific poem is the 'Lament
for Mejías'.

The murder of Lorca seems symbolic. It is just one of the
most terrible and significant things that has happened to us: I
find myself repeating it over and over again.

[1] This was probably the edition in English of Lorca's poems translated by
Stephen Spender and J. L. Gili, published by The Dolphin in 1939.

I was so delighted by your letter.—Lady Crewe is beside herself with pleasure about the prospective reading. She telephoned and told Osbert. We long to know all the proposed details.

I have received from the gentleman who owns the Blue Book Press, South Croydon, a letter assuring me that he has 'noted' that I am 'interested in poetry'. He has, it seems, written a book of poems entitled *In my Garden*. This work, 'although it has received quite a nice notice from the *Publishers Gazette*, has not received a notice from the bigger papers, such as *The Times Literary Supplement*.' If, on reading this work, I 'care to increase its sales by getting for it the right kind of publicity', its author will be 'glad to recognise your services'.

'Now, then, will you be tempted?' as an old lady wrote to me when she asked me to a tea party to meet the great-niece of a former editor of the *Wide World Magazine*,—will you come in with me on this? I suppose we shall have to hand over part of our rake-in to the Editor of the *T.L.S.* . . . Still, the author is evidently going to make it worth one's while. The only snag is, I see his business telephone has been cut off, which looks sinister. . . . He says his sister in New Zealand thinks it is a lovely book.

Oh, dear, it is so sad.

We long to hear all about your adventures at Dorothy Wellesley's reading. It takes place on Wednesday or Thursday, if I mistake not. I hope she will have a great success, poor woman. . . . Incidentally, Walter Turner is really exceeding himself. Stephen Tennant has written me a very nice letter, covered with a design of roses painted by himself. I am about to answer this. What an extraordinary book Einstein's is;[1] thank you for telling me about it. I am looking forward with the greatest excitement to seeing the sonnets. I do hope they are nearly finished.

Osbert's best wishes. Love to Natasha. Affectionately, Edith.

[1] Probably *Greatness in Music* by Alfred Einstein (1941).

72. *To Ree Gorer*

21 June 1943   Renishaw Hall

Darling Ree,

I miss you and Geoffrey more and more, if such a thing were possible. I can't tell you what it is like being in London, and your not being there. After all, the moment I arrived, the very first thing I always did was to telephone to you. A, take off my hat, B, telephone to you,—the hat being taken off first because I am not good at telephoning and cannot hear if I have anything over my ears!

Oh how much I wish you were here, for a million reasons. One being that I have so much to say that is difficult to write, [another] being a very funny joke that loses its flavour on paper.

Osbert and I are living a sort of Robinson Crusoe existence, with one very aged, fearfully bad-tempered good Man Friday. Good Man Friday has the temperament of a prima donna, and nearly as great a hatred of the arts. The diatribes of certain women journalists against anyone possessed of intelligence, have a fearful effect on him, and he and his daughter, with her piano, have started a kind of reign of terror. I wish the Government would put a tax on pianos for the incompetent.

However, Osbert has brought off a coup about pianos with the gardener's wife, who has recently purchased a piano to be hit by her four-year-old daughter. Osbert, with his eyes starting out of his head, told the proud mother that the Death Watch Beetle had got into the piano, and that it must be returned *immediately* to the manufacturers, otherwise the whole of the furniture will start ticking. The advice was effectual. But I can't believe it will be lasting.

Did I tell you about the fearful row there was when I was in London? I may have, but I also may not, for time had to elapse before I could bear to speak of it. It was after the reading. A certain excitable lady got over-excited, tried to go for me, was prevented by two editors and a famous M.P., smacked the

M.P.'s face, and was taken outside, where of course no taxi could be found. She therefore sat on the pavement and proceeded to raise Cain again. I was dreadfully sorry for her, poor thing, for I think she is very unhappy owing to various causes. The repercussions seemed endless, but I think they are now dying down.

I've been given the most wonderful presents lately, as a tribute to my *Street Songs*: three Swinburne manuscripts, and *Macbeth* from the 2nd Folio. The Folio was an incomplete one, and was therefore taken to pieces.

73. *To Alec Guinness*

1 August 1943   Renishaw Hall

. . . It was so good to get news of you, *from* you. May you soon be back in England, and may we soon be going to a new First Night of yours, my dear. I cannot help feeling that the war *must* be over soon.

Merula sent me a photograph of Matthew, who looks like a sweet angel. But you'll have to keep him in a monastery: he has too much charm, evidently, and charm in Saints has died out with St Francis, I think. You can't have him grow arid. Besides, he couldn't!

I long to see you and to have a talk. Having begun to write again, I shall now write far more often: but my letters will be dull, because anything that I say must be spun out of my head, and from nothing outside, as I live a cloistered life.

I am sending you, *under separate cover*, today (it is all ready to go) my *A Poet's Notebook*, which has the notes on Shakespeare (considerably extended) which appeared in that American magazine. I've kept a first edition to send to you (it is now going into its third edition, though it only came out at the end of April). It is going by separate post, because, although I *hope* it may be possible to send it by air mail, I am not sure, and I want this letter to go by air.

How I long to discuss with you the way in which *Iago* ought to be acted. (I'm working on the play now, for I'm going to write a book on Shakespeare.) Do you notice how extraordinarily flat and dead all his speeches are? and shrunken in sound? Shakespeare never did anything by mistake, and he meant (I am certain), Iago to be small as the serpent that bruised the heel of Adam, that terrified Eve to her fall. It is very odd that that great critic Swinburne behaved as if Iago was a gigantic character. . . . Criminals, I am convinced—(*born* criminals) have no *colour* sense in morals—everything is on a dead level with no shading, and this is what we have, for the first time, with Iago. Don't you think so? I am expressing myself very badly, because I only began working on the play two days ago.

Then, too, I've got five million ideas about Lear. Oh, yes, and that amount about Othello himself, leaving Iago aside. Do you read Italian? I was reading Dante the other day, and thought this exactly described what Othello's hours must have been after Iago dropped his poison.

> Né *o*, sì tosto mai né *i* si scrisse,
> com'el s'accese e arse, e cener tutto
> convenne che cascando divenisse;
> e poi che fu a terra sì distrutto,
> la polver si raccolse per se stessa,
> e 'n quel medesmo ritornò di butto.

(in Laurence Binyon's translation):

> Never *O* nor *I* was written in such a gust
> Of speed as he took fire with, all allumed,
> But then must needs drop into ash and dust
> When down to the very ground he was consumed,
> Of its own motion re-combining there,
> The dust straightway its former shape resumed.

Terrific, isn't it? And there is a phrase which (from another Canto) exactly suits the daughters of Lear, who are always being compared to dogs: 'Dog-visaged from the cold.' Oh how tremendous that is! They *are* beings of the ultimate cold, are they not—Goneril and Regan?

By the way have you ever read Lancelot Andrewes' Sermons?

In one of the Sermons on the Nativity, he said that the *meaning* of the name Bethlehem, is 'the House of Bread'—one can hardly surpass *that* for splendour, can one?

74. *To Lord Keynes*

1 August 1943   Renishaw Hall

Dear Maynard,
I am at once almost too aghast and too touched at your kindness to know what to say.[1] When Osbert showed me your letter my feelings entered into an all-in wrestling match which is still going on. He *told* me he had written to you—but I didn't believe him.

I do not know what I can say to show my gratitude to you. I think I have never heard of anything so kind and so generous in all my life. And I feel it is not fair to accept it, but at the same time it would be ungracious not to. I do indeed thank you.

I had wanted the book so wildly for this reason. I have a particular feeling for Swinburne partly because, when I was seventeen, I ran away from my grandmother in Bournemouth, in order to put roses and pour libations of milk (and put a honeycomb) on Swinburne's grave in the Isle of Wight. This, of course, was in the days when, at seventeen, one must be clamped to an older female, or one's name was mud. Now I have several Swinburne manuscripts.

Then, too, I have written a poem in which I have incorporated a line of Ben Jonson's: *Out danced the babioun.* I am going to look out that poem of mine, and the workings of it, have them bound, and send them to you. This will take some little time, I suppose, but I shall see to it at once. With the very greatest gratitude and appreciation of your quite extraordinary kindness, Yours very sincerely, Edith Sitwell.

Osbert says I am one of the Gold-Diggers of 1943!!

[1] Lord Keynes had given E.S. a first edition of a volume of Swinburne, possibly inspired by her quotations from Swinburne in *A Poet's Notebook*.

75. *To Stephen Spender*

30 September 1943   Renishaw Hall

Dear Stephen,

I have been thinking so much of you and Natasha, all these days
since I have been back here.

I can't *bear* to think of her being ill, and of your both being
so worried and unhappy. I am saying this to you instead of to
her, because if one is ill, sometimes it is a terrible disturbance of
one's being to have it spoken of to oneself.—The more I know
her, and the more I think of her, I realise her—what she is like
—the more. That brightness, in the original real meaning of
the word—like a flower's or a jewel's brightness.

I really *do* feel her being ill as I should feel it if it happened
to a member of my family for whom I cared.

This is only a note. I shall be writing again in a few days about
the anthology. What we never settled was: are the poems to be
famous poems, or are they to be less well known poems?

In our *Sound* section, don't you think we might have
Skelton's 'Lullaby', and that thing on the House of Sleep, out
of Gower.—And if we are including famous poems, is not 'The
Eve of St Agnes' a transcendental example. Among small lesser
known poems, are not Peele's 'Bethsabe's Song' and the 'Song
at the Well' lovely examples? Do let us have a *long* anthology.

In re *Images*. I never quite know what is meant by an Image
—though it may sound idiotic. If it is what I think, shouldn't
those lines from Hopkins's 'May Magnificat' that I quoted in
the *Notebook*, and that lovely fragment about a boy whose hair
was like a sheaf of bluebells, go in? People *will* like Hopkins for
his rheumatic joints and swellings. I can't think why.

Oh, I've found such a *lovely* sentence in Ben Jonson's *Dis-
coveries*. I am sure you know it—but if you don't: 'It is said of
the incomparable Virgil, that he brought forth his verses like a
Beare, and after form'd them with licking.' It made me think of
the sentence of Cocteau's I quoted in my *Notebook*: 'We

become drunk with a strong honey, and that honey must sometimes be gathered from the paw of a very young bear.' It made me think of Mr Day-Lewis's wonderful translation, dedicated to you. (What a work of heaven that is, really.) I shall speak of all that in connection with each other in my next *Notebook.*

By the way, do you or don't you, think we ought to have lovely examples of translations in our book? They do enrich the country's poetry.

It isn't possible to work today, as the noise is transcendental, two poor deaf people having been added to the household. They, of course, can't hear the noise *they* are making, and it gives the others the excuse to roar like a flock of bulls. In addition, Mr —— ——, in spite of setbacks, is trying to get into the house. I know it is inhuman—but I *hate* bad poets, and when they interrupt me in work I could *kill* them. Love to you and Natasha from Osbert and me, Edith.

76. *To Colin Hampton*

3 November 1943   Renishaw Hall

Dear Mr Hampton,
Thank you so much for your very kind letter. I may say at this point that it has taken five days—yes, five—to reach here, for it is dated the 28th, and I've just this moment got it.

I cannot tell you what Osbert and I feel—hearing that there is a hope that the wonderful day when you came here may be repeated, perhaps when you are next in Sheffield. Nor can I tell you how great is our appreciation and our gratitude.[1]

It was an experience to be remembered always—hearing the Britten quartet for the first time under such circumstances: and the thought of hearing the Bloch quartet in such a manner is a tremendous prospect.—The Britten has an extraordinary explosive force. In spite of the fact that I've just had a most

[1] Colin Hampton was the 'cellist of the Griller Quartet, which had played privately for the Sitwells at Renishaw.

debilitating cold, it is still exploding in my head with a blinding light followed by new ideas, points of view, even new vision. I'm not sure that Britten hasn't been, spiritually, where Coleridge went before he wrote *The Ancient Mariner*—to those polar regions. (Have you read Professor Lowes's *The Road to Xanadu?*) Only Britten saw it, I think, from a freezing height, like a bird—very, very high up. And Coleridge saw it from the sea.

In a few days I shall be sending you an anthology (it was composed specially for reading in trains, and when marooned in hotels).[1] We look forward more than we can say to your next visit. We can *never* say what we feel about your great kindness. Yours very sincerely, Edith Sitwell.

77. *To Stephen Spender*

1 December 1943   Renishaw Hall

Dear Stephen,
So very many thanks for your letter.

I am so distressed to know what you are going through, and have gone through, with fatigue. I had better not begin to say what I feel about your being caught up and imprisoned in this miserable machine, when you ought to have your whole life for poetry. It is monstrous, and you must get out of it. Oh, if only that plan I told you about would materialise. But it has to go through department after department, and will take months and months. I *hope* it will come about. But hoping isn't much use when you are so tired as this, and longing for release. I hope you didn't have horrible experiences.

Do remember you must *never* write to me when it is difficult for you to do so, because of fatigue, or because poetry is waiting to be written. I said that before, and I could not mean anything more. I know what letter-writing can be, and how it is often the last straw.

I am very sad about our anthology; but sad as I am, the most important thing is that you should do your original work; and

[1] *Edith Sitwell's Anthology* (1940).

nothing must be allowed to take up your time when it is a question of that.

When, and if, we ever do the anthology, I've got suggestions to make, such as: (*Pattern*) Compare the feminine endings of 'Strephon and Klaius' with Keats's feminine endings: 'Sleep and Poetry' (first lines) and the 'Dark Lady's Song'. (That I had begun to do in other books, but I have now worked it out far more elaborately.) Compare these again with those endings of Pope's which could hardly be called 'feminine endings', but which have the faintest shadow falling from the last syllable.

Compare the lovely 'My truest treasure so traitorly was taken', with the ghastly 'The Assyrian came down', and go into the reasons for the difference: the slowness of 'My truest treasure', the alliteration—the awfulness caused by the 4-syllable Assyrian which makes the whole verse slippery. Compare these with Baudelaire; show how his alexandrines move with the slow unearthly pomp of great serpents.

Speak of very early poetry: show how in 'Under the Leavës Greene' the line 'Who but I? who but I? who but I?' has the exact sound of a certain bird-note. Thrushes shout it here from dawn to dusk in spring. I expect they are saying the same thing.

Compare some of Crashaw's *images* with some of Hopkins's. The 'primrose's pale cheek' (compared with the saint's) has the same strangeness as certain of Hopkins.

(Incidentally: I am convinced that Hopkins is a more important image-maker than prosodist. As far as other people are concerned, prosodical copies of him seem to me fatal.)

Ballads, and how they have led up to such wonders as 'For we'll go no more a-roving' and the splendours of that wonderful couplet in Burns 'Open the door to me-oh!':

> 'The wan moon is setting behind the white wave,
> And time is setting with me, oh!'

I'm *delighted* to hear about the novel, and extremely interested to hear about your new plan, though I always have a horror of anyone going away. Odd, considering how much I have lived out of England.

Will you soon be sitting on a committee with me as another

fellow-member? I hope so. Personally I look on the whole thing partly as a party. I'm hoarding up two poems I've done, to send to you. But *not* yet. I've had one for some time; but I think you should be rationed, or rather, one should ration oneself in the amount one sends you; for it is not fair to send too much. It takes you from your work. Oh my hands are almost too cold to form the letters of the words.

I comfort myself by reading Barents's *Voyage to Spitzbergen in 1596*, and other works of the same kind, like Van der Brugge. 'On October the 26, we saw the shadow of the glorious sun, for the last time.'

And that description of how their tent was blown down and they had nowhere to go excepting an open boat, among the ice, stared at by walruses and polar bears.

I've also been reading Le Corbusier's *Towards a New Architecture*, which is full of remarks applicable to modern poetry:

'The happy towns are those that have an architecture. Architecture can be found in the telephone and in the Parthenon.'

'Machinery includes economy as an essential factor leading to minute selection. There is a moral sentiment in the feeling for mechanics.'

I am using these in my new *Notebook*, which is progressing. Love to you and Natasha from Osbert and Edith.

78. *To Stephen Spender*

14 December 1943   Renishaw Hall

Dear Stephen,

I was more than delighted and happy to receive the lovely 'Spiritual Exercises', some of which I am proud to have known before they reached their maturity—lovely then, and lovely now. They have an extraordinary perfection of sense and form. You have, really, a genius for producing a form and spirit that are one,—a form 'arising out of the properties of the material.'

Nobody who was not a poet could guess that any *making* went to the poems. They seem to spring from you perfectly naturally like leaves from a bough, by a natural growth.

I find these poems start one on many different roads. Poetry ought to make one live, in one's own way, and these poems, like all your poems, make me live in my own way. Very few poets pack their lines with meaning as you do, and yet keep a universe of air round them. The lines are never breathless. Each meaning has its life of air. I hope I am explaining what I feel about them—which is much, and deep. I am *very* tired and despondent, and so find it difficult to express what I feel.

Realising that Christmas is upon us, and that you will therefore, probably, be unable to work at anything you want to,—I am sending you the poems I had been keeping back, so as not to interrupt you. *But you are not to read them until you feel inclined, and have nothing else to do.*

I sent you and Natasha, yesterday, my *Pleasures of Poetry*, which has *at last* turned up (a very old work). But it isn't my real Christmas card to you both.

That will be Sachie's new book, which I am expecting at any moment.[1] It *should* reach you before Xmas. I hope it will. It has some really gigantic things in it about the blitzes,—and one of the most extraordinary things about madness I have ever read. Also terrific things about beggars. It is a book of black sadness, but has a quality of greatness.

I hope you are not being driven mad by this wretched fireman's work. Really, looking at those poems, my blood boils as I think of it. . . .

Love to you and Natasha (to whom I am writing by the same post). 'They' now lose *all* letters, but I trust both will arrive. Edith.

And best wishes for Christmas. I hope you both gargle and take great care against the 'flu.

---

[1] *Splendours and Miseries*, published on 17 December.

79. *To John Lehmann*

December 14, 1943   Renishaw Hall

Dear John,

Thank you so much for your most kind, charming letter—one of the most charming I have ever received. I can't tell you how much pleasure it gave me, and it came (yesterday afternoon) at a moment when I was feeling nearly dead with depression, and changed everything for me completely.

Well, about that poem 'One Day in Spring', at last, I have got a reply from my poor afflicted Ann Pearn, my agent (who has been having shingles in the head, and consequent agony).

I told her exactly how many lines I'd taken from old poems, and she says if she were me—us—she *wouldn't* write to Duckworths. But just print the poem with a nice word, thanking them. I should think something like 'Certain lines in this poem appeared, originally, in my *Selected Poems* published by Messrs Gerald Duckworth, to whom grateful thanks are due for permission to reprint them.'

I am *certain* that will be *perfectly* all right. They always allow me to reprint, and are always kindness itself. Miss Pearn says it will be all right, and as she is more timid than any rabbit before a rattlesnake, if she says it is all right, *we* needn't bother. I have every intention of doing the same thing in my forthcoming book, which is nearly finished.

I always consult Miss Pearn about whom I have to ask, and if I have to ask them, about copyright.

I am particularly happy for that poem to appear with you.

I do hope your mother is better: I am so sorry to hear of her illness: and hope she will be very careful not to go out too soon. It is very dangerous. Here, at Sheffield and in the district, the flu is very, very bad indeed—a worse epidemic than in London; the military have had to be called in. Our Sheffield doctor was, at the beginning, very alarmed, as he had several cases of a very 'odd' type, which he was watching with great care. *All* the epidemics start from here—including small-pox

and meningitis. We began a lovely 'spotted fever' one in this
village three years ago, but after a flare-up it died down. But it
was heaven while it lasted. And there is a village called Clowne
three miles away which had small-pox endemically for years!!!
What a macabre Dekker-ish letter. I feel macabre. Nobody
knows what I am going through with my various invalids.—
Take as much care of yourself as you can. Hot drinks at night
should be your rule, and *do* put Benger's balsam up your nose.
It is wonderful. Yours ever, Edith S.

80. *To Denton Welch*

22 December 1943   Renishaw Hall

My dear Denton,
I call you this, and hope you will call me Edith,—I could not
possibly express how much delight your *exquisite* present has
given me. It is one of the most lovely rings I have ever seen.
And I really think you *must* have second sight—for I have
always longed for a pale topaz ring of that particular description and strangeness. But I couldn't have imagined this one,
which has a singular exquisiteness of workmanship, imagina-
tion and colour. It really *is* a *beauty*. It fits the first finger of my
left hand, as if it had been made for it. In fact it looks rather
as if we had been born together. (Perhaps we were, several
centuries ago.)

I do not know which has given me the most happiness, your
sweetness in giving it to me, and in having thought of it for
me,—or the intensive beauty of it. Both seem part of each
other.

I haven't, in this letter, given the faintest idea of the pleasure
it has given me. It is the one thing which has given me a feeling
of happiness, that has happened for ages.

I am so delighted *Maiden Voyage* has had such a great success. It deserved it thoroughly. But not all books that deserve
a success get it.—Elizabeth Bowen was full of admiration for
it—(she is a friend of mine, and spoke enthusiastically to me).

And I tell you who wrote to me with enthusiasm also—Mr Roger Senhouse, of Secker and Warburg. (I said 'spoke' but I should have said wrote,—at the end of a business letter about copyright.) *That* may be useful, in the long run. It is always as well to have two publishers on a lead.

I long to see the new book, and to hear more about it. Do, when you have time, tell me about it.

There has been a long gap of silence, but I've been very much under the weather. I came to London, and read at a Poetry Reading, but was taken miserably ill with the lowest possible blood pressure, no pulse, etc., lingered there a few days, and then returned. So I only saw the few people who were on the spot, and were either at the Reading so could be got hold of then, or who could have messages conveyed to them.

But I am hoping to be in London early in the spring, and I hope then you will come and spend the day with me, i.e. lunch first, and in the afternoon I'll get together a giant tea party. I'll write and arrange it with you well beforehand.

All the above-chronicled woes were brought on me by the events consequent on my father's death. We had a very unhappy family life, and his death (or rather, what we found out after) was entirely in character.[1]

I long to know more about your letter from your school-master. Of course, I can see he would be *furious*.

Poor Osbert had an awful thing happen to him. He described in an admirable short story, the crammer's where he was, when a boy (locality, house, etc.).[2] All the characters were imaginary, and he bestowed upon the crammer an imaginary wife. Alas! the imaginary wife was separated from her husband, and was a little mad. Little did Osbert know that the actual crammer's wife (whom he had never seen) was separated from the crammer and was a little odd. The lady brought a libel action, settled out of court with a payment of a large sum, and the book had to be withdrawn.

Osbert and I are really insistent that you should meet

[1] Sir George Sitwell died in Switzerland on 8 July 1943.
[2] 'Happy Endings' in *Dumb-Animal* (1930).

Wyndham Lewis. When and if he returns to England. We want a record of the meeting, in the style of the Sickert meeting.

I've got a book of poems half finished, and a notebook in progress.[1] Very best wishes for a happy Christmas–New Year.

Most touched, and most grateful and appreciative thanks, Yours ever, Edith S.

81. *To Stephen Spender*

6 January 1944   Renishaw Hall

Dear Stephen,

I cannot tell you how much pleasure your letter gave me. It is a very great happiness to me to know that you like those poems ... indeed it is all the encouragement I need: it makes me feel as if I could work with more fortitude.

Your letter gave me a happiness that I much needed, especially at this time. I've now finished the book of poems, and sent it off to the publishers. In a few days I shall be sending you two more poems to look at,—*but to be kept until you feel like reading them.* I've run out of paper (foolscap) or they would have been sent today. Never have I heard anything to equal your adventure at that interview. If it were not so terrifying, it would be extremely funny. But it isn't funny, because it throws too powerful a light. I hope there is going to be a terrible row about it. Where on earth can these officials come from?

Osbert and I were furious at not being able to hear Natasha's broadcast owing to the machine breaking down. (It is a very old one). It never, incidentally, breaks down when male choirs are singing the *March of the Men of Harlech*, or Mr Sandy Macpherson is oozing out warm treacle. But it did the same thing when a play of Osbert's was being broadcast. I do hope it was a great success, and I hope our telegram arrived in time.

You write wonderful letters. What you said in this last letter about events being 'a slurred and hideously misused language

[1] *Green Song* (1944) and *A Notebook on William Shakespeare* (1948).

of human life, and that this language can be understood and is not irremediable',—and that all poets can do is to point this out, is most poignantly true; and though it is so poignant, it has a comfort about it, a nobility. It has that quality of feeding goodness, like bread, that I say you have, always, in all utterances . . .

This seems to be the season when the Indians begin asking questions and producing manuscripts. One day, ages ago, meeting Tom [Eliot], I asked him 'How are the Poets?' 'The Indians,' he said, 'are peculiarly persistent.' I've been reading William James's *Principles of Psychology* lately—(I've got very much the night-school nature, and try to educate myself). I expect you have read it. Osbert says I am always discovering books that everyone knew during their infancy.—Anyway, I do think it contains some wonderful things, such as 'The first time we see light, in Condillac's phrase, we *are* it rather than see it. But all our later optical knowledge is about what the experience gives.'

So now I am going to read Condillac on the sensations,[1] although I know the London Library will pretend it is out.

Then I've been reading Coleridge's letters, which make me unhappy. How dreadful his [mésalliance?] is. I am so angry with Wordsworth for not helping him, but adding to his sense of guilt.

I found such a wonderful phrase in *Moby Dick*, which might be about Coleridge's poetry. 'It was noon. Silence reigned over the before tumultuous but now deserted deck. An intense copper calm, like a universal yellow lotus, was more and more unfolding its noiseless measureless leaves upon the sea.'

One could go to sleep by it, couldn't one?

Speaking about *Moby Dick*—if you see the connection—Beryl is here. There is something very marine about her nose, which always seems pointing at something, as fish point. My new teacher William James says paranoiac conditions are explained by 'a laming of the association organ'. Mine are explained by the organ in question being far too active. Love from Osbert and me to you and Natasha, Edith.

[1] *Traité des sensations* by Étienne de Condillac (1754).

82. *To Maurice Bowra*

January 24, 1944   Renishaw Hall

. . . It would be quite impossible for me even to begin to say what great pleasure your essay on my war poems has given, and is giving, me, or how profoundly grateful I am to you.

I wish I could express what it means to me to have my poetry so understood—understood so richly and completely. It is a great happiness to me.

There is so much to say, and so much to be grateful for, that I scarcely know where to begin. What you say about my technique fills me with gratitude. It must surely now enter the heads of your readers that perhaps someone who could work so hard—work with such endurance and patience,—may have something to say. I am very glad that you chose my poem 'Poor Young Simpleton' to speak about in that connection. It was extremely difficult to manage—or would have been if I hadn't got my technical muscular system under control.

I am deeply grateful to you for pointing out that my vocabulary is deliberately unpretentious and my poetry simple. Oh, what I feel when I hear the words 'Russian ballet' used in connection with my poems! I could really commit an act of violence. I am happy that your essay will correct this nonsense once and for all. Women's poetry, with the exception of Sappho (I have no Greek and speak with great humility on that subject) and with the exception of 'Goblin Market' and a few deep and concentrated, but fearfully incompetent poems of Emily Dickinson, is *simply awful*—incompetent, floppy, whining, arch, trivial, self-pitying,—and any woman learning to write, if she is going to be any good at all, would, until she had made a technique for herself (and one has to forge it for oneself, there is no help to be got) write in as hard and glittering a manner as possible, and with as strange images as possible—strange, but believed in. Anything to avoid that ghastly wallowing . . .

I see that at last 'Street Song' is going to be made clear to readers. It is a poem that for some reason gives me a pang—

again, as though I had just written it. I think it is one of the saddest of all the poems, in spite of the ending.

It is a dangerous thing to say, but I can say it to you. Sometimes, when I begin a poem, it is almost like automatic writing. Then I use my mind on it afterwards. It was so here. For that reason, partly, it means several things to me, whilst being deeply experienced. Sometimes I think a barrel organ was playing in a street, and a young woman passing it hears, through it, the voice of her dead lover, killed in battle, and buried—a little hopeless sound. Or else she hears it just in the sounds of the street, of the children playing, and the people selling and buying. In any case it is meant to be a love song from a dead man to a living woman, or from a man who is about to die,—but I think dead—and seeing the world as it is now, and seeing the woman who had been his peace and his night of rest. Then he sinks back into his deeper night, and she realises that the counsel of despair, sounding through the words of love, was perhaps only that of the (mind) world speaking, as you so finely say: 'It is possible that the cry is really from the depths of the human heart as some brutal tyranny pursues its relentless way; but it is no less possible that the present agony is some little understood process of change in the world.'

What you say of my 'assertion of positive values' is very true, and it has been very rarely understood. Your sentence: 'the earth is more than a garment of God: it is a manifestation of God Himself' is wonderful, and it is the truth that lies beneath all my poetry. I said before, but must repeat again, I do *not* know how to express my gratitude to you, or the happiness your essay gives me, and the feeling of strength it gives me . . . the thought of it, the encouragement it gives, makes me inflexibly determined to work as hard as I have ever worked. It wouldn't be possible to work harder, or I should do it.

83. *To John Lehmann*

February 28, 1944   Renishaw Hall

Dear John,
I've been hearing dreadful stories of the bombing, and I feel I
must write you one word to say how much I feel for you,—for
it must have been horrible. No matter how brave one is, there is
the feeling of being completely helpless against an appalling
wickedness, and in addition there is the strain of that cataclys-
mic noise, and the weariness of having no sleep.

Is it true that Stephen and Natasha have been bombed out?
It is horrible to think of—but more horrible far to think of the
unspeakable thing which *might* have happened.

I would be most awfully grateful if you could let me have
news of them,—where they are, etc. I know how busy you are,
but I would be deeply grateful.

This isn't a letter, it is only a note. Yours ever, Edith.

84. *To John Lehmann*

March 9, 1944   Renishaw Hall

Dear John,
Thank you so much for your letter. I am distressed beyond
words about poor Demetrios. I simply cannot *bear* to think
what he is enduring, and that there seems to be no hope. It is
too terrible, and it wrings one's heart.[1]

I feel for you so much: it must be perfectly dreadful for you.
I helped nurse poor Helen Rootham who had brought me up
from a child, and who was like my mother, through cancer
of the spine, in a tiny flat. She used to watch one's face closely
for any sign. So I know just what you are going through.

How good you were to think of that cable for him.

[1] The Greek poet, Demetrios Capetanakis, to whom E.S. had become very
much attached, had been seriously ill in Westminster Hospital for some time.
He died on the day this letter was written.

What do you mean, by saying you will not send me any more poems for the present? You do not know what pleasure it gives me, and how much I look forward to getting poems from those of my friends who *are* poets. I ask myself what I can have done to make you say that. Please relent and send me any you have, always.

We are having the most awful time, in a minor way, for we are having to look through every paper we have in order to find things for family solicitors! Which means that one is always smothered in dust, and that we can do no work!

I am delighted those poems are coming in *Penguin New Writing* No. 20, with my '[Girl and] Butterfly'. I can see you are not yet inured to the goings on of the *Nation*. I must say it does seem to me most odd, but *nothing* surprises me with them.

Please heed what I say about poems. Yours ever, Edith.

85. *To John Lehmann*

15 March 1944   Renishaw Hall

Dear John,

Your letter came by the *second* post yesterday, when it was too late for me to get an answer off to you. You have never been out of my thoughts, with the nightmare of pain and bewilderment, the feeling of blind waste, that you are enduring. One is helpless against such pain.

I *still* cannot believe it, for I never thought it would happen, —one *could* not believe it, somehow.

How well I know that feeling that one must deaden the pain somehow, temporarily. I think you are an extremely courageous person—otherwise I would warn you '*don't* try to deaden it', for if you do, you will never be the same person again; for if one deadens anguish, some part of one remains numb. But I do not think that will be so with you: I do not dread it for you, in the very least.

How thankful I am that you were spared that last afternoon: it would only have been an anguishing memory for you.—

Osbert, who has seen a great many men die, says he believes
all people want, at that moment, is, not to be surrounded. No
human contact can appear to them real, and it is only an added
cruelty. . . .

86. *To John Lehmann*

29 March 1944   Renishaw Hall

. . . To go back to what we said about being with people when
they die. *I know* they wish one not to be. One holds them back,
and they have to go through it all again, just when they were
going peacefully. Poor Helen Rootham, who brought me up
and shielded me as much as she could in my wretched childhood
—she was like a mother to me—died of cancer of the spine. I
helped her sister nurse her. Three days before she died, some
good religious friend of hers came and sat beside her, and called
her. She seemed to be dying at the moment. But she revived,
because of that. Afterwards, she said to me, with a frightful
despair, with infinite bitterness: 'You know, Edith, I was in
such peace. I was just going. And that *poor good fool* brought
me back.' Even people one cares for do that, I am convinced.
Such humiliating things happen to one's poor body when one
is dying,—and one looks so beautiful afterwards,—so beautiful
and noble.—Of course one wants the people one cares for to
see one—not humiliated, but beautiful and noble, which is
what one really is. . . .

87. *To John Lehmann*

May 22, 1944   Renishaw Hall

Dear John,
Thank you so much for your letter. I *do* sympathise with you.
It is a kind of torture like that inflicted in the most scientific
prisons, to be interrupted when one has a poem 'coming

through'. I am afraid I usually hate the people who do this to me. But interruption from people ordinarily is a different matter from the disruption caused by being caught up in a machine. As you are at present, as Sachie is. (You and Sachie haven't met yet, I think: I do particularly want you to meet, as I have a feeling that each would get on so well with the other. I shall try to arrange it this summer when I am in London). Poor Sachie has the same H[ome] G[uard] adventures. Every night of the week he is up till the middle of the night, lying in a bog or something of the sort; and he seems never to have a decent meal, all his work is interrupted, or he is too worn out to do it. But he doesn't, of course, get pestered by MSS in addition. Or only in the degree that all authors do get pestered. To be an editor in addition just must, at moments, be *hell*, when one is wanting to get on with one's own work.

Can't you ask your secretary to tell authors that they'll get answers all in good time: in other words, to get the hell out of it? I am very happy that you like the essay on Demetrios.[1] But how horribly sad one felt, writing it.

Oh, about Mr Reed's article on my poetry.[2] What I understand from your letter disturbed me a little; but perhaps I misunderstood it. I am extremely anxious that the public, at this moment, should be led to contemplate my *latest* poetry (written since this war), until, in the course of time, and through getting to understand this later poetry, they are able to understand the earlier.

Heavens, what I have been through in the past! In the first place, neither the sadness nor the gaiety of those early poems has been understood,—nor any underlying meaning. It is always so, I think, with any new poetry, unless there is a layer of meaning on top—which *can* happen with very good poetry; but it is not the only way of writing good poetry.—Then there are the technical problems. I practised for years, like a pianist, meticulously, with infinite patience. I am very anxious that people should get accustomed to my later poetry; and then,

[1] For *New Writing and Daylight* (Autumn 1944).
[2] Henry Reed's article 'Edith Sitwell', appeared in *Penguin New Writing*, no. 21 (1944).

when they realise I am not in the least the person they supposed
me to be, they will at last understand what I have done in my
earlier poetry. I think it dangerous, at the moment, to lay most
stress on the earlier.

I am so delighted to hear you like *The Pleasures of Poetry*.
The complete volume is out of print now (bombing, bless
them!) but I believe the three separate volumes are still to be
found; and I am going to get them for you, if they *are* still
available. I would like for you to have your own copy.

But I am very glad, too, that you have Demetrios's notes.

Oh, *how* much I shall miss him when I come to London. Do,
indeed, miss the thought of him every day. But how can *you*
miss him? It isn't to be thought of, how much.

I was tortured, all the time I was writing the essay about
him, by fearing I wasn't doing the right thing. But I *think* I
was; and am now utterly reassured by you.

I do hope you are going to have time to let those poems
grow. It is a dreadful thought that this is happening to them.
Yours ever, Edith.

88. *To John Lehmann*

28 August 1944   Renishaw Hall

... I have begun your poem, which is going to be about
Eurydice. I have many ideas, and some lines. The poem, I
think, will begin with

> Then from the chrysalis of my thin sleep
> That lay like light or dew upon my skin,
> I rose and wrapped my wings about me,—went
> From that porphyrian darkness like a rose.

(but I don't know. I dare say it will begin differently).[1]—I've
put it aside for a few days, because I mustn't touch it at the
moment. A week ago we heard the terrible news that the only
child of my first cousin who is like a sister to me, was killed

[1] 'Eurydice' did not contain these lines in its final version, dedicated to John
Lehmann and published in *Horizon*, August 1945.

fighting.[1] Poor boy—22 years old. . . . She, my cousin, is one of those very rare people, now, who is a born mother. And I daren't think of her,—although of course I do, every moment of the day. If I could hear she had died in the night, I could almost be happy again. But I think it is quite probable she will go mad.

That is why I have to wait to get on with the poem until the *first* shock of the horror has left my mind. It shrivels one's emotions, and, too, in a strange way, one's language.

To leave that horror, and speak about something else. Did I tell you that a woman I know in America has written to say that her Autobiography has just been accepted by publishers. There are to be *800 pages about her life before she went to school.* She is sending this masterpiece over to *me* in order that I may 'read it, criticise it, make suggestions, and cross out in red pencil anything that won't do.' She adds 'The poor censors. It will take them 6 weeks to read it', and continues that she has *not* shown it to her husband, 'because I am afraid it might bore him. He reads Dante and Aeschylus in the original.'

89. *To John Lehmann*

2 September 1944   Renishaw Hall

My dear John,
I cannot tell you how grateful I am to you for sending me the poems of Hölderlin. It is a great and wonderful experience to read such a poet for the first time. What nobility, and how ennobling! They have a deep effect on one, of making the horizon wider, and of removing noise and littleness.

The poems only arrived on Thursday afternoon, and I do not nearly *know* them yet, although I have read them all. But at first sight I think 'Descend, descend, fair sun', 'Diotima', and

[1] David Gilliat, the son of Frank and Veronica Gilliat, mentioned in Letter 28, was killed in action on the day before his twenty-third birthday.

'Often while still a boy' are among the most wonderful. But I am deeply moved and impressed by all. . . .

The wind has started one of its non-stop rages—howling like a universe of wild beasts. We are near the Wuthering Heights country, and that is the atmosphere at the moment. Sachie has lent me a book called *London Labour and the London Poor*, by Henry Mayhew (published 1851) that has nearly reduced me to committing suicide. But I have turned from him (Mayhew) to Hölderlin, and he has calmed me. All the same, the Mayhew book makes me want to go and hit the Archbishop of Canterbury very hard in the face. I know it isn't *quite* fair, because this book was published over ninety years ago, but still he ought to be hit because of his predecessor's smugness. Melville's *Redburn* made me feel the same when I read it. I have put a shawl over my head to shut out the noise of the wind, and Robins's dog howling. (Robins is our Old Retainer, and at moments he is exactly like Heathcliff's servant in *Wuthering Heights*.) Robins likes his dog to howl. He says it is 'what dogs are for'. Mr Agate has made a long fresh attack on Osbert in the *Daily Express*, because O. has dared to say that it would not have helped the world much if Mozart, Shelley and Keats had been conscripted into the various services. Mr A. thinks it would have been grand for them all to be killed.[1] Oh the blockhead! . . .

90. *To William Plomer*

September 5, 1944   Renishaw Hall

Dear William,

I was delighted to get your letter. We wish you were still here, and hope you will return before very long, although I must say it would be purely to *our* advantage. At the moment life is one long hell.

[1] James Agate reviewed Osbert Sitwell's *A Letter to my Son* adversely in the *Daily Express* on 12 August 1944. He renewed the attack in the *Daily Express* on 2 September and in a pamphlet, *Noblesse Oblige: Another Letter to Another Son*, which Osbert Sitwell in turn reviewed in the *Daily Express* on 2 December.

The old man like something out of *Peer Gynt*, whom you may have seen lumbering about, has taken to standing for hours just underneath my room, and haranguing distant multitudes. ... It is exactly like listening to the loudspeaker in railway stations. Smut, Robins's dog, upset by the fact that an alien dog has walked in the park, has barked without stopping for seven hours. The clergyman says he is lonely and has asked Osbert to go to tea *any* day he likes. Mr Agate has made a fresh violent attack upon Osbert, and Osbert is going to hit him back. I can hardly be restrained, when I think of Dingy Desmond's latest poetical discovery, crowned by him in the *Sunday Times*. Nobody to whom one writes answers any letters—but strangers in shoals from all over England send one poems. The bell-ringers are practising, and it is raining like a cloudburst. ...

As against that, I am writing a poem with which I am pleased, and may, no doubt, finish it one of these days, if Smut and the old gentleman with the loudspeaker calm down. Robins says it is the function of dogs to bark and howl. But ever since the flower-show Smut (upset by the sight of Mr Middleton and others) has taken to biting people, and it is thought this may end badly, with his own execution.

Do you know William Law's sermons? They are so wonderful. I've just got them out of the Library. It will take me months to read them—but how worthwhile! They are full of fire and light.

I do—(knowing nothing, naturally, but humbly, from instinct)—believe that all this ghastly horror of death and cruelty will soon be over. But you, who have worked so hard and so incessantly, will be very tired, I am afraid. You will need that long holiday which consists of doing what one likes best—one's own work!!

I do hope to see you again soon. Yours ever, Edith.

91. *To Stephen Spender*

30 January 1945   Renishaw Hall

Dear Stephen,
I have been thinking of you and Natasha so much, as always,
and have wanted to write every day since I got back, but the
frightful cold has a most extraordinary numbing devitalising
effect on me, so that by the time I had finished copying those
poems for Dr Bowra, I found the time had flown by without
my realising it.

I can't tell you how happy it has made me to see so much of
you and Natasha lately, and to know that if all goes well I
shall be doing so again in April.

The more I read what you have written about Macbeth, the
more enthralled I am by your Time theory.[1] It is truly wonderful. Not only because it explains much of Macbeth's agony, but
because it tells one what every criminal excepting the most base,
must suffer.—Am I not right in thinking Shakespeare was the
first to explore the character and mind of the criminal? Macbeth
of course was not born criminal, but in Iago he surely produced
the exact reason for the criminality born in the man—that
frightful *deadness* which Bradley and others have spoken of,
and which I am sure is the hallmark of the born criminal. I
suppose Macbeth's tragedy was that he was *born* with a noble
mind.

I think your Macbeth criticism is a really great piece of
criticism. It is wonderful, the part where you say 'There is no
Amen nor night of sleep which will ever end that moment
which opens wider and wider as the play proceeds,'—and the
passage where you say 'The play seems to spread out, burning
up and destroying a wider and wider area, without moving
forward' is terrific. So is the part about Macbeth reminding
himself 'of the exact time of night, and this calms him.' It is
most moving, and most terrible, and makes me realise, more

[1] Spender's article, 'Time, Violence and *Macbeth*' appeared in *Penguin New
Writing*, no. 3 (1941).

than anything I have ever read about Macbeth, his frightful suffering.

I do hope you are going to reprint this wonderful essay, soon, in book form.

Here is what I have written about Lear. At least, what is going into *New Writing*. It will be longer in the book, because it will have added to it what I wrote in my *Poet's Notebook*.

I am most deeply anxious to know what you feel about it.

How is Natasha? Please give her my best love. I do hope this loathsome cold doesn't make her feel ill.

I returned here without my luggage, which contained my fur coat, and two hot-water bottles,—to find the boiler had gone wrong so that we could have no hot water, and that we were knee-deep in snow. Now we are waist-deep, but my luggage is recovered, and the boiler mended.

I can hardly bear to think of the poor birds. But I *daren't* think of other things. Simply daren't.—I think I realise more than ever, just now, the complete *horror* of the time. I don't know how we endure it mentally.

I have got no news, excepting that the Man with the Wig said to my club at large, after my last tea party, that he had enjoyed it because his dear old friend Stephen Spender and his charming wife were there! *Are* you his dear old friend? Poor wigs! Really, he is a very kind old thing, and his main fault is writing that awful verse, and insisting on reciting it to one in the midst of a large concourse, when people are talking about something quite different. Best love to you and Natasha from Osbert and Edith.

92. *To Maurice Bowra*

March 17, 1945   Renishaw Hall

Dear Dr Bowra,

I have been reading that extraordinary electric battery, Apollinaire, with the greatest interest, enlightenment, and pleasure

... I have inhabited Apollinaire's poetry, ever since you sent me the book, and now I am beginning to feel at home in it. They are curiously vitalising, and at the same time, one can see in them many living roots, from which later poetry, painting, and even music, has sprung. As soon as I began to know his poetry at all, the images made an impact on my mind—almost like a blow, perhaps because of the hard sharpness of the best of them—their sharpness and poignancy is such that they make one relive an experience as a scent does, although, in a way, they are so natural.

I think it is the poetry of a man who has sprung from an uncertain and unhappy past. Even when his poetry seems to arise from triumph, or to speak of triumph, one knows that first there is something to overcome,—and that in spite of the great vitality and driving force of his images.

What an amazing life of the senses he lived—(I had put 'led', but I don't mean 'led'!) What a passionate vitality! I am overcome by admiration for 'Les Collines'—so packed with life—packed, but never overcrowded: a dynamo, giving one fresh life—for the extraordinary 'Chef de Section', for 'Le Chant d'Amour' and for the last part of 'Vendemiaire'—that which begins with the line

'L'univers tout entier concentre dans ce vin ...'

As you say in the Preface, 'He might well claim "*Je suis ivre d'avoir tout l'univers*".' I admire very greatly, too, in a quite different way, 'L'Emigrant de Landor Road' and the strange 'La Blanche Neige'—which is like one of Stravinsky's *Chansons Plaisants*, I think, don't you? It has an odd beauty. I feel in all these poems '*la rumeur sourde des sêves montantes*'

93. *To William Plomer*

April 2, 1945   Renishaw Hall

Dear William,
I cannot tell you how much your delightful letter pleased and enchanted me.

It arrived at a moment when I was considering cutting my throat with my left hand because I couldn't use my right hand sufficiently to do any work. But I changed my mind immediately, though I still write with an uncertain hand, as you can see.

You are in the great tradition of writers who can also write living and perfect letters.

How beautiful that Coster's cry is, you quoted: 'Growing, growing, growing, all the glory going!' It really might be part of a song by Shakespeare. It seems to belong to him, I think it is quite wonderful, and am so grateful to you. I did not know it.

I agree with you about the 'Rubaiyat' being a beautiful poem. To me it is a splendour and I think only foolish snobs could under-rate it. You are one of those people who, like myself, can read a work as if no one had ever read it before, and so realise its full worth.—I can read the 'Lucy' poems like that,—and Tennyson's exquisite simple early poems, 'Where Claribel low-lieth' etc. But the 'Rubaiyat' of course is more wonderful than those.

This is partly to say how much your letter delighted me, and, also, to say how much I look forward to seeing you when I am in London. Please do try to come to my tea party on *Tuesday the 17th* at the Sesame Club, 49 Grosvenor Street, and also to lunch with me on *Sunday the 22nd* at 1 o'clock—also at the Club.

I do hope so much you will be able to come. I tried to make one of these arrangements for a Thursday,— but an old friend has arranged a meeting on that day, at which I have to make a speech,—and the whole club is given up to this horror. Yours ever, Edith.

94. *To Stephen Spender*

6 April 1945   Renishaw Hall

Dear Stephen,
I was so rejoiced to get your letter, and to know that you and

Natasha and Matthew can come on the 17th. It is quite impossible for me to tell you how much I look forward to seeing you all three. It is so exciting, really!

There is a great deal to say, and I hardly know where to begin. It is very wonderful to think of you and Natasha having this great happiness. This is always in my thoughts, and makes me very happy too. Those last days of waiting before Matthew was born were terrible days of anxiety. I cannot tell you what we felt when the telegram came saying he was in the world. Such a sense of profound relief and calm comfort. Your description of the time when the first birth-pains began was profoundly moving. How brave Natasha is! I am told a baby has more vitality if it is born when the mother is conscious, —but I don't know if it is true. I *long* to see the dear little creature.

It is very good that you are in your new house. Because you begin Matthew's life, not with the memories of past anxieties, about Natasha, and about many things. Oh, if *only* you are very soon freed from your slave-labour! It really makes me so furiously angry when I think of it.

Your letter to Osbert about his book,[1] and what you said to me about the book, filled him with happiness. Of *all* the letters he has received, yours has made him the most happy. It was a very wonderful praise and sympathy and understanding. He is writing to you, as soon as he has recovered from the dazed state into which the appearance of the book, and all the repercussions from it, have thrown him. I believe, too, that it is a masterpiece, and of a wonderful shape and order and beauty. And the portrait of my father is quite terrific. Of my mother I can only say that her physical beauty was far greater than that of the Richmond portrait in the book. But my life as a child and a girl was a squalid *hell*: it was no question of 'misunderstanding' or severity or anything of that kind. There was something very seriously wrong, and I bore the whole brunt. I may say at this point, that Osbert has been the best brother in the world, of course. In this wonderful book, I feel something has been made of my parents' useless lives. And I remember that I shall

[1] *Left Hand, Right Hand!*

never see them again. And that I am intensely proud of the book.

To go to something else. There is one thing I want to ask. If Mr George Barker is in London now, will you bring him to see me? I want particularly to meet him, for I think him a wonderful poet.

I do *not* think Mr Harry Brown ought to transform and maim two of your greatest lines, as, to judge from the review in *The Times Literary Supplement*, he has done. But I have not seen the book yet.

The telegram I received (you'll be amused to hear) from you was repeated to me as saying you and Natasha could *not* come on the 17th, and this caused considerable alarm and despondency until I got the confirmation of the exact opposite.

I am longing to see all three, and shall be writing to Natasha to whom my best love and also Osbert's. How exciting it is to think how very soon I shall be seeing you. Yours affectionately, Edith.

95. *To T. S. Eliot*

1 July 1945   Renishaw Hall

Dear Tom,

Osbert and I were so very disappointed you could not come on Tuesday. But you are not out of the wood yet. Osbert is determined—and I am equally determined—to go to any lengths to induce you to come and stay here. He is about to write to you on the subject.

If you hate paying visits—as I do—let me assure you that this can *not* be considered in the light of paying a visit, because you do whatever you want to, with no interference. Nobody ever comes down to breakfast—people disappear for hours on end if they want to, go out by themselves if they want to, or stop in by themselves. They go away to work, if they feel like it, or for siestas that last for hours. Nobody is ever hurried or badgered. There are wonderful places in the district to which we can motor. In short, you will be simply in your own home.

The Indian world has not yet claimed us ... nor, I fancy,

ever will. But, as against that, I am the Wedding Guest to every
Ancient Mariner, and am now bent permanently sideways,
with my right ear almost touching the ground, because, for
seven hours at a stretch, I had to remain with the ear in question clamped to the mouth of an old lady who cannot hear, and
won't speak above the faintest murmur. One can neither get
anything out of her or anything into her. But she stops and
won't go away.

Then on top of that, I had to look after an old gentleman in
the train. 'Put me opposite to that lady', he said to an attendant.
'*She will look after me.*' . . .

96. *To John Lehmann*

29 August 1945   Renishaw Hall

Do forgive the scratchings out on the next page. Robins
keeps coming in and out, badgering me about a strap for
my trunk. These things excite him unduly, and he will
give me no peace.

My dear John,
Thank you a thousand times for your most kind, most understanding and sympathetic letter. It did me a great deal of good.

You always understand everything,—with such intuition
and heart.

. . . I have my small family allowance. . . . I had great charges
of honour and gratitude, and so have had, in the past, and still
have, to pay out a part of my income. But I have the house in
Bath (a present), and I have an allowance, and I can earn money.
And I never—never mention the charges I have spoken of,—
because it is so terribly painful to the helpless, generous and
noble-minded person concerned,—and was to the one who is
now dead. I should have been lost if it had not been for them.

When do you go to Paris? I don't want to bother you about
poor Evelyn Wiel, and if you have not time to see her, I shall

more than understand. If you *do* go, No 129 rue Saint-Dominique is between the Avenue Bosquet and the Avenue de la
Bourdonnais. The house is exactly above the Fountain (a
landmark). The flat is the top right-hand one.

Evelyn Wiel is one of the most wonderful women I know.
(I lived in the flat before the war, and she looked after me like a
mother. She is the sister of my dear Helen Rootham, who
brought me up, and who is now dead). E.W. may startle you
by her *maquillage* effects. These are worn to prove to herself
that *nothing* can conquer her,—neither having starved in the
past (she used to live on *25 shillings a week*),—*nor* having had
frightful operations, (*not* cancer but terrible, anyhow),—*nor*
being in constant pain, *nor* being old, (she is nearly seventy, if
not quite)—nor having been beaten and then deserted by her
Norwegian husband, who was at the Legation in Paris—
deserted with no money.

She is terrifically brave, and is covered with decorations for
bravery as a nurse in the last war. The Germans bombed a
hospital full of liquid-fire cases. All the nurses and doctors ran
for their lives, excepting Evelyn and two doctors who remained
with the delirious patients.

She has no brain in particular, but a heart of gold, and one of
the most lovely natures I have ever known.

I shall be in London rather longer than I thought: till about
the 26th, so I am *hoping* there will be some chance of seeing
you. Is there any likelihood of your being back in London by
Thursday the 13th (you mentioned the 15th to me in a letter).
If there is, will you lunch to meet Tom Eliot, and also Sachie,
whom I think you have only just exchanged a few words with.
I *do* hope to see you. We are so excited to hear 'the men' are
already in your new house, and we are longing to see it. Yours
ever, Edith.

97. *To T. S. Eliot*

30 October 1945   Renishaw Hall

Dear Tom,

I should have written before, but returned here the day after the party at which Violet Woodhouse played, and I caught a wretched chill in the train.

We were so very disappointed not to see you while we were in London, but hope to be there again soon. We only came up for a few days, to see Osbert's play performed, at a theatre the size of a postage stamp.[1]

I cannot think what the people at the theatre were doing, not to send you a notice about the first night, which was on Tuesday of last week. They seem to have sent no notices—but yours should have gone first of all. *That* would have been all right: but *we* did not write to you about it, because we think quite enough people make your life a burden to you, and that it is intolerable to do so.

Which reminds me, has Mr ——— ——— crossed your path? If one lives in the country and will not let him into the house, he offers to come and read his poetry to one in the general waiting-room of the station at the nearest town, 'if only for an hour'.

This threat was uttered some time ago, but he has now had a poem accepted by a new magazine, and I can see there will be fresh trouble.

The general waiting room at Chesterfield has a quality all its own.

I dread this terrible winter, and think with sadness of everyone. Yours ever, Edith.

---

[1] *Gentle Caesar*, written with R. J. Minney.

98. *To the Editor of The Times Literary Supplement*

[2 February 1946]

Sir,

In the last number of *New Writing and Daylight* appeared an extract from a book on which I am at work.[1] The extract referred to *King Lear*, and in it there was a passage relating to Edgar's line

'Nero is an angler in the lake of darknesse.'

The implication in this sentence is even greater than I had supposed.

I have just read for the first time Pausanius's Description of Greece (translated by Sir James Frazer). In Book II, Chapter xxxvii, occurs this passage:

I saw also a spring, called the spring of Amphiaraus and the Alcyonian Lake. Through this lake, the Argives say, Dionysus went to hell to fetch up Semele; and they say that Polymnus showed him this way down to hell. The lake is bottomless. I never heard of anyone who was able to sound its depth. Nero himself made the experiment, taking every precaution to ensure success. He had lines made many furlongs long: these he joined together and weighted with lead, but he could find no bottom. I was told, too, that smooth and still as the water of the lake looks to the eye, it yet has the property of sucking down any one who is rash enough to swim in it: the water catches him, and sweeps him down into the depths.

The reference in Shakespeare's line would seem, I suggest with humility, to point to this passage, or to the story from which it was taken.

And the meaning is of an appalling greatness and terror.

'The lake of darkness'—the bottomless depths of human nature, in which Lear (in that world in which child turns

[1] *A Notebook on William Shakespeare.*

against parent, Nature against man) and Nero, the matricide, find blackness after blackness, depth beyond depth. Edith Sitwell.

99. *To Stephen Spender*

16 March 1946 Renishaw Hall

Dear Stephen,

Thank you so much for your most kind, sweet letter, and for the essay, which reached me yesterday afternoon.[1]

Nothing could please me more. Of course, one expected you to seize every aspect of poetry that is in the poet's mind. But that isn't all. You do, in this essay, definitely give me, for one among the poets you have written about, something to think over and to work on. You show me where I go wrong, and where I go right. Nothing could possibly be more valuable to me. It is *constructive* criticism, the whole way. When I was young, I suffered terribly from having nobody who could give me the real poet's advice. This essay does. I am never tired of working, never tired of learning and of trying to expand and to clarify,—and to prune. (Pruning, actually, I have always been pretty apt at.)

Not only what you say about my own poetry, but also what you say about Robert Graves and Mr Auden is excessively valuable to *me*—so what can it be to *them?*

I am now asking myself this question: you say, about Graves 'There has only been a purifying down of a wider less discriminating poetic creative impulse into something within very strict limits.'

I am asking myself whether *I* ought to go in, now, for a strict 'purifying down'. But on the whole, I don't think so, because a woman's problem in writing poetry is different to a man's. That is why I've been such a hell of a time learning to get out my poetry. There was no one to point the way. I had to learn everything—learn, amongst other things, not to be

[1] 'Poetry for Poetry's Sake and Poetry beyond Poetry', *Horizon*, April 1946.

timid. And that was one of the most difficult things of all. And I think that if I started getting the thing into very strict limits it might bear the marks of a return to timidity.

I cannot tell you how valuable that whole essay is to me. I am profoundly grateful to you, my dear Stephen, for so many reasons connected with this: not only for explaining my poetry to the *Horizon* public in a way which really no one could fail to understand, but also for helping me with my own problems.

I think you are deeply right in what you say about the horizontal line and the vertical image. Oh it gives me a great deal to think about.

How strange it is, what you say (and you have said it before, to me) about the Spanish character of some of my poetry. I had a far-back Spanish ancestress, and I have always felt a strong physical affinity with the Spanish nature. I like hardness and fire, and detest milkiness and softness.

Please can I keep the essay! There is a great deal I want to think over.

It arrived the day after I had been put in my place by a young gentleman in the *Granta*, who described me as a Poetaster (his exact term). The poison was rather taken out of the reproach by the fact that his name was foreign, and he wrote Babu English.

I don't know why Cambridge is always so much more offensive than Oxford. He made the most disgusting remarks about Dylan Thomas.

It is perfect that you and Natasha are going to be in London after all during our visit. Will you both—*A—lunch on Thursday the 11th—and stop on for the tea party. B—Come to the Reading on Sunday* (I'll get tickets) and *C—Lunch on Monday?* I look forward more than I can say to seeing you both, also Matthew.

I am very excited to hear you are at work on a new play, and look forward to it tremendously. Also it is most exciting to hear you are at work on an Anthology of the Romantics. I am hoping it will get some of the bosh out of people's heads about Shelley. Our dear Tom has set people wrong about several great poets. How foolish it is not to recognise Shelley as one of the greatest (though not one of the most perfect *invariably*).

But Tom is another great poet, and can do no wrong in my eyes excepting in this one matter.

Oh, dear, this is a stupid letter.

Best love to all three, and my deepest gratitude. Osbert's best love too. Yours affectionately, Edith.

100. *To T. S. Eliot*

4 April 1946   Renishaw Hall

My dear Tom,

Thank you so much for your letter. I am overcome with horror at this dreadful thing, and of course have signed the appeal at once.[1]

I can't bear to think of the man, and I can't bear to think of the poet—I mean of his misery. But of course I *have* thought of it continually. I've never allowed anyone to speak against him in my presence.

Even if he is not tried, what on earth will his future be like?

The extracts from the affidavit are quite unbearable. Yours ever, Edith.

101. *To Maurice Bowra*

8 May 1946   Renishaw Hall

My dear Maurice,

I was so excited to receive your letter and the Inaugural Lecture yesterday morning. I am *very* grateful to you for sending it to me. I cannot imagine anything more likely to revive poetry in England, to bring about a real poetic renaissance, than the fact that you are now Professor of Poetry at Oxford. I can still hardly believe poetry *could* have such luck. However, there we

---

[1] In February 1946 a Federal District Court in Washington found Ezra Pound mentally unsound and unfit to stand trial on charges of treason arising out of broadcasts made during the war from his home in Italy. Pound was later incarcerated in a mental home in Washington.

are. It has happened. And I really see a renaissance ahead of us. . . .

I am so glad Dylan Thomas is being introduced to you. I had hoped to do so, and am very sad that someone else has got in first. He—Dylan—was lunching with me that day I had hoped you could come when I was in London last time—but you were in Paris.

I believe him to be one of the greatest poets—really great, a genius, not a poet of talent—that we have had for the last hundred years, and I am extremely fond of him as a person: he is most sweet and lovable as a character, and I feel a kind of maternal pride in him, for I fought his battles every week for about two months in the *Sunday Times*, when he was beginning. And a pretty savage fight it was! I have just seen him again, to my great joy, after a long time.

If only we had Sidney Keyes. I cannot bear to think of our loss. With him and Dylan, to what might we not look forward. There is a great deal of high talent about—but these were two high geniuses. Now there is one.

I wish I could convey anything of the sense of a new vitalisation that the Inaugural Lecture gives me. 'The pioneer task has been done. The language has been revived. . . . Enough experiments have been made, and the gravity of the time demands a more disciplined verse and a more exalted outlook.' I feel that helps everyone. Both the people who are trying to understand what was being done twenty years ago, and us who are now working in that more disciplined verse.

I see the taste of the time embracing, for the first time, *real* poetry.

With most grateful thanks for allowing me the great privilege of reading the Inaugural Lecture. I do hope you do not want me to return it. With all best wishes, Yours very sincerely, Edith Sitwell

I have just finished an extremely long poem—about two pages[1]—which, *if* you like it, I want to be allowed to dedicate to you. I shall begin to copy it this afternoon, and hope to send

---

[1] 'The Shadow of Cain.'

it (in spite of a sprained right wrist) before I leave for London tomorrow. I shall be there for a week.

102. *To Maurice Bowra*

May 21, 1946   Renishaw Hall

I was so happy to receive your letter, and know you will allow me to dedicate that poem to you. It will be coming out in America (first of all) in the autumn. Because a young man is bringing out a number of a paper devoted to my work, and so I must let him have the most important new poem I have. There are, I think, several things to be done to it yet. I am not quite sure. But as soon as I *am* sure, I'll copy the poem itself, and its principal workings, and have them bound and send them to you.

I only received your letter on my return here,—the servants, for some inscrutable reason, having chosen not to forward that letter alone among my letters. I sometimes wonder what governs their choice in these matters. They seem to have an infallible instinct as to what letter it could annoy me most to have kept back, and would most like to have.

I do wish I had been at the Inaugural Lecture; as I said before, I think it is the most important thing that has happened for poetry, in my memory, that you should be Professor of Poetry at Oxford. I do not wonder that you felt like tears when thinking of Sidney Keyes, and that wicked, senseless loss. I feel the occasion of this lecture was one of the utmost importance. I see a whole new race of young intelligences properly trained to love poetry in a fiery way, instead of damply and tepidly.

When I saw Dylan Thomas, he was under the impression that he was seeing you on *Saturday.* He told me so. I repeat it, in case there was a mistake and he didn't appear—His recital of the 'Tyger' was one of the greatest, the most impressive, the most truly wonderful things I have ever heard or witnessed.

I am writing under some difficulties, as a band of ten cows

are holding a kind of mother's meeting under my window. Poor girls, I am sure they have grievances—but oh, if they would only go and voice them somewhere else! . . .

P.S.—It is amazing how the *New Statesmen* boys *hate* poetry. It fills one with a despairing wonder.

103. *To William Plomer*

July 26, 1946   Renishaw Hall

My dear William,

A mysterious telegram reached me yesterday (I am holding the fort alone, Osbert still being away)—saying 'Pioneer broadcasting, Dylan Thomas reciting'—and a lot more. I came to the conclusion that this must mean that somebody or other was broadcasting about pioneer poetry,—so returned to Higham (whence the telegram came) an amiable reply saying that I shall be delighted for Dylan Thomas to recite these poems; (there was one other muddle in the telegram: i.e., 'Do the fish still glitter in the waterfall' was ascribed to me, instead of to Sachie).

Imagine my delight when I received David Higham's letter this morning, and find that Pioneer is—*you*! So I am telegraphing to *you*, now, to say how happy I am.

Oh!!! Higham takes—or seems to take—a gloomy view about our being able to listen in. He says it is on the Overseas Service. Why is *everything* one wants to listen to on the Overseas Service? What have Overseas done to deserve it? I *am* happy to know you are broadcasting about us. So will Osbert and Sachie be. I shall be really *furious* and so will they be—if we can't hear the broadcast, which I understand is on the 7th of September, (but that it is being recorded today). I really shall be so angry and disappointed. I would give anything to hear it.

How are you, my dear William? It seems so very long since I saw you or heard from you.

I have only been in London for that terrible Poetry Reading

got up by the Poet Laureate, and for one other Reading—just,
as one might say, up, and then down. But I am coming up to
London on the 2nd of September for a fortnight. Evelyn Wiel
is coming over from Paris to stay with me. I intend to have a
large lunch party to which I hope you will come.

I seem to have no news at all. Are you able to work? I am
not, but am *trying* to finish my book on Shakespeare. It seems
almost hopeless to try to get people not to interrupt one the
whole time.

Please do let me know some details about the broadcast. I
long for them. I also long to hear how Dylan is faring. He has
wandered away again, and renounced me and won't have
anything to do with me. Love from Yours ever Edith.

104. *To Maurice Bowra*

November 18, 1946　　　　　　　　　　　　　　Renishaw Hall

My dear Maurice,

Thank you so much for your letter, which delighted me. I am
now going to ask a great kindness from you—a kindness for
Dylan Thomas. I know only too well how busy you are, and I
know only too well what an extra letter to write must mean to
you. But I wouldn't ask you if I didn't think it tremendously
important for poetry.

Dylan is talking of going to America with his family to live
for a while, because the eldest child is delicate, and it is supposed the American air would cure him.

On *no* account must Dylan go there to *live*, without the
possibility of coming back, if he doesn't like it there, and if it
doesn't suit him.

He has been offered a house, somewhere in the wilds, but he
must not start off in this harum-scarum manner to *live* there,
without seeing the house.

So I suggested to him he should go and lecture and read
there (so as to look round) taking Caitlin, but not the children,
with him. This would mean that their fares were paid, there and

back. They must be. I have got a number of addresses of people who would be of use, from Diana Reeve, the American girl you met at lunch with me. Amongst those people, she suggests that one should write to Professor Theodore Spencer, Harvard University, Cambridge, Massachusetts, saying Diana Reeve (who I suppose knows him; but perhaps it would be better to omit mentioning her) said she was sure Dylan would be wanted to read his poems for the Morris Grey Fund.

Now, unfortunately, I cut less than no ice with Professor Theodore Spencer, who says I am Hell, and why can't I write nibbling rat-like little books like Lytton Strachey (of course the language is mine—but still, the sentiments are his.) If *I* write to Professor Spencer, Dylan is doomed.

Dare I—may I—*beg* of you to do so, saying that Dylan is coming over soon (the date depends on when he can get a passage) and could he be invited to give this reading (mentioning, too, that he has no money, and must have some). The word from you that Dylan is a great poet—and also recites poetry greatly—would carry him through. I don't suppose Professor Spencer has ever heard of Dylan.

Please forgive me for troubling you. In order to save you trouble as far as *I* am concerned, I enclose a questionnaire, so that you have only to scratch out the wrong answer! Yours ever, Edith Sitwell.

P.S. Dylan seems very worried about the child's delicacy.

105. *To John Lehmann*

Friday [11 December 1946]   Renishaw Hall

Dear John,
I am so ashamed not to have written, and not to have returned the Grigsoniana before. But *A* I've been having blinding headaches—due to oil lamps with as much light as that given by a cigar—and *B* dear Mrs W. B. Yeats sent down a young American who is writing a book about Mr Yeats.

I wonder if she has any idea of what he is *really* up to! His

one interest (if one can call it one, as several ladies are involved)
is exactly what terms Mr Y was [on] with Mrs Maud Gonne and
others. He says he is going to base the book on the effect this
had on his poetry!!! Oh, oh, oh!! Is it not *awful* that every
great man has got to be exhumed and nailed down on the
crossroads with a stake through his heart? I think I shall write a
poem about it. The young man was quite well-intentioned. He
just doesn't understand a great man has a right to protect
himself from the crowd.

Before I get on to the subject of the Anthology—which is a
real and great delight and excitement—in re *Dylan and the
Fund.*[1]

A. I think, in fact I am sure, John, that Dylan ought to be
the *sole* beneficiary. We are not likely to get another man of
such genius—such *great* genius—(between ourselves George
Barker, the one other runner-up, had just got a Bursary Fund,
—Osbert has something to do with it, only that is private to
you and me).

The Anonymous Donor does *not* wish *journalists* or people
of minor talent to get it. She wants the greatest artist in poetry
or prose who can be found.

*B. The danger of the use of the money doing harm to his creative
work.* I worry about a certain habit, terribly. But that is because
I am terrified of it harming him *physically.* It obviously does
not harm his work, because his latest book of poems is infinitely
greater than anything else he has done. We don't want what
happened to Swinburne to happen to him.

And I think he has a fabulous physique. That does not mean
I do not wish to God that he would stop it.—Only he would
have (for that to be any good) to stop it of his own accord—not
to *be* stopped. I need hardly say that I know the moral point of
view is not what you are considering—but I'd rather give the
fund to Coleridge than to Southey.

C. America. I was aghast when I heard he was going there.

---

[1] This Fund had been started by an anonymous donor in 1943 in order to
provide a yearly 'travelling scholarship' after the war for an author, young or
old, who might benefit from the experience. It is administered by the Society
of Authors through a Committee of Management.

I've tried *everything*—imploring, owl-like prognostigations of disaster,—saying that Caitlin will have a rotten time because she isn't rich. *Nothing* sways him. And his hostess at Oxford, Mrs Taylor, the wife of a don, says it is like measles—you have to have it and get over it—I mean this mania to go to America.

I am terrified of the family going there with *no* money, and that is why I am so anxious Dylan should have the whole of the Fund. If he will go—(and it is certainly necessary the eldest child should be taken out of this climate) then I feel we must do our best for him. And he has real nobility. I know he will try not to let us down.

I suggested to Raymond [Mortimer]—in answer to his letter, that the *men* members of the Committee should try and get Dylan to go to Switzerland instead of America—on the plea of wonderful food, and cheapness. I had better not go on about it, because he will simply think me a fussy old lady.

He says—and Caitlin says—that they have been found a house somewhere in the mountain wilds, and that *Dylan wants to go there to get away from people and work.*

I *implore* you to help me get him the whole of the fund. Also, it is urgent, because I think he will be going soon. . . .

106. *To John Gielgud*

15 December 1946   Renishaw Hall

Dear Mr Gielgud,

I waited to thank you for your most delightful letter and for your kindness in sending me Mr Shaw's enchanting article, until I thought you might have returned from Portugal. Letters get lost, and then one appears ungrateful and impolite. I am registering the letter for the same reason. . . .

I am convinced you are right in what you say about minding the cruelty of certain aspects of the Comedies today, but not at the time when they were written. Then, nobody was in the least squeamish about the delicacies of behaviour and of moral issues. And yet the other world was so real, and so important to those people that they would go to the stake for the minutiae of their beliefs.

My mind is still fixed on *King Lear* ... I think Goneril and Regan are deprived of half their terror and grandeur by the fact that they are fixed to one point of time by their costumes, where all the same they are turned into superior and arty secretaries to business men by those plaits over the ears,—changed from Furies out of Hell into young women one sees shopping every day in the High Street Kensington. Why does nobody make use of the terrific Fuseli drawings of evil women like ghosts out of Hell, like phantoms from Thebes or Pompeii —beings with immense feathered headdresses and featureless faces,—beings outside Time.

I hope you enjoyed your holiday in Portugal, and had all the sun you needed, and feel rested. I hope so much to see you before you go to America.

I shall be going through London in January, on my way to Switzerland, and hope that if you are not too appallingly busy, you will come and see me. I am being driven demented by the fact that no answer comes from the people who are seeing to our reservations, but as soon as I know exactly when I am coming, I will write in the hope that you will be able to come and lunch.

I enjoyed our three-cornered talk with John Piper so much that I will see if he can't come and lunch also. This has to be done in a certain amount of secrecy, as I shall be in hiding from certain ladies. (By the way, do you think they have their secret service agents posted at all the railway stations, and in all the post offices, opening one's letters? I think they must. Nothing else could account for how they get to know things.) Ever yours very sincerely, Edith Sitwell.

107. *To Ronald Bottrall*

February 25, 1947   Grand Hotel, Locarno, Switzerland

I have been meaning to write to you for ages, but since I

arrived in Switzerland have been able to do nothing. I just sit in mute surprise, staring at the pre-war conditions. It seems, too, so odd to see anyone smile.

I see practically no papers here. What of the *Selected Poems*, and of the anthology?[1] Before I left England, I saw a review of the poems in *Time and Tide*, but beyond that have seen nothing that anybody has written about anything. I do hope both the books, and *especially* the former, are having the greatest possible success.

Dylan Thomas and his family (wife and two children) will be going to Italy shortly, for him to write poems. I *think* he should be going in April, but the actual time isn't settled yet, nor is it yet settled where he will stay.

When he comes, will you be an angel and get him lectures and readings in public to do? It is absolutely essential that he should, as you will understand.[2]

Have you heard him read? It is a *very* great experience—absolutely terrific. I've never heard anything like it.

He is a most enchanting creature—wildly funny and very charming, and she is a darling too. I am writing this under the assumption that you don't know each other, because I believe you don't, although you have other mutual friends besides me. You are bound to be friends. May I tell him to communicate with you when—or before—he arrives? . . .

Give Margaret my love and tell her that the young American woman turned out to be really sweet—I like her enormously. But she terrified all the Great Panjandrums by asking them to lunch and dinner. They became alarmed as to what would happen to her if she pursued this reckless course. At last, Tom [Eliot] had to give out that he was absent from London. Before that, he confided to me, at lunch, that he was 'seriously disturbed' about her. But just when he was going to tell me why, everyone at the lunch table, seeing my enthralled face, stopped talking in order to listen to what we were saying, so

[1] Ronald Bottrall's *Selected Poems* was published in November 1946 with a Preface by E.S. The anthology was *Selected English Verse* edited by Ronald and Margaret Bottrall (1946).
[2] Mr Bottrall was Representative of the British Council in Italy at the time.

Tom stopped too. The invitations, I may say, were based
purely on literary interest, but we felt it might be the Queen
next.

108. *To Maurice Bowra*

March 24, 1947   Sesame Club, 49 Grosvenor Street, W.1

My dear Maurice,

What *can* you think of me for not answering your perfect letter
before! But first of all, it was delayed at Renishaw, where
Robins is so sunk in despondency and snow that he only
forwards things from time to time (remembering that an outside world exists)—and that when it did reach me, I was
starting one of the worst chills I ever remember having.

Chill or no chill, I was entranced by your description of the
Chevalier's activities, and by the sinister note at the end, in re
the various ladies 'going out to earn'.

All the same, though it is very funny, it is also very shocking
that the Chevalier should have the impertinence to contradict
you in matters of poetry. It springs from this idea that the
dilettante is always right! . . .

It horrifies me to hear that you had had no further news
about Dylan and his plans. *I thought you had been told*—that
was firmly in my mind, or *of course* I should have told you, in
my letter. I blame myself very much for not having done so,
but really I did think you had been told.

After endless discussions, it has been decided now that the
Authors' Society Fund had better be given to Dylan to go to
Italy instead of the U.S.A.—it being held, and I think very
rightly, that America might be exceedingly dangerous for him.
I do beg your pardon for not having, myself, told you this—
especially after your very great kindness in writing to Professor
Spencer. And you should have been told, anyhow, quite apart
from that.

Dylan, I think, has been very ill with 'flu. I saw him last

night, when I crawled out to attend the Apollo Society meeting—an awful affair at which he read superbly. He told me he had been walking about with icicles hanging from his cough, and they seemed to have frozen all energy in him.

Your kindness and goodness in writing to Professor Spencer was very great, and I, for one, and certainly he too, are *very* grateful. And I am very ashamed to have put you to all this trouble—as I know he will be. I had no chance to talk to him really, last night, because there were a good many other people and one could have no separate talk. .... Have you seen Mr Grigson's attack on Dylan in *Polemic?* The editor has had the temerity to ask me, of all people in the world, to answer it! I am returning his letter to him, with a few very sinister remarks.

With the subsidence of floods, I shall leave next Monday, for Renishaw. I didn't dare ask anyone to lunch before I returned and found if the food was even vaguely eatable. It is. So if, by any happy chance, you should be able to lunch with me, if you are going to be in London before that day, do please let me know. It would be so delightful if you could.

With all best wishes from Osbert and me, Yours ever, Edith Sitwell.

109. *To Maurice Carpenter*

11 April 1947   Renishaw Hall

Dear Maurice Carpenter,
Many thanks for your letter. This is only the briefest note, because I am in the middle of a piece of work which I must not put down.

I do hope to hear from you very soon that you have won the Atlantic Award, and that all is well about *that* problem.

This is to beg you *not* to seek a job on the British Council *if* you are wishing to go abroad as an official. Believe me, it would be most impracticable, and would only lead to your being very unhappy. First of all, I am sure you would not get it. They need a completely different type of person—one who omits *all your* virtues, and who has quite a different set of virtues. (You see, I have known a good many of them). What they need is someone who combines the character of an Ambassador with the character of an all-in wrestler!!!!

And that life!! You would neither of you stand it! It is one long round of *social* engagements—and when I say social, I do not mean lunches and teas to or with people one wants to *talk* to, but simply people who are *socially* eminent,—one long round of *entertaining*, and perpetual va-et-vient with the Embassy and its officials and *other* embassies and *their* officials.

You wouldn't stand it for a month!—But even more important is the fact that I am as certain as I can be of anything in this world, that you would never, *never* get the appointment. It is simply waste of time your asking for it. I am used to British Council officials in foreign parts . . . the B.C. in foreign terms is simply an off-shoot of the Embassy, although no doubt the B.C. wouldn't say so.

No, no. Something else. *Not* that. Give your wife and my godson my love. Yours very sincerely, Edith Sitwell.

110. *To Raymond Marriott*

June 7, 1947   Renishaw Hall

Dear Raymond,

I am sorry that I cannot do as you ask about your novel. I have had to make it an *invariable* rule *never* to read manuscripts. (And this is also the invariable rule of every other writer of any standing.) I have not the time.

This is the *second* letter I have had to write about your novel, and I must not be asked to write any more. I am extremely busy and have no secretary (Messrs Dobson wrote to me about your book). However, I shall be writing about another matter to a member of the firm of Messrs Nicholson and Watson, in the course of the next few days, and I will strongly recommend that the book shall be very seriously considered.

If they do not take it,—or in case they do not take it—I will mention to a friend of mine at Jonathan Cape *when I see him*, that you may be sending him a novel, and will make the same request.

But this I do under the strict understanding that you are not, under any circumstances, to start worrying the people in question, or making inroads on their time.

Again, I cannot be perpetually disturbed, every time I come to London, by some fresh request or another. I do not like to be telephoned to, so please do not ring me up. And please do not telephone to my brothers' houses either. And do not, now, start apologising and giving me a fresh letter to write. Just behave, in future, like anyone else, and have a proper consideration for my time, which belongs to my work. Nobody else behaves as you do. If Messrs Nicholson and Watson do not take the book, (I hope they will) please drop me a line. I will have the MSS returned to you as soon as anyone goes to the Post Office—it is a three-mile walk there and back. I wish you a great success with the book. Yours, Edith Sitwell.

111. *To Stephen Spender*

Monday [Autumn 1947]   Renishaw Hall

Dearest Stephen,

I was at once very happy to get your letter this morning, and *very* miserable to think you will have gone to America before I have a chance of seeing you. It really is very wretched. I *shall*, thank goodness, unless you have changed your plans, catch Natasha before she goes too, but even so, she will be on the point of going, I suppose.

Everything seems extremely disorganised in our lives, and this departure of yours to America is the most disorganising and unhappy of all.—Although I feel exceedingly melancholy about it, I try to comfort myself by thinking and saying to myself what wonderful work you will be doing for poetry out there—but it is one of those high-minded comforts which doesn't really work, and, let us face it, we shall miss you and Natasha horribly, and next September, when I suppose you will be coming home again, seems a very long way off.

I should have written to both you and Natasha long ago, but haven't been well.—I was dreadfully disappointed to miss that last afternoon with Natasha, but I hadn't slept for three nights, and was made really ill by it and had to go to bed. Will you please give her my best love and tell her I am coming up on the 1st, and she will be the first person I shall want to see.

Thank you *so* much, dear Stephen, both for your essay in the book, and for your review in *Time and Tide*. (The latter I am holding up as an example to the multitudinous people who are making my life hell about 'The Shadow of Cain'. I cannot tell you how grateful I am, and the lateness of my thanks is due not to knowing how to get hold of you (as Natasha, I understood, took a gloomy view of anything reaching you), otherwise I should have telegraphed. Oh, you don't know, you can't conceive, the *rubbish* that is being written about that unfortunate little effort of mine. Mr Something-or-other Fausset, in the *Manchester Guardian*, says it is about Primitive Man and Miss Sitwell's recent mania for esoteric writings. I suppose he never heard of an event that took place at fifteen minutes past eight, on the morning of Monday the 6th of August, 1945!

As against that, an Irish reviewer, who also has never heard of the event, says it is about the Fall of Man. *There* he is right, —but *which* Fall?

I enclose a poem, which, as no doubt they would point out, is about the Fall of Napoleon the Third, and Jenner's discovery of inoculation against smallpox.

The B.B.C. is trying to recite my poem 'Still Falls the Rain' with an introduction saying it has Miss S.'s usual wit and irony!!! I have written saying that I never thought of the Crucifixion as being in any way funny or the subject for wit, and that anyway I loathe wit. I said I didn't know the bombing was funny, either. They really are terrifying. How do you suppose the grey matter in their heads—when it exists—works?

I saw the most wonderful beasts yesterday, at a show in the park. The prize-bull of all England—he was like the power of

Gravity . . . oh, terrific! and the most marvellous horse I have ever seen—a roan, all fire and air, like the horse of the Dauphin. Then there were shining dray-horses, with their manes and harness all twisted with flowers and ribbons. The pride of them all was heavenly. Best love to you both. I can't bear to think of the 20th. Also best love from Osbert, Yours affectionately, Edith.

112. *To Maurice Levinson*

2 October 1947   as from Renishaw Hall

Dear Mr Levinson,

Thank you very much for sending me *The Trouble with Yesterday*.[1] I am profoundly moved by it, not only because of the story of struggle and of a noble heart and mind, but because you really *can* write.

The portrait of your mother is beautiful and moving. That terrible episode of Max Stubey and his mother,—starvation, death, madness, *could* not have been written more beautifully. Then there is that strange encounter with the very old man: that, too, could not be bettered. The life at the orphanage, the description of that, is so real it nearly chokes one.

It is a book with which you have every reason to feel satisfied.

If you have written anything that is not published yet, will you not submit it to my friend John Lehmann. He is the editor of the famous *Penguin New Writing*, and I have been talking to him about your book. When and if you send him a manuscript, will you tell him I suggested to you that you should. He is *very* important to young writers.

I am very glad to have met you. And we shall certainly meet again. For one thing, next time I am in London I shall write and ask you if you will be so kind as to let me know what day you would be 'off duty'. So that I could ask you to have luncheon

---

[1] Mr Levinson had sent E.S. a copy of his first novel after he had picked her up as a passenger in his taxi.

with me, and I would invite, also, Mr Lehmann, who is one of the nicest men in the world.

I cannot bear to think that anybody like you should have suffered as you have. (Indeed, I cannot bear it that anybody should suffer so.) I hope your future will be very happy, and that you will have a great success.

Please let me tell you *I know* you have been forgiven for what a little boy of four years old did, long ago. Don't you see —it was the result of some terrible cruelty inflicted, I think, on some member of your family—as upon your grandfather—that made that little child do that. Forget it now.

The address at the top of this paper is my home address. I return there on Monday. I shall not be in London for some time, but I will not forget to let you know and invite you when I do come. Should you by any chance change your address, please let me know.

Meanwhile, let me tell you again that I think *The Trouble with Yesterday* is a beautiful book; and I wish you success, and I wish you happiness. Yours sincerely, Edith Sitwell.

I hope my *The Song of the Cold* has reached you safely.

113. *To William Plomer*

December 20, 1947   Renishaw Hall

My dear William,

This is just to wish you a very happy Christmas and New Year.

Personally, I loathe Christmas, in spite of being very greedy. But in the new year, one always hopes it can't be quite as bad as the previous one, although one's hopes are never realised.

I am so grateful to you, William, for having so kindly said you liked my 'Shadow of Cain', in *Horizon*. You are one of the only people who understand the poem. I send you, herewith, my two other Atomic Bomb poems. 'The Canticle of the Rose' was written after reading that vegetation is beginning to sprout at Hiroshima.

I went to London for two days, to see Osbert given the *Sunday Times* prize—but two days was quite enough for me. The luncheon party at the prize-giving was delightful, however. There was a man there who began talking to me by saying he knew you. I think I have got his name wrong, but it was either Frazer or Fleming, I think the latter.[1] I thought at first, from his manner with her, that he was Lady Cunard's social secretary, but realised afterwards that she would scarcely have employed him in that capacity. He told me he was 'very amused' to see that you had put my 'Shadow of Cain' first on your *Horizon* list. He ran no immediate risk in saying this, as we were both guests at a luncheon party given in honour of Osbert. He then, until I was at last released from him, expatiated on the other 'amusing' and 'surprising' choices.

I shall be coming up at Easter for about ten days, to look after Evelyn Wiel. I do hope you will be there, even if it is only for part of the time. I am proposing to have a giant luncheon party the Tuesday before Easter. But I'll write to you about that nearer the time.

Love, and all best Christmas wishes from Edith.

114. *To T. S. Eliot*

1 January 1948   Renishaw Hall

Dear Tom,

All Osbert's and my warmest and most delighted congratulations.[2] It was so exciting to be woken up this morning with the news, and it has begun the year so happily, that I, for one, realise the Government can't be one single giant fool, as I had thought. But anything but a fool.

I had never hoped to see the greatest poet of our time properly honoured and reverenced. Well, I have.

Robins—Osbert's old soldier servant—rushed into our

---

[1] Ian Fleming.

[2] T. S. Eliot was appointed to the Order of Merit in the New Year's Honours.

rooms with the news, panting. He is an extraordinary man. Though nurtured on football, and inured by his daughter to crooning on the wireless—(I mean to listening to the horror)— the names T. S. Eliot, Stravinsky and Picasso are part of his vocabulary. He is always bringing them out, with an air of pride. Osbert and S. always jump violently when he does. We feel like the people in Saki's story 'Tobermory' when the cat began to speak—excepting that Robins is a fox terrier, not a cat.

Love from Osbert, Yours affectionately, Edith.

115. *To Richard Eberhart*

11 January 1948   The Hotel St Regis, New York

Dear Richard Eberhart,

I am writing for both of us, because Osbert has gone galloping off to Virginia to lecture (and be badgered by —— —— who are not exactly lower grade mental defectives, but something like).

We are both most delighted to have the poems. They are curiously alive, curiously your own, and their rhythms, which are integral, are very living, and very much a part of your personality. If I had seen them, anywhere, unsigned, I think I would have known immediately that they were yours. I say 'I think.' But I *know*. I have always wanted to tell you that I admire your work, and here is the opportunity.

The book you so kindly sent has not arrived, alas. Can my publishers have foreclosed on it? My *Shakespeare Notebook* has just reached *me*, and will soon reach *you*. I am sending it express.

I can't tell you how much I enjoyed our evening with you, and so did Osbert. We agreed afterwards that it was one of the happiest we have spent anywhere at all. The moment we got inside your door we knew exactly what we felt, not only about you both, but about all your family. Do let us meet again very soon.

You will be receiving an invitation to you both to come to the dress rehearsal of my *Façade*, which is going to be at the Museum of Modern Art (in the Auditorium)—11 West 53rd Street, on Monday the 17th, at 11.30. Is there any happy chance of your being in New York? It would be such fun if you could be there. I am reciting it myself; it is fearfully difficult, and I am nearly dead with fatigue. But it is, at least, great fun.

Mrs —— ——, the lady who drew 'my other brother', is *real*. Yes, she is!! Apparently she is the terror of all who knew her, and is addicted to clinging to bars. (I don't mean that she is an acrobat). I am going into her dossier, but it is, so far, incomplete. Still, she lives. And that is something.

With all best wishes from us both to you both, Yours, Edith Sitwell.

116. *To John Lehmann*

18 January [1948]   Renishaw Hall

My dear John,

Thank you a *thousand* times for sending me this early copy of *Orpheus*.[1] I do hope my telegram arrived safely. I am more than enthusiastic—really think you have surpassed yourself. It is a most exciting and inspiring work.

I admire particularly 'The Man Who Learnt to Walk Naked'. (What a wonderful title, and for what a subject! You write grandly about that great poet)—and the really magnificent translations of the Seferis and Elytis poems. What great poets they are, and how superbly and with what beauty their translators have treated them. I am very excited about both these poets, and think they must be amongst the finest poets living, and that everyone who cares for poetry must be deeply grateful to you for making them available to us. If you have a

---

[1] *Orpheus* was an illustrated 'Symposium of the Arts', the two volumes of which appeared in 1948 and 1949. The first included two contributions by E.S. as well as 'The Thrush' by George Seferis translated by Rex Warner and 'Body of Summer' and 'Sadness in the Ægean' by Odysseus Elytis translated by Nanos Valaoritis.

chance, will you please tell the translators from me how deeply impressed I am by the beautiful English poems they have produced from the Greek poems.

As Osbert and David insisted on seeing the book, I have only just got it back, and therefore do not nearly know it yet. The reproduction of Mexican paintings look very exciting, and Harold Acton's article about them seems admirable. But I am *most* impressed by your essay, and the beautiful translations from the Greek, which really are heaven.

Osbert on dear Arnold gives me a full feeling of that extraordinary man's life.[1] How exciting it is that the book is out, and that it surpasses all one's expectations. (I say 'out'—of course it isn't until the 5th of February: but still it is visible.) I *do* congratulate you, John. I don't see how you could help being proud of the book, from every point of view.

I am so grateful to you for so kindly letting me have this early copy. . . .

117. *To William Plomer*

April 29, 1948   Renishaw Hall

My dear William,

Thank you so much for your letter. Of course I would love to lunch with you when I come up in June. But as the same time I think you and Mr Fleming ought to lunch with *me*, because I got in first. But we can arrange all that nearer the time. I am not trying to bully you, but I shall try and insist. Nobody could have written me two nicer letters than Mr Fleming did.

. Oh dear! how your description of your reaction to poor —— made me laugh. It makes me think of a fearful lunch party when I sat between Sir Edward Marsh and Sam Courtauld. The first made me feel like a dock policeman with an extra size in boots. The second made me feel unpardonably flippant—just a

---

[1] Osbert Sitwell contributed 'A Short Character of Arnold Bennett' to the first issue of *Orpheus*.

wisp of chiffon drifting toward the Great Beyond and the Judgement Day.

—— thinks one has to be screwed up to the pitch at which one writes, the *whole* time,—otherwise one isn't a writer. I told her if one was always at that pitch, one would have died a long time ago. And that I, personally, am an incredibly lazy (physically), greedy, platitudinous person, liking sleep and comfort in my off moments. And that I advised her to be the same. I understand that she is now making Arthur's[1] life hell, and that Bobbysoxer Beryl[2] is furious. Poor girl, and there is something very nice about her, really. Love from Edith.

Yes, do become one of my patients.[3] The great thing would be, I should always advise my patients to do exactly as they like— which would result in an almost immediate cure.

118. *To Bonamy Dobrée*

9 May 1948   Renishaw Hall

Dear Professor Dobrée,
I am most deeply grateful to you. Of course I am perfectly aware that I owe this honour to you. I can only say it could not have been conferred on anyone more appreciative and grateful.

Friday was the proudest and happiest day of my life—quite unflawed by anything. I can't conceive why it didn't rain, in order to make everything look black instead of golden, and glamorous in the original, not film-star, sense of the word. Even my shyness couldn't spoil the day. . . .

I am sending you and her [Mrs Dobrée] under separate cover, a poem of mine about the Atomic Bomb on Hiroshima, and the state of the world that led up to it. A goosey-gander, writing in the *Manchester Guardian*, said it was 'about Miss

[1] Arthur Waley.
[2] Beryl de Zoete.
[3] William Plomer had told E.S. that if she was to become a doctor (Hon. D. Litt. at Leeds University), he would register with her under the National Health Service.

Sitwell's interest in Alchemical writing.' I suppose he thought the part about the cloud shaped like the hand of man, and the splitting of the world, was a description of a boys' cricket match spoiled by a slight shower!

I hope to see you and Mrs Dobrée soon. All my most grateful thanks. I do indeed appreciate your kindness. Yours very sincerely, Edith Sitwell.

119. *To John Lehmann*

15 June 1948   Renishaw Hall

My dear John,

The moment has now come to plague and badger you. (You are used to that, but, I trust, not from me).

I shall probably die—not that it matters—if I can't have lots of advance copies of *I Live Under a Black Sun*[1] by the beginning of September. I beg. I really *implore* that I may, as I want to get the book really started from my point of view (I mean amongst those people who like my work) before I leave for America. And that would take about six weeks. I do hope you will say it is possible. I don't care a bit if it hasn't got its jacket on.

It really is my ewe lamb, and I feel about it as I do about my poetry—I mean, a personal feeling, as if it was part of myself. I don't care about any of my other prose, excepting works *about* poetry.

Have you ever thought of publishing, in the Chiltern Library, Wagner's transcendental short book about Beethoven—to me one of the greatest books about an art that has ever been written? I don't know if you know it. I quoted from it largely in my *Poet's Notebook*.

If you don't know it,—it was translated by Dannreuther, and published by a bookshop called William Reeves. I should think it must have appeared years and years ago. Anyhow, do

[1] E.S.'s novel, first published in 1937, which John Lehmann was re-publishing in his 'Holiday Library'.

have a look at it. (The London Library has a copy.) I thought lunch on Thursday was *hell* . . . there was a general coldness . . .

Next day, an old hag called Lady ——, perhaps hag isn't the right word, she is a large pink woman blooming in the midst of a lot of imitation pink roses,—stopped and said to me 'We were so *amused* by your luncheon party yesterday.' I said 'I am am so glad. We put on the Act to give you a good laugh, and I'm glad it did.' She said '*We* are *never* allowed a party of more than *eight*.' (She thinks I go in for black magic.) She then said, peering at me: 'Are you ill? You are so pale.' I said 'I always go as white as a sheet when I am bored' (which is true). She then went away.

I am enjoying the Seferis very greatly. Thank you so much, John, for giving it to me. Love, Edith.

120. *To Jack Lindsay*

July 23, 1948   Renishaw Hall

I have been wanting to write to you for days . . . but Tom Eliot has just written to ask me for a poem for a new continental magazine got up by a friend of his, and I have got to try to finish this (without an idea in my head) *and* write two broadcasts, before the 15th of August. This has made me nervous, because, to quote Tchelitchew on the subject of his own likeness to the gait of his pet tortoise, 'I crowl and I crowl.' He referred, as do I, to the speed at which he works. Sometimes I work at lightning speed, but now I have got to drag something out of the depths into the light, and it doesn't like coming. Do you work like that? Perhaps not, because you have an amazing and unchained energy. . . .

I hope you will not curse when you read what I have to say. James Laughlin, the American publisher,—the publisher of *New Directions*—is about to bring out, in America, in the early autumn, a collection of essays about my poetry.[1] He asked me who I would most wish to write about me now (the other

[1] *A Celebration for Edith Sitwell*, edited by José Garcia Villa (1948).

essays were collected three years ago, and then mislaid!)—and I said, of course, *you*.

Please do not be angry.

I would be more grateful, more deeply grateful, than I could say—and I know what I am asking, because I know how busy you are,—if you could possibly find time to add, perhaps, a little to your review of *The Shadow of Cain*, so as to make the essay longer (could some of the new book be added?) and send it to James Laughlin, New Directions, 500 Fifth Avenue, New York City 8. It would mean a very great deal to me, and to the success of the book.

I am afraid it would mean a swift despatch of the essay, because I imagine the book is going to press almost at once.

Its history is too extraordinary, and there has been a kind of tug-of-war about it, interspersed with frequent mislayings of the manuscript between the various combatants, for three years, and there have been moments when I have been driven to the verge of dementia by the cross-currents in the case. Now such of it as exists is safe in the hands of Mr Laughlin, a strong silent American. . . .

It was wonderful, what you said about the exquisite creature who looks at you with those eyes made wise by the centuries. Strangely enough, I have such a communicant here. The stone head of a boy, sculptured by Michael Angelo's teacher. I have never seen anything of such a heavenly youth and divine yet earthy innocence. I watch him always when I am in the room. He shames wickedness.

121. *To Barbara Cooper*

[September 1948]   Renishaw Hall

My dear Miss Cooper,
How *very* kind and sweet of you to write and tell me about dear Demetrios's headstone, and about your visit.[1] How much I wish I had been there. Do you think one day when I am in

[1] Demetrios Capetanakis was buried in the Greek Cemetery at Norwood.

London, we could go and put flowers there together? I would particularly like to go with you, and then perhaps you would come back and lunch with me afterwards. I have long wanted to ask you.

It will be a great relief to John to know the stone is there at last. What a terribly long time it has been.

One never ceases to miss Demetrios. I thought what you wrote about him was very beautiful.

With all best wishes, Yours very sincerely, Edith Sitwell.

122. *To John Lehmann*

January 6, 1949   The Hotel St Regis, New York

My dear John,

I do hope you have received my letter by now, and realise to what my long silence was due. I do hope to hear from you soon. I miss you very much.

I hope the new year is going to be a very happy one for you, and better for me, too. This last one was hell, and I have written no poetry.

We spent Christmas at Boston. It was deep in snow, and everything we touched gave us an electric shock. Flames, blue and livid, sprang from keyholes when keys were put into them. David, touching Osbert's forehead to show him where he had a smut, received (and communicated) such a shock that his left arm was useless for the rest of the day, and Osbert gave a piercing howl. I touched nothing excepting through the medium of a glove.

We read poems at the Cambridge school, and I had a short sharp row with a psychiatrist. He said to me, 'I prefer your early poems to your late ones. Am I wrong?' I said 'Actually you are.' He said, 'I don't like to find you writing so much about Christ, as if you had to rely on Him.' 'Oh, isn't He good enough for you?' I enquired. 'What do you want me to substitute for Him—the goodness of the Atomic Bomb? Is *that* what I ought to urge people to rely on?' 'I would like to see you writing about the Dignity of Man', he replied pompously! I don't know what he thinks I am writing about, inter alia, when I write about Christ, if *not* that. And apart from Christ, I don't think the Dignity of Man is on a very high level at this moment. And I said so. We parted with no feeling of friendliness. . . .

Dear me, how much I *do* like the Americans. Anyone who doesn't, must really be mad.

This is a very boring letter, for which I apologise. I do hope to hear from you very soon. Much love, Edith.

PPS. Poor little Denton, I am filled with sadness about him.[1] Not thirty, and so gifted as a prose writer. I do think the short story 'Brave and Cruel' is extraordinary. I had a letter from him a few days before he died.

123. *To John Lehmann*

12 April 1949   Renishaw Hall

My dear John,

I telegraphed to you yesterday, begging you to be an angel and send me *Orpheus* No. 1,—because the servants have gone and lost my copies while I was away—I *told* them *not* to touch a certain drawer where I kept it, so of course they raked it out from top to bottom and threw away everything they felt like throwing away. I need it *urgently*, because it contains my *only* copy of my 'Notes on the Making of a Poem', and I am needing to quote something in my Preface for the American edition of my *Selected Poems*.

I am having, at the moment, hell with the American Anthology.[2] Heavens! There is practically not a living poet, excepting Tom, Ezra, Marianne, E. E. Cummings, Wystan, and José Villa. There is, however, a really magnificent poem by Robert Lowell, 'The Ghost'. Do you know it? I think that on the

---

[1] Denton Welch died on 30 December 1948.
[2] *The American Genius* was eventually published by John Lehmann in 1951.

highest level, one may very nearly call it a really great poem. It has a despair about it, and a haunting wickedness.

There are also very few dead poets either!! Still, the only thing to do is to give a large representation, of those who *are* good poets,—our wonderful Whitman, of course, some Poe, some Emily Dickinson, and Wystan's discovery, the early Taylor. Wystan also pointed out to me a very fine poem by Melville.

For the prose, I shall have a great deal from *Moby Dick*, and Whitman's *Prefaces*, etc.

Can you find out, please, if Ezra's Pisan Cantos *have been published in England?*[1] I have the American edition. There is (amongst a great deal that is quite mad) one perfectly *wonderful* poem, which we will have.

I shall be in fearful trouble with all the Americans for not putting them all in. I shall therefore say in my Preface that this is the First Volume only, and that of course they will all come in the Second. And then there will be *no* Second!! That will jolly them all along, and I shall say to them, if I ever go to America again, that the Second Volume is coming. . . .

124. *To Humphrey Searle*

26 May 1949   Renishaw Hall

Dear Humphrey,

Are you beginning to recover?—For four days I lay like a crocodile on the bank of a river, one hand upraised (as is their habit) in the hope of food being put into it; but otherwise making no sign of life.

You have caused a fearful disturbance here, with that Work to amuse the Kiddies.[2] Robins (Osbert's old soldier servant, who has been with us for thirty years, and is now the butler) kept on waking his wife up, on the night of the performance, by shouting 'Miss Edith is dead'. And his wife, when she saw

---

[1] The *Pisan Cantos* were published in Britain by Faber in July 1949.
[2] Humphrey Searle's setting of *Gold Coast Customs*.

me (she is the cook) said 'Oh-*Miss*', and tittered nervously.
Ooh-er. We *did* have nightmares! The young housemaid
creeps in and out of my room, sideways, like a crab, and looks
at me as if I were going to bite, and the whole of Sheffield is in a
turmoil.

I have just written to the Vice-President of the Columbia
Records, in New York, to say what a great work it is. And I
think that presently we must get started on Mr Stokowski. I
should think he would be mad about it.

I do hope it is going to be done again.

... There cannot be the slighest doubt that you have produced a work of genius. I am more excited about it than I can
possibly say. Am, indeed, completely overwhelmed by it. It is
terrible, awe-inspiring, and noble, even in its horror. And it has
produced the dreadful *loneliness* and broken-heartedness of it in
a way I could not have believed possible. By that, I mean, that
there should have been such an *exact identity* of feeling.

It must have been terrible to do. It is terrible to feel that, let
alone bring it out of oneself. I think you are capable of anything.
What are you going to do next?

I shall be coming to London on the 13th, to see the various
people concerned about the script for the film of the *Midsummer
Night's Dream*. I shall be there for three days, and as soon as I
know when I have to see them, I will write to you, and I hope
you will come and lunch. (I shall be in hiding, due to lack of
time, so don't tell anyone). Yours ever, Edith Sitwell.

125. *To John Lehmann*

7 June 1949   Renishaw Hall

My dear John,
Thank you so much for your postcard.

Holiday time here is one long hell, and one is practically
incarcerated, with no means of reaching the outer world until
it is over—and if one *does* attempt to reach the O.W. the post
simply loses one's attempts. The post also leaves at crack of

dawn, so there is no hope of posting this today. So I shall get it expressed tomorrow.

I *do* hope you will at least have *some* things to enjoy in your South American tour. Oh how I envy you for most things,— but not, of course, the air-journeys. We shall all be thoroughly relieved when you are home again. And what on earth will poor Carlotta[1] do? Howl and howl, I suppose. All song frozen on her lips, poor girl.

This is a very dull letter, but I am not very well, and am appallingly tired. Though you are not the person to whom I should say it, considering the fatigue you will, I am afraid, go through.

Osbert and I are having a fearful row with an Indian. We are, I hope, terrifying him out of his wits.

He pestered me last year to give him an interview, as he wished to write about me. I answered very politely, saying I regretted I could not ever give interviews, as I did not like my *personality* being discussed. He replied he was not an 'ordinary reporter' (the words were *his*) but a D. Litt. and a friend of Tom Eliot's, and that he was going to write about my poetry, not my personality. I therefore let him come and see me. I was very polite to him. But because I would not lunch with him, and could not read the proofs of a book he had written, he has written insufferably about me in the *Continental Daily Mail*, and has said that Osbert's, Sachie's, and my 'fame' exceeds our popularity. We are, it seems, *not* popular in England, and I told him I had no time to waste on reporters!!! He has done his best to injure us. Osbert telegraphed to him yesterday, asking for the name of his lawyers. He keeps on ringing up, and we won't go to the telephone. He appears terrified. Oh dear, I am very unhappy you don't like the second version of 'Medusa' as well as the first. I must look at it again. I thought the second one better technically.

All best wishes for a safe journey, dear John, from Osbert and me. Do try to protect yourself a little against getting too worn out. Love from Edith.

[1] John Lehmann's spaniel.

126. *To Rache Lovat Dickson*

14 July 1949   Renishaw Hall

My dear Rache,

I am very grateful to you for having rescued me from that cover.[1] It really would have been *disastrous*.

Osbert, Sachie, and I are extremely displeased when we are treated as if our works are a *mass* production. We do not like to be treated as if we were an aggregate Indian god, with three sets of legs and arms, but otherwise indivisible. I should have been extremely annoyed if this 'Sitwelliana' idea had appeared on the cover of my *magnum opus*. We have all three suffered very much from this. It vulgarises and cheapens everything, and deprives all the work of its importance. People don't mean to be impertinent, but it *is very* impertinent to lump us all together indiscriminately. We are individual artists, and the fact that we are two brothers and a sister is the business of nobody else considering our work.

I shall be very grateful, too, if you will delete the part about Dr Leavis from that particular place. I *should* like it to appear among the press cuttings. Dr Leavis is certainly *not* of sufficient importance to place him in the blurb. But I *would* like the remark of his quoted among the press cuttings. Please may I have a look at the press cuttings before they are put on—just in case I could think of anything else.

Once again, really, Rache, I am so *very* grateful to you about this.

As you know, we are one of the most devoted families that has ever been, and are *extremely* proud of each other's work. But we don't like being treated as a hive, because it diminishes the importance of each individual.

I shall be in London for ages in September, and do look forward to seeing you.

In great haste, with love, yours ever, Edith.

[1] Lovat Dickson of Macmillan had sent her a proof of the dust-cover of *The Canticle of the Rose* (1949) which contained a reference to herself and her brothers with the general title 'Sitwelliana'.

127. *To John Lehmann*

19 December 1949   Renishaw Hall

My dear John,

A very happy Christmas and a happy and most successful New Year to you.

I must say I hope the coming year will be better than the last one, which, I think, was sheer *hell*.

I found your letter about the Anthology waiting for me when I got back here, and I should have answered it before. But I was in such a state of exhaustion I had to take to my bed. *Gold Coast Customs* is *very* tiring. (In five days I had close on 10 hours of shouting above orchestra. Of course Constant[1] did a lot of it, but there was a good deal of strain waiting for cues.) . . .

In re the Anthology. You know I think José Villa a really fine poet. I, too, think his *experiments* are bosh,—especially the comma one. But he is a Filipino, and Osbert says his heart will be broken if we don't put in those explanations. I, too, agree with what you say about them. But it is very difficult. Because José began to weep at 5.30 on the evening before I left, when he came to say goodbye; and although somebody took him out to dinner afterwards, tears rolled down his dark green cheeks, like large pearls, throughout the evening. This makes it difficult for me to hit him about his experiments. Because he says he *has* to have the poems accompanied by the explanations.

Charles Ford I think a curiously interesting poet. And there I am in an awkward position, too, because I told him I would put those poems in. Kenneth Patchen I think has great gifts. I don't think he always works properly. But he is *literally starving*. I have had a *terrible* letter from his wife about their state, and a letter from James Laughlin imploring me to do something to help.—As for Wystan, I do feel he ought to go in. Anyhow, it seems to me to make a lovely book. And is—or

---

[1] Constant Lambert, who was conducting Humphrey Searle's musical setting of *Gold Coast Customs*.

are—the public lucky for once to get an anthology with *beautiful* American poetry in it? I have written to Tom.

I have read Mr Thompson's[1] poems. Two seem to me quite *magnificent*—very strange. Others also are very beautiful. Not all are equal in value. I am having really *magnificent* notices in America of my American edition of *The Canticle of the Rose*. The *Herald-Tribune* gave it the *whole of the front page and* what amounts to 2 extra full columns of praise. The *New York Times* was also very long and laudatory. . . .

Please stroke Carlotta from me, wish her a Happy Christmas, with plenty of hunting, and thank her for singing so beautifully at my ghastly supper party. (The date of the day and almost each hour in the day will be found engraved on my heart, like the name Calais on the heart of B. Mary, after my death.)

All best wishes once again for Christmas and the New Year. Love, Edith.

128. *To John Lehmann*

Castello di Montegufoni, Val di Pesa, Florence, Italy
10 May 1950

My dear John,
I was so delighted to get your letter of the 5th, last night—(the posts arrive at 6 o'clock in the evening; there isn't a morning one).

How much I wish you were here. Today everything is grey, but yesterday we lunched out amongst lemon-trees just beginning to flower, and we dined out again, lit by fireflies.

I had a hideous journey—(but perhaps I told you about that) and left a trail of nervous breakdown and desolation from Victoria to Pisa. At Victoria I lost a permit, which was found with difficulty. Boarding the Blue Train I lost my porter and my luggage (again retrieved with difficulty). In the afternoon I awoke from a sleep of exhaustion to find —— —— (whom I had met once, five years ago) sitting in my compartment

[1] Dunstan Thompson, American poet.

staring at me. I thought he was an official, and gave him my ticket and passport. At the frontier, I had a hideous battle in the snow with the Customs House officials, who asked me if I was opening a shop.—At Pisa there was no motor to meet me, and my luggage was (again) lost. It is a 2½-hour motor drive, over the mountains, from Pisa to Montegufoni, I can speak no Italian, don't know the way, there was a thick mist, and night was falling. I started off in a taxi, expecting to spend the night in the mountains, but was, eventually, rescued.

Have you received, among your press cuttings, one from the *Isis?* I am really *most* indignant. You remember the afternoon when we played over the *Façade* and *Gold Coast Customs* records? The young people you saw, had come to consult me about *Façade*. They are nice, but they recite *horribly*. *They* were invited. But with them came, *uninvited*, the lout who, taking advantage of my kindness and hospitality, wrote of me as 'the doyenne of drawing-room letters'!!

Naturally, it does not matter what this moronic pip-squeak says in that paper for baby-boys. What *does* matter is that a person can come, uninvited, into my presence, and then behave in such a manner. It is made all the worse by the fact that I never receive journalists who wish to write about me personally. I think it is an outrage. And I think a complaint ought to be made to his college. Unfortunately, I don't know which it is.

An old gentleman, aged 92 ,who was a friend of my father's, came to a lunch party here two days ago, and broke down and sobbed at lunch because his pet hen is dead. This bird used to sleep in his bed, and was in the habit of kissing him goodnight. There were also rows at hotels, because he would bring her into the dining-room. . . .

129. *To C. J. Purnell*

June 29, 1950   Renishaw Hall

Dear Mr Purnell,
Very many thanks for your letter, which I only received yesterday evening, on my return home.

First of all, I must speak of the *very* deep regret we must all feel, that you are going away from us.[1] I know that every member of the Library will miss you very greatly. The London Library is one of the most important inspirations in our life—(I shall never forget the dreadful blank after it had been bombed) and your learning, kindness, and great courtesy have been a part of our lives that nothing and nobody could replace.

Of course I shall be only too happy to move one of the resolutions in the Agenda at the Annual Meeting. I expect I will do it very badly,—but I shall mean well. You speak of a short speech. But I imagine, *not* from me. *If* from me, will you please be very kind and tell me, so that I may prepare it.

With best wishes, Believe me, Yours very sincerely, Edith Sitwell.

130. *To John Lehmann*

17 January 1951   Fairmont Hotel, San Francisco

My dear John,

I was so delighted to get your letter. (I never got the previous one). A very happy new year to you, if such a thing is possible at this awful time.

I am very distressed to hear about the proofs and the expense of the American anthology. Now look here. I have for a very long time wanted to make a present to the firm of Messrs Lehmann. Please allow me to make a present of this book. By which I mean, with the exception of David Higham's fee, I don't want a penny from the book. In fact I won't take one. All I shall want will be Higham's fee paying.

I've been awfully ill. I got amoebic dysentery in Mexico, and really thought I was dying. However I didn't die. As soon as I was up again, long before I was fit to travel, I had to spend three days and three nights (and fourteen hours extra because the Mexican train was late) in the train, because of the infernal

[1] Purnell was retiring as Secretary and Librarian of the London Library.

fussing of the man who had engaged us to speak in Los Angeles.

As a result of fatigue, I got bronchitis, for the second time in three months. I had to give three readings here, coughing my head off. However, the reading in Hollywood was a great success, I do think. Lots of film stars, including Harpo Marx, came. And during my reading of the *Macbeth* sleep-walking scene, I was just announcing that Hell is murky, when a poor gentleman in the audience uttered the most piercing shrieks, and was carried out by four men, foaming at the mouth. As one of the spectators said to me, 'You ought to be awfully pleased. It was one of the most flattering things I have ever seen.'

I've made records of that scene, the pillow scene from *Othello*, Cleopatra's death-scene, etc., for the Columbia records. There will be *rough* copies ready by the time we return, and I'll bring them with me.

In Hollywood I got into a Laocoon entanglement with Miss Mary Pickford, that lasted for ¾ of an hour. Miss P . . . discoursed to me of her role as Little Lord Fauntleroy, and said she always regarded herself as a Spiritual Beacon. We also met Miss Ethel Barrymore, who was delightful, although Osbert ascribes my bronchitis to her, as she was breathing heavily.—I must say I couldn't have enjoyed Hollywood more. We think all the waiters at the hotel there were suffering from the effects of smoking marijuana, their conduct was so strange. They would shriek with laughter suddenly, join in the conversations, and lean on the sofas on which we sat for our meals, putting their heads between ours. . . .

131. *To Sir Maurice Bowra*

5 March 1951   The Hotel St Regis, New York

My dear Maurice,
Once again, I really do *not* know how to express my deep gratitude to you. There is nothing I could say that would be in

the very least adequate. I can only say that the 20th June will be the proudest and happiest day of my life.[1]

Needless to say, I shall love to stay with you for the night before, and the night after.

I look forward to the ceremony with pride and trepidation, and shall be most grateful if you will coach me about it. It is perfect that you can lunch on Wednesday the 28th. I look forward enormously to seeing you.

Even if you *do* have to have clergymen to stay with you, I still think it is most exciting that you are going to be Vice-Chancellor, although you say it is 'a hideous job' involving ceaseless committees. . . .

This is a fearfully dull letter, as nothing ever seems to happen except meetings with Political Hostesses.

I forget if I told you I had my hand kissed by a gorilla? (If I did, forgive me for repeating it). It has made me very vain, for I can't believe many people can boast of this. The gorilla fondled my hand (going over each finger in turn) and then kissed the palm over and over again. She then flung her arms round my neck and pressed her cheek against mine.

With the deepest gratitude, and with love from Osbert and me, Yours affectionately Edith.

132. *To John Lehmann*

21 May 1951   Renishaw Hall

My dear John,
Thank you so *very* much for your letter.

I am very touched that you should suggest my writing my Autobiography, and I have been thinking over very carefully what you said,

There are many reasons why I *might* have wanted to. But after long thought, I don't think I must. One reason is, I think it might upset Osbert. His Autobiography is in one way his

[1] On 20 June, E.S. was to receive an Hon. D. Litt. at Oxford.

greatest life work. And I couldn't bear for him to feel I was trying in any way to rival him over that. (I couldn't, anyhow, because it is a masterpiece, and I can't write prose excepting when I am writing about poetry.) That is the principal reason. The second reason is that I should be asking for death at the hands of the critics, who would ask why the hell a second member of the family had got to do it, when there *had* been a masterpiece of that kind by another member.

What I *do* propose doing, is keeping an elaborate diary, which should produce a feeling of characterisation without telling the inner side of my life. . . .

But thank you, dear John, for suggesting to me that I should do it for you. If I felt I could, I would indeed. . . .

133. *To John Lehmann*

[*c.* 13 June 1951]   As from the Sesame Club.

My dear John,
Thank you very much for your most kind letter. I am so happy to know that you are at work on this book which with such great kindness and goodness you are writing about me.[1]—I do hope it is not being a worry to you. In re my development. Some poets who have not even been among those whom I love most, have yet had an influence on me technically. Baudelaire is one of the poets whom I think the greatest, but I do not know that I have been *influenced* by him.

I think my far-back (but very copious) French blood has had a great influence on me; also my one drop of Spanish blood. I don't know, really, that I *am* very English.

When I was 13, I learned the whole of *The Rape of the Lock* by heart, but I don't think I've been influenced by Pope.

I had an absolute mania for Swinburne as a girl, and learned a lot about vowel-technique from him.

[1] A monograph on E.S., published by the British Council and the National Book League in 1952.

I think on the whole I 'have found' (to quote you) 'poets and poetry in every age that are equally important to me.'

I find sometimes a kinship with poets I have only read very late in life: Sappho, Claudel, Lorca.

I don't know if this is of the faintest use to you. . . .

134. *To Sir Maurice Bowra*

June 21, 1951   The Sesame Club

My dear Maurice,

Nothing that I could say or write would begin to express, in any way adequately, my profound gratitude to you. For what you have done for my poetry. And for your quite extraordinary personal kindness and sweetness to me. And for the two days which have been the most wonderful days of my life (which has had many days of wonder, but of a different and remote wonder).

The day my ten-page book *The Mother* appeared seemed to me then the summit of happiness. But it was the beginning of the journey. And this is the arrival at my destination.

I never did for one moment think, dream, or hope, that this could have happened to me. And I know I owe it entirely to you.

So what can I say?

Whilst I was at Oxford, I was most truly too moved to speak.

Then there was the really fantastic visual beauty. I couldn't have imagined that night-garden and, literally, the most marvellous tree I have ever seen. And then, next day, the undimmed splendour of the proceedings, against the grandeur of such a background.

And your ceaseless kindness. . . .

How much I wish that you could lunch tomorrow. I think, however, that you are, as far as *you* are concerned, well out of it, for I think it is going to be undiluted Hell. . . .

The party on the evening we arrived was great and happy

fun. I think you are the kindest host I have ever known. With my deep gratitude, Yours affectionately, Edith.

A Mrs Mackintosh, from a number that apparently belongs to Mappin and Webb (who say they have never heard of her) rang up twice yesterday and once today. Mackintosh. Can it be Maclean? What makes it much more sinister, is that the parent firm of Mappin and Webb is in Sheffield. . . .

135. *To William Plomer*

January 2, 1952   Hotel San Domenico, Taormina, Sicily

My dear William,

Thank you so much for your most charming and delightful letter. And I am more grateful to you than I can say for so kindly sending me Colonel van der Post's most remarkable, most noble, and beautiful, book.

But before I go any further, I wish you a very happy new year, dear William. And this would have been written before, but for the last fortnight we have had nothing but news of dreadful illnesses—one after another, culminating in the fact that poor Susan Robins, who has been with us for 35 years, has inoperable cancer. (Only please do *not* mention that to Osbert, if you should be writing to him.)

Venture to the Interior is one of the most remarkable books I have read for a very long time. The beauty is quite extraordinary, and the nobility of outlook, the warmth of heart and spirit, very great. And what *verbal* greatness! 'The intolerable and fanatic sun of the Nyasaland summers.' 'The grey, old, prehuman world about us.' The flowers 'sizzling with colour and sun-fire like Catherine wheels at a fair', the honey with 'a royal, antique flavour, a wild, sharp, uninhibited sweetness all its own'.

Extraordinary, and exquisite. But it is the nobility and fire of the spirit that gives the book a real greatness. He seems to me a most truly extraordinary writer. . . .

I am having a good deal of trouble with the poets at present, owing to the fact that I arranged a 'Personal Anthology' for the B.B.C. One old gentleman told me (I am *not* exaggerating) that he was going to send *390* poems which would form part of his Collected Poems, and that I had to read them all, criticise them at length, and find him a publisher. He had had a previous volume, entitled *Songs to Circe* published by Messrs Thompson and Parkins of Wolverhampton, but these, by some strange mischance, had only been reviewed in one paper, the *Wolverhampton Herald*. Could I throw any light upon this. The new 390 were to be called *Songs of the Spirit*—which seems to me to tell one all, without there being any necessity for the fatigue of reading them.

I told him that I was, regretfully, unable to spare the time to read them. Whereupon he replied that he quite understood, and sent me *Songs to Circe*, a book which contains 286 poems!

I should be most awfully grateful, if you could be an angel and tell me, some time, Ian's address in Jamaica.[1] He thinks I am annoyed with him because he had to chuck lunching with me. And I want to tell him I am not. I don't want to bother you. Just a postcard.

Love, and once again all very best wishes from Osbert and me for the new year, and so many grateful thanks for *Venture to the Interior*. Edith.

Please forgive this paper. I came away without writing paper, and the hotel's is the size of a postage stamp.

136. *To Jack Lindsay*

May 21, 1952   The Sesame Club

I should have written yesterday; but had very unpleasant experiences at the 'dress rehearsal' on Monday—which was not a rehearsal at all, as the people concerned had not troubled to

---

[1] Ian Fleming.

see to a microphone for me!!! So I could not rehearse more than two items!! I was very angry, and this, and the heat, made me ill. I thought I was going to faint at the performance.

I only tell you this to explain why I am late in writing.

I *cannot* be grateful enough to you for lending me, not only the proofs of this very great book, but also for sending me the terrific opening of the *Herakliad,* and the wonderfully lovely *St Sophia.* My goodness, have you opened a new world for me—and for how many thousands of others!!![1]

But first, I must speak of your letter.

I am made *ill* by the thought of atrocities—no matter by whom they are committed. I am unable to see that it matters who is the victim—peasant, Jew, nun, Negro, priest, aristocrat. An atrocity committed on any of them is equally infamous. I am horrified at, and terrified by, warmongering propaganda. The persons who are responsible for it will be responsible, before they have done, for millions of deaths. All we can hope for is to keep calm, and fight this with a sane mind. I think there *must* be a mistake about our men: I cannot see them doing such things. And I think, also, that the story about germ warfare must be one of those atrocity stories that whip up hatred against opponents in every war.

But you know, dear Jack, that I am incapable of understanding political questions. I was (I believe, even, as well as hope) born to be a poet; and nobody can be that who does not care for great human problems. But I am unable to understand the mechanism of politics. . . .

137. *To Harriet Cohen*

[29 July 1952] The Sesame Club

Darling Harriet,
I would have adored to come—but *alas*! I am in the wars! I've

---

[1] The book was *Byzantium into Europe* by Jack Lindsay, published in the autumn of 1952. He also sent E.S. his translations of the *Herakliad* (which is the opening of George of Pisidia's *Hexameron*) and a poem of Paul the Silentiary on St Sophia.

got a chill, *and* a sprained foot (having barked it against my luggage). On top of this, I have to meet a stone-deaf old lady (very sweet) off the Golden Arrow, and move from this club to Durrants Hotel, where she is staying with me, as this is closed. I *am* sorry. Will you be in London during August? Do let us meet. I was rather battered morally after my tea party, as somebody went mad at lunch. And when I say mad, I mean mad. I wonder if *you* had trouble with him at tea—a tall, fairish young man like a superannuated choirboy.

At one moment I thought he was going to commit suicide over the balcony. I should have been delighted excepting that I suppose I should have had to behave well, cancel the tea party, and attend the inquest. He made 'advances' of an unusual character to one elderly lady of a pristine purity, one young girl, one young married woman, and Jane Clark. (The young married woman being Gillen Searle.)

I am more than disappointed about Thursday. Love, Edith.

138. *To Geoffrey Gorer*

27 September 1952   Castello di Montegufoni

Dearest Geoffrey,

I am afraid we shall have to chose another theme for the opera if we do it—not Anne Boleyn,—because I have just had a letter from George Cukor, who, with the greatest kindness, has got his agent to make a rough draft of what my contract ought to be with Columbia, with whom I am to work, and one of the clauses says that Columbia will have all rights in the book[1] if they take the film.

So I am thinking out another theme for the opera. At the minute I am wondering whether an opera called *The Adventurers*, about the discovery of America, might not be a good idea.

The President of Columbia, when tackled by George, at once said he would put down 5,000 dollars for my transit and

---

[1] *Fanfare for Elizabeth.*

keep in Hollywood (this being my option on the film). George says he is a very hard-headed go-ahead tough businessman, so if he is willing to risk that, I think it looks very hopeful.

George says 'the prospects are exceedingly rosy.'

His agent suggest that *if* Columbia takes the film, I should be paid 45,000 dollars *over and above* the 5,000,—which is not so dusty! (Of course I don't know if Columbia will agree to that, but George's agent must know what he is doing, as he will have enormous experience).

I am very excited by the prospect of this. For it really would be rather nice to have some money just for once. I feel poor David Higham will be very disappointed if I get this, as he told me all I should get at most would be about £5,000! Osbert was so overcome he couldn't sleep, and says he feels he will never sleep again. . . .

I am just reading the Life of Hugh Walpole[1]—a wonderful human document. Perhaps the best part is about that treacherous old beast Lady Colvin, who wrote and told Hugh that Galsworthy was the man who was the most like to Christ of anyone she had ever known, 'without being the least bit of a prig'. She did not, however, like the hero of his *Loyalties*. 'I could not feel much interest in a hero who steals money; *any* other crime one might forgive, but not that.'

139. *To T. S. Eliot*

30 December 1952   As from the Bel Air Hotel, Los Angeles

My dear Tom,

. . . I cannot remember, now, how many pages Mr Heath-Stubbs suggested should be devoted to my poems. So I send, on a separate sheet, various suggestions from which, if he liked, he could select, according to the number of pages needed.[2]

I do hope you are keeping well, and that no wretch has

---

[1] By Rupert Hart-Davis (1952).
[2] *The Faber Book of Twentieth Century verse*, edited by John Heath-Stubbs and David Wright, included six poems by E.S. when it appeared it 1953.

managed to give you, or *will* manage to give you, bronchitis or influenza.

We go to Los Angeles on the 1st—for five glorious days of luxury among the—as we suspect—marijuana-smoking inhabitants . . .—and then to a flat that George Cukor has very kindly found. I looked forward immensely to being in Hollywood, but everyone I have met has done his or her best to terrify me. I was told yesterday that people of my height are frequently *drowned* walking along the street, by a sudden downpour of rain.

Wystan and I, who for some reason often share the same cross, have recently shared a very heavy one. I admit that Wystan bore the heaviest part of the burden, but mine, also, had a certain weight. The cross is in a very odd state—taking off his coat and collar and tie, and reciting while dancing wildly and plunging like runaway horses. Opinions vary. Some say he is under the influence of the god, and has been to too many parties. Others say not. I had three quarters of an hour alone with this—having seen him but once before. He is enormous, and I feared a plunge through the window, in which I would have been unable to hold him. Two days after, he rang up at 2.30 A.M. and said I must give him something to make him sleep. Then I really did swear. Wystan—who really has a saintly character—came round next day and got him a doctor, at the request of the cross—who is sweet when he isn't being a cross, and, I think, a good poet, so nothing must be held in evidence against him.

Wystan also suffers from a girl of 20 who tries to get into his flat at 2 A.M. . . .

140. *To T. S. Eliot*

Sunset Tower, 8358, Sunset Boulevard,
Hollywood 46, California

22 January 1953

My dear Tom,
So very many thanks for your letter. Yes, I certainly like that selection very much.

I do hope you are keeping well. Here everybody is sporting influenza-germs like a herd of sea-elephants.

My principal entrancements here are the columns of the lady gossip-writers, which I read with avidity. . . . Unable to get at me—because I wouldn't see them—one wrote 'A *little* old lady' (my italics) 'has just come to Hollywood: Edith Sitwell.' A man reporter asked me on the telephone: 'Is it true you are 78?' I replied: 'No. Eighty-two.' 'But I read last week that you are 78.' 'Yes, but that was *last* week. *This* week I'm 82.'

Osbert sends his love. Affectionately, Edith.

141. *To John Gielgud*

12 May 1953 Renishaw Hall

Dear John,
Very many thanks for your letter, which I should have answered before, but was in agonies with sciatica.

I am *very* proud that next month we shall be partners in the same 'practice'—i.e., Oxford.[1] Personally, I feel that the Oxford doctorate is the one thing most worth having. Fools are made knights and dames—and anyhow, who would want to walk through doors in Heaven ahead of William Shakespeare?—Fools are made doctors by other fools in other universities, but no fool has ever been given an Hon. D. Litt. by Oxford.

[1] John Gielgud was made an Hon. D. Litt. of Oxford on 24 June 1953.

I shall think of you so much on the 24th of next month. I
wonder where you will be staying.

It is most exciting about *Venice Preserv'd*; I look forward
eagerly to seeing it. I shall be coming to London in the middle
of July and I do hope that then you will not be too busy to
lunch with me one day.

I long to talk to you about Hollywood. Oh, how right you
were! I wonder if you met that appalling woman Hedda
Hopper? I had trouble with her, so I've told everybody that
I heard on the best authority that the very bad outbreak of
rabies in Hollywood was due to the fact that Miss Hopper had
pursued the dogs and succeeded in biting them. I added that
personally I didn't believe a word of it—for, after all, they run
very fast!

With very best admiration, Yours, Edith Sitwell.

142. *To Alberto de Lacerda*

22 May 1953   Renishaw Hall

Dear Alberto,

So very many thanks for your letter, for the lovely new poem,
which I like *very* much, and for those beautiful poems of Jean
Cocteau's. The one in memory of Lorca is most moving and
beautiful.

I should have written before, but have been having a terrible
time with my film-treatment, now restored to me to be worked
at, after dear —— has wreaked his will on it. *Please tell nobody
about this, excepting Gordon,*[1] *whom I am telling, as I do not want
my troubles going all round London, and being discussed in
potato queues.*

The film now opens with what would seem to be a sort of
pillow-fight in the 'dorm' of the 6th form at St Winifred's
(Anne's awakening): When the atmosphere isn't that of *Young
Bess* or *The Tudor Wench*, it is that of *Forever Amber* or *Sweet
Nell of Old Drury*. There is a lot of 'rough stuff'. George

[1] Gordon Watson, Australian pianist.

Boleyn comes into Anne's room when she is in a bath-towel!
Henry is always either rolling drunk on the floor, or roaming
about in his night-clothes, or snoring in bed. George acts as
pander between Anne (*his sister!!*) and the King. —— has
endowed the King and Anne with napkin rings!! marked H.R.
and A.B. (after she is Queen) and Elizabeth's governess says
'Give the girl some cookies!' Oh, heavens above!!! . . .

I have had a miserable letter from Tennessee Williams. His
very great play *Camino Real* has been taken off. It is a terrific
work. I wrote to the *Herald-Tribune* protesting against the way
it has been treated.

I am thinking of having a book of *Collected Poems*. Do you
think this is a good idea?

Several people are trying to get into the house. An Italian
woman wants to interview me, and if I won't go to London, she
will come here. What a hope! And a woman I have never heard
of says she is coming down here to draw me,—and will do so
while I am writing!!!

My temper is like a rhinoceros's. I must soon indulge in a
tug-of-war with ——. There will have been nothing like it
since the battles between the Ichthyosaurus and the Pleiohippus.
But if I don't win, it will have to be the river for me.

The Russian lunatic says he will bother Dr Leavis.

Oh, how much I want to get back to poetry! I am no writer
for *Sweet Nell of Old Drury*. They should get a genius, if they
want that sort of thing.

All best wishes, Yours as ever, Edith.

143. *To Lady Bantock*

18 August 1953   Renishaw Hall

Dear Lady Bantock,
Your most charming letter and very kind wish that I should
read your poems touched me very greatly.

Please believe that only the really *terrible* pressure of work that is on me at this time prevents me from having what I know would have been a very real pleasure.

I am having to forgo all reading outside that with which my work is involved, at this time. For two reasons. I am obliged to finish a film for which I have a time-limit. *And* I am about to compile an anthology of 2,000 pages! The latter involves endless reading, and I have to devote all the time left over from the film, to that. So far I have reached the date 1350!!

So you see how I am placed.

It is with the greatest regret that I am forced to forgo the pleasures of other reading.

But of one thing I am certain. You should indeed republish your poems. They will give great pleasure, it is most easy to see.

Thank you again for your very delightful letter.

Yours sincerely, Edith Sitwell.

144. *To Sir Maurice Bowra*

November 25 1953   Sunset Boulevard

I cannot be grateful enough to you for your very wonderful letter, which was *the only thing* that made the first ten days here endurable. It was a great comfort to me. And I should have written before, but have not been very well.

The whole story of Dylan's death is a most terrible one. Caitlin had not wanted him to come, and of course (apart from the opera he was to write with Mr Stravinsky) she was quite right, because he did know the most awful people here.

I got a cable on the boat to say that Dylan had died; then, from the moment we set foot in New York, the rows and accusations started. There were moments when I simply did not know *where* they would lead, and I was seriously alarmed. As though it was not terrible enough to have that great loss—frightful loss—to poetry *and* one's grief, for I was deeply attached to him. . . .

Leaving aside the terrible, dreadful sadness, I was nearly

worried out of my wits because everybody, including complete strangers, kept on ringing me up and denouncing each
other to me, trying hard to involve me in barren and ugly
rows. That awful man Mr —— ——, whom I don't know,
rang me up 19 times in two days. I refused to see him. He had
been a *very* bad influence on Dylan, and an absolute nuisance
all the way round.

That poor, most dear, and most wonderful poet! I still feel
absolutely numb, which was the state I fell into after the first
dreadful knowledge both of that death and the manner of it.
What young poet can begin to compare with him? And he was
a most endearing creature, like a sweet and affectionate child. I
can't bear to think how we shall miss him.

145. *To Tom Driberg*

4 February 1954   Sunset Boulevard

Dear Tom,
I do not know when I have been so moved as by your most
chivalrous and noble defence of me in the *New Statesman*. I am
very deeply grateful to you. I shall not, believe me, forget it.[1]

I thought the attack particularly mean, and that it was actu-
ated by personal hatred and, probably, envy. We have been
having trouble with the *New Statesman* for some time. A
person named Ustinov produced a play called *No Sign of the
Dove* about Osbert and me. (Several papers said so in as many
words.) In this we were given the name of *D'Urt* and were
represented as sex maniacs!!! One paper said our 'greedy
sensual lives were rebuked' (it mentioned us by name). One of
the only two papers that *praised* the play was the *New Statesman*, that went into raptures over it, not once but twice.

I am here writing a film. At the moment it is frightful, owing
to the fact that my dear good collaborator wants to make it

---

[1] The *New Statesman* published a satirical profile of 'Queen Edith' on
23 January 1954. This drew replies from Tom Driberg and John Pudney on
30 January, and from E.S. herself on 13 February.

naturalistic, as he calls it. One can't contradict him, because if one does he shrieks like a regiment of horses that has been mowed down by cannon. It is exactly like a battle-picture by Géricault transformed into sound. Luckily the director, George Cukor, who is on my side, has a will of iron.

I shall be glad to leave in some ways, though the weather is heavenly. It has been 86 for five days!

I know how terribly busy you are, but when I return, at Easter, I do hope you and your wife will come and lunch with me.

My deep and unforgettable gratitude to you. All best wishes, Yours ever, Edith (Sitwell).

146. *To John Lehmann*

February 5, 1954   Sunset Boulevard

My dear John,

Thank you so much for your letter. I am *rejoiced* to hear this splendid news about the *London Magazine*. I am [*illegible*] but surprised, but I am more than delighted. Once again, can I ask you to have someone send me a subscription form. There will then be 28,501 subscribers.[1]

I should have written before to thank you for your review in the *Sunday Times*, but I've been feeling deathly ill, and have had to work 8 hours a day, including Sundays. (This has stopped for a few days, but I've got to do the whole damned thing again; for reasons which I will tell you later.) The review pleased me very much. I am, and always shall be, *deeply* grateful to you for what you have done for my poetry. . . .

Oh God, what I am going through here, and now, in spite of the heavenly weather (it is *86*—imagine)! I long to be back (if only I could take the weather with me.)

—— (my collaborator) was determined from the beginning that the atmosphere of Henry's Court should be a cross

---

[1] The first number of the *London Magazine* was dated February 1954, but was on sale in January.

between that of Le Nid and Mon Repos in Surbiton, and that of the sixth form dormitory at St Winifred's. Anne Boleyn eats chocs behind a pillar, and pinches Jane Seymour's bottom behind Cardinal Wolsey's back. She is frequently addressed by her brother as either 'Sister mine' or 'Little sister'. ——'s obstinacy has to be seen—or rather heard—to be believed. When contradicted—(which is once in a blue moon, because I can't get a word in edgeways) he shrieks so piercingly that, although I am on the 10th floor, he can be heard on the 4th. It is exactly like a battle picture from Géricault transformed into sound (a cavalry regiment complete with horses, mowed down by cannon, and uttering their death shrieks). 'Dr Sidwell,' said Mrs Pastor, the sweet elderly Hungarian who cooks for me, 'dose shrieks dey heard down the lift shaft on de fourth floor, and doze people dey crowd round de lift wid their eyes raised to heaven.'

George says he won't have the atmosphere of Le Nid or Mon Repos—but *he* will have to do the fighting as I want my voice for reciting, and my iron will has got very badly dented.

Much love to you and Carlotta—tell her I have a friend here who is a poodle, but she comes first. Edith.

147. *To John Lehmann*

3 April 1954   Hotel St Regis, New York

I have been very ill, or should have written before. This is just to say we start for England on Saturday the 10th, arriving on Maundy Thursday. Do let me know, please, the first day you can come and lunch. I shall be in London till about the 3rd of May, when I start for Montegufoni.

I am *not* feeling very matey—which is scarcely surprising—and you are one of the *only* people I intend to see.

The poem I sent you is the last I shall ever have published in England, so I think it is very suitable that it should be published by you.[1]

---

[1] The first of the 'Two Songs of Queen Anne Boleyn' was published as 'A Young Girl's Song' in the *London Magazine*, no. 4, May 1954.

I have altered the end slightly. It now runs:

> 'Then the heart that was the Burning Bush
> May change to a Nessus-robe of flame
> That wraps not only its true-love
> But all the gibbering ghosts that came:
> That flame then dies to a winter candle,
> Lightless, guttering down,
> And the soul that was the root of Being
> Changes to Nothing-town.'

(All the same verse.) . . .

The London Magazine (three numbers) has appeared, and I am deep in it. I am particularly glad you have published a poem by Charles Causley. He is *the only* young poet of talent that I have seen. Did you discover him? I think the only young poet since Laurie Lee . . .

a dog

Give Carlotta my love, and stroke her ears. Tell her I have heard no music since I reached America—excepting for that awful day and night when the radio was turned on in my compartment on my way back from Hollywood—playing the same very bad programme over and over again. It was 24 hours before it was discovered that the noise was actually in my bedroom!

148. *To Sir Malcolm Bullock*

18 June 1954   The Sesame Club

. . . I have only just found (I was packing at the time I wrote to you) my letter to you, thanking you for that really enthralling book about Rasputin, *in my hat-box*!! It must have got slipped in there somehow. I do apologise. The description of the murder is one of the most terrifying things I have ever read.

Now. In re the pull-over. The measurements you sent me are tailor's measurements, not for use by knitters. Can you please ask your cook to measure you and send me the following: measurement round the hips. Measurement from bottom of pull-over to where the neck opening comes. Measurement from bottom (at side) to under the arm. Measurement from under the arm to where the arm-hole ends. All this to Renishaw. Then I'll begin. Yours affectionately, Edith.

Will she please measure a *pull-over*, not you, as one must make allowance for it being properly loose.

149. *To Benjamin Britten*

26 April 1955   As from Castello di Montegufoni
My dear Ben,
I am so haunted and so alone with that wonderful music and its wonderful performance that I was incapable of writing before now. I had no sleep at all on the night of the performance. And I can think of nothing else.[1]

It was certainly one of the greatest experiences in all my life as an artist.

During the performance, I felt as if I were dead—killed in the raid—yet with all my powers of feeling still alive. Most terrible and most moving—the appalling loneliness, for all that it was a communal experience one was alone, each being was alone, with space and eternity and the terror of death, and then God.

What a very great composer you are! and what a very great singer Peter is.

I can never begin to thank you for the glory you have given my poem. . . .

150. *To Father Philip Caraman*

7 May 1955   Castello di Montegufoni
Dear Father Caraman,
My most grateful,—indeed grateful—thanks for your letter,

---

[1] Benjamin Britten's setting of 'Still Falls the Rain' was sung by Peter Pears at the Wigmore Hall on 23 April 1955.

which I found waiting for me on my arrival on Thursday. It gave me great happiness, a feeling of hope.

I believe, and trust with all my heart, that I am on the threshold of a new life. But I shall have to be born again. And I have a whole world to see, as it were for the first time, and to understand as far as my capacities will let me.

Prayer has always been a difficulty for me. By which I mean only that I feel very far away, as if I were speaking into the darkness. But I hope this will be cured. When I *think* of God, I do not feel far away. . . .

I am at this time reading St Thomas Aquinas, and shall read, daily, in the Missal. . . .

With my deep gratitude to you for your great kindness to me, and your infinite help, Yours very sincerely, Edith Sitwell.

151. *To Benjamin Britten*

11 May 1955   Castello di Montegufoni

My dear Ben,

Your wonderful letter to me *just* missed me in London, and was forwarded to me here. I can only say that it has filled me with pride. I am full of excitement and wonder at the thought of what those months in which you are going away will bring.

I am so happy to know that if it is possible, you and Peter will give us, again, the great experience of hearing 'Still Falls the Rain', at the Festival Hall. I am very grateful.

I can't tell you how much Osbert and I are looking forward to *The Turn of the Screw* . . . and we are happy to think that you, Peter, and Mr Douglas will be lunching with us here on the 5th. We will have you fetched (I'll let you know at what time later, because I never *can* remember how long it takes to get here). I hope it will be fine so that we can lunch on the terrace, which is looking very lovely just now. Until today it has been burning hot, and we have lunched out almost every day, and dined out often. . . .

Love to you and Peter from Osbert and Edith.

P.S. I do wish the village band had not disrupted, owing to warring political factions. I would have liked you to hear them. They played with an incredible rhythmical elegance, and, as they never by any chance played the right notes for more than two bars running, they gave the impression that the waltzes, etc., had been written by Satie.

152. *To Sir Maurice Bowra*

May 30, 1955   Castello di Montegufoni

My dear Maurice

It would be most delightful if you could lunch with me on Wednesday the 22nd of June, at the Sesame (12.30). I am going to ask Kenneth and Jane,[1] and Mr David Jones, whom I do not know, but I think he is a really great poet. Do you agree? (I have been in correspondence with him about my giant anthology.) I do *hope* you will be able to come. It is such ages since we have seen you, and we have missed you very much.

My first week in London is going to be very *mouvementé*, and I shall probably be a stretcher case. First I go to recite at Cambridge (which may end in my being lynched). Then I rehearse for *Façade*, and finally read my later poems for forty minutes and then recite *Façade* at the Festival Hall on the 15th. Ben Britten has composed a most wonderful setting of my *Still Falls the Rain*, for tenor, piano, and horn, and he, Peter Pears and Mr Dennis Brain are performing it also on the 15th.

I am in bad trouble in Leamington Spa literary circles. A lady unknown to me, who lives there, has written to tell me that her relatives 'had no right whatsoever' to 'allow' me to think that I might use her poems 'The Thrushes' Lullaby', 'Mr Tittlewit's Zoo', and 'The Mouse's Wedding'. Apparently not only have I pirated these, and am masquerading as their author, but, philistine that I am, I have actually had the effrontery to make certain alterations in them. This, says the

[1] Sir Kenneth and Lady Clark.

lady, has 'damaged her terribly', and she is heartbroken, also, at 'the liberty that has been taken'.

I have written to reassure her, and have told her that I am *not* masquerading as the author of these works, but that it is evident that *someone, somewhere,* has been behaving very badly about something.

I advised her to write to Dr Leavis, and tell him everything, keeping nothing back—for I am certain that *he* knows what is at the back of it all. I said I remembered distinctly the very loud and laudatory essay by him in *Scrutiny* on the subject of her work—he being particularly enthusiastic about 'The Mouse's Wedding' and 'The Thrushes' Lullaby'. I told her to *insist* on an answer, and to *insist* on his sending her the essay. I said 'He is very remiss about answering. Just keep on till he *does* answer.' I think we may get good results.

Osbert sends his love, and so do I. Yours affectionately, Edith.

153. *To Father Philip Caraman*

3 June 1955 Castello di Montegufoni

Dear Father Caraman,

You told me I might write to you on the subject of the books I have been directed by you to read, and so I do. I only hope the letter will reach you, for I see that the posts are most uncertain owing to the strike.

I cannot express to you my gratitude for having recommended these books to me. The first feeling they give me is one of absolute certainty. They—and especially the wonderful writings of St Thomas Aquinas, and Father D'Arcy's *The Nature of Belief,* make one see doubt—perhaps I am not expressing this properly—as a complete failure of intellect. Then again I see that purely intellectual belief is not enough: one must not only *think* one is believing, but *know* one is believing. There has to be a sixth sense in faith.

How wonderful that passage is in *The Nature of Belief* about 'looking through the appearances at reality. Once this is granted the existence of God must be admitted without more ado. . . . If there is anything there, then there must be something fully real.' And this passage: 'The evil of unbelief is that it must shut its eye to the forms and patterns of truth inscribed in the universe, and retire to the inner sanctuary of the mind, there to rest in uncertainty, in the presence of a fugitive self and the broken idols of its hopes.'

When I was a very small child, I began to see the patterns of the world, the images of wonder. And I asked myself why those patterns should be repeated—the feather and the fern and rose and acorn in the patterns of frost on the window—pattern after pattern repeated again and again. And even then I knew that this was telling us something. I founded my poetry upon it. Did you, I wonder, know Dr Hubble, of the Expanding Universe—one of the greatest men I ever knew. One day, in California, he showed me slides of universes unseen by the naked eye, and millions of light-years away. I said to him 'How terrifying!' 'Only when you are not used to them,' he replied. 'When you *are* used to them, they are comforting. For then you know that there is nothing to worry about—nothing at all!'

That was a few months before he died. And so I suppose now that he knows how truly he spoke. I was most deeply moved by that. I could never cease to be so.

With my deep gratitude, Yours very sincerely, Edith Sitwell.

This is a most inadequate letter. For some reason I cannot express myself in the slightest at present.

154. *To Father Philip Caraman*

9 July 1955   Renishaw Hall

Dear Father Caraman,
I am most *deeply* grateful to you for your great goodness in giving up your most valuable time to come here and instruct me.

I do not, indeed, know how to thank you. I am so ashamed that owing to my incredible stupidity, you were not met in Sheffield. Please believe me when I say that I would not have had it happen for anything, and, also, that I hope it is not usual for me to be so careless and so (apparently, but not in reality) ungrateful.

I enjoyed our meeting so greatly, and look forward to the next.

Have you seen Evelyn's onslaught on two would-be invaders of privacy, in the *Spectator*.[1] It is in his best vein. Isn't it strange how, with the best prose-writers, you can hear the sound of their voice? 'Artists of all kinds form part of the battle-training of green reporters. "Don't lounge about the office, lad," the editors say, "sit up and insult an artist!" '—I can hear Evelyn's actual voice in that. I wonder what the Beaverbrook Press will try to do to him in revenge, and what will be their resultant fate.

I am still looking for the drug-addict's lingo of which I spoke and will send it to you with the other notes, when found.

With my deepest gratitude, and best wishes, Yours very sincerely, Edith Sitwell.

Please give Father D'Arcy my best wishes.

155. *To William Plomer*

July 9, 1955   Renishaw Hall

My dear William,

It would be quite impossible for me to tell you what *enormous* pleasure your letter gave me.

I shall be *deeply* proud and happy to have the Ballad dedicated to me.[2] I long to see it, and hope John will send it immediately. I think it is most sadistic of you not to have sent it with your letter.

---

[1] In 'Awake my Soul! It is a Lord' (*Spectator*, 8 July 1957) Evelyn Waugh got his own back on Lord Noel-Buxton and Nancy Spain for calling uninvited.
[2] 'Palmyra'.

I am *so excited* at the thought of the dedication. Thank you a thousand times, William.

I don't think I have any news. I am feeling slightly battered after last week's University and Master Cutler's beanos in Sheffield, and after tramping for miles with a Doctor's hat precariously perched on my head (and too small for me). The only relief was Lord Goddard's speech at the Master Cutler's. He had had a very tiring week at the Assizes, and, from time to time sank into a coma that seemed to me to last for ten minutes —but of course it can't have been quite so long. This happened several times, and once I thought he must have died in his sleep. But he awoke (eventually) and said 'Is this the Master Cutler's Feast? Yes, of course it is—and here I am!' He then continued his discourse.

Osbert and I saw him immediately before, and immediately after, and he was then in fine trim, so I think perhaps he was doing it for fun.

I have just been re-reading (for the hundredth time, I should say) 'Ula Masondo'. What a *great* short story. It is *most* magnificent! All the stories in that wonderful book *Four Countries* are! Every time I read them, I am overcome. The dedication of the Ballad is the one happy thing that has happened to me since I can remember—that and Ben Britten's great setting of 'Still Falls the Rain' and his, and Peter's great kindness to me.

I have a book for you. Having not heard from several people to whom I had asked my American publishers to send my *Collected Poems*, I sent for a list of people to whom they *did* send it. Your name was on my list, but not on theirs, so I am sending the book to you. It will not be appearing in England.[1]

Love, and deep gratitude, from Edith.

---

[1] E.S.'s *Collected Poems* were in fact published in England by Macmillan in 1957.

156. *To Geoffrey Singleton*

11 July 1955   Renishaw Hall

Private and Confidential

Dear Mr Singleton,

Many thanks for your letters and for showing me the manuscript of your book, most of which has, indeed, given me very
great pleasure and aroused my gratitude.

With what care you have gone into everything; thought
about everything, and written about everything! I am indeed
grateful. And it is in a spirit of gratitude that I am about to put
right such very few and small errors that naturally, in a book of
such size, written away from the subject of it, have crept in. I
will take these as they occur.

Miss Rootham did indeed nurture my innate love of the arts.
But my poetry has *always* been my own, my particular tastes
have *always* been my own, and nobody else's. Nobody *could*
influence my taste in poetry. I am, and always have been from
babyhood, a woman of my métier. I was born to be so. My
dedications to Helen Rootham were made because she was
such a wonderful friend to me during my childhood and youth.
She protected me against my mother—which needed some
doing. (It was my mother, and not my father, who made my
childhood and youth a living hell,—and I am not exaggerating.)

Helen Rootham did *not* come with me on my flight
to Swinburne's grave. That would have been delightfully
respectable (and completely devoid of any interest) but it
did not happen. She had nothing to do with it. I took my
maid.

I shall be glad if you will be careful about all that, because
the Rootham family are, to say the least of it, difficult. Their
late brother shovelled any responsibility for Miss Rootham and
her still-living sister Madame Wiel on to me. His cynical
impudence was beyond belief. I shouldered and shoulder the
responsibility gladly, loving them, but it does not excuse him,
as to do so, I have to *work*.

By the way, I did *not* praise Mrs Meynell. Please erase that. She is *hopelessly* bad. And I do not remember praising Dowson. He is limp and lifeless.

Pages 303, 304 et seq. I now admire Day Lewis and Spender, and they are close personal friends of mine. So I would be grateful if you will omit any passages quoting me as having written in detriment of them in the past, as it would endanger our relations, which I value greatly.

I like MacNeice personally (though he is not a close personal friend like Spender and Day-Lewis) but the only poems of his I like are 'Brother Fire' and 'The Streets of Laredo'. I *cannot* see that the quotation of page 305 has any merit. As for *great* poetry!!! Good ideas, yes. But are these enough to make great poetry?

I do *not* like *The Last Party*. I had to write it to make money.

How right you are about Mary Wollstonecraft. What an *awful* woman. But I did not say she was great. I put her in that book as an example. Virginia Woolf, I enjoyed talking to her, but thought *nothing* of her writing. I considered her 'a beautiful little knitter'.

Page 331. My God! Why Enid Blyton? For heaven's sake! Or is it a joke?

Page 352. The poem 'A Song of the Cold' (the beginning, about Winter being a time for comfort and for food) were *indirectly* inspired by Rimbaud, *not* by Eliot. That is most definitely *not* so. One line 'Allayed the fever of the bone' *has* influenced me. But that is all—enormously as I admire him, and long as I have known him personally (since 1917). *Gold Coast Customs* was not inspired by him. Mostly that poem was the result of things I have actually witnessed, or have been told. ('The rat-eaten bones of a god that never lived', I quote from memory, was the result of a frightful thing I was told in youth about an illegal operation;—which shocked me appallingly.) As for the part about the wind beating 'on the heart of Sal'— during the time of the hunger-marches, I saw, in a procession *three* times, a ragged creature, with nothing under his outer suit, unspeakably famished looking, and with a face that looked as if it had been ravaged (I imagine from T.B.) beating on an empty food tin with a bone. That is *where* that passage came from.

I now admire Lawrence *very* much, but not *technically*. Vachel Lindsay is, technically, a simply *horrible* poet, and the Congo poem is the worst of the lot. (I like *The Golden Whales of California*; but his technique is always ghastly. He has had *no* influence on me whatever.)

P. 434. I love Clare, but *not* his winter poems. And Thomson would have been completely out of key for my Winter book. I was making a banquet, not a catalogue. . . .

I admire Faulkner greatly.

Well, it is an extremely interesting book, and I am extremely grateful to you. I will return it one day this week.

Is there any chance that you will be in London any time during August? If so, do let me know and come and lunch with me. My address in London will be The Sesame Club, 49 Grosvenor Street, W.1 until the 12th., and then Durrants Hotel, George Street, Manchester Square. All best wishes and much appreciation, Edith Sitwell.

P.S. Would you please substitute *Dame* Edith for Dr Sitwell. The Queen has honoured my poetry by making me a Dame, so that is now my name.

P.P.S. Oh, I forgot. I have never heard of my Coronation Ode!!! It is probably part of my famous friendship with Miss Marilyn Monroe—whom I met exactly once, for half an hour or so, in February 1954, and have not seen since.

P.P.P.S. I was between 12 and 13 when I learnt *The Rape of the Lock* by heart—for my own pleasure. I was not told to do so.

157. *To Roy Campbell*

14 July 1955   Renishaw Hall

My dear Roy,

I was so *deeply* distressed and unhappy to get your note and realise how ill you still are. Osbert and I feel so much for you and for dear Mary in your illness. We have hoped with all our hearts to hear that you are better. And I had gained the impression from Mr Regnery[1] that you were. So that it is a great blow that you are not.

I got your letter rather late—only a day or two ago—owing to the fact that I had stayed a few days longer than I had intended, and so my letters were kept.

William Empson is now Professor of Poetry at Sheffield, and he lunched here the other day. We talked of you, with all our warm affection, for you and Mary. And yesterday I had a letter from him asking for your address. How *miserable* it is that you are ill, dear Roy. You, of all people in the world. We do pray that you will soon be better.

I hope to be received into the Church, as your and Mary's god-daughter, next month.[2] I do not know, yet, who will act for you both. I am being instructed by Father Caraman, whom you know, do you not? Because Father D'Arcy was in America at the time I began being instructed. I have no news, excepting that the Forum Club . . . has written to say will I choose *any* day (the letter came, naturally, well before this) in the past June, July, October *or* November, to lunch *or* dine with them, and give them a lecture without payment. That means 244 invitations, as it would be difficult for anyone devoid of my grim determination, to help accepting one of them. Osbert suggested that I should reply that unfortunately I can accept no invitation for the next three years, as I am expecting 'an urgent call from Sweden, Turkey, or some such country'.

Our love to you and dear Mary. We think of you so much.

[1] Henry Regnery, Campbell's American publisher.
[2] E.S. was received into the Roman Catholic Church by Fr Philip Caraman, S.J., at Farm Street on 4 August 1955.

Please ask her if she will be an angel and give us news of you.
How *deeply* we hope to hear you are better. Yours affectionately, Edith.

158. *To T. S. Eliot*

1 November 1955   Castello di Montegufoni

My dear Tom,
I think Messrs Faber and Faber will have received, some days
ago, a letter from my secretary Miss Fraser, begging for permission to include *The Waste Land* and *Sweeney Agonistes* in
my new anthology, to be published by Little Brown in America
and, I suppose, here,—and consulting them about fees.[1] I
should be most *deeply* grateful to you—I could never say how
grateful.

I should have written to you immediately, but have been
wretchedly ill with a nice new form of influenza (which
attacks one's throat and bones and gives one a very high
temperature). I felt so ill for a few days after it was over, that I
could do nothing.

It was a great struggle with me to know which poems to ask
for. I know Messrs Faber won't let me have the Collected
Edition in toto!! At last, I felt that if I am allowed these, I
shall have the entire root of the present and future poetry, and
that is why I ask for these.

I have just received what I can only describe as a thoughtful
letter from a gentleman living at Colorado Springs. He tells me
he has heard of the splitting of the Atom! But that in his
opinion 'thinkers should seek the quintessential mental and/or
spiritual atom, which belongs to the universal pulse, that
invests Man with his uniqueness.'

'Assuming, then, that an instrument were devised capable of
splitting an Idea into its components.—I. What pervasive and
historically influential Idea' (he asks) 'would you wish to see
separated into its fundamental particles? II. Why would you so

[1] *The Atlantic Book of British and American Poetry* edited by E.S.

choose? III. How do you feel that mankind would be benefited thereby?'

Don't you think Dr Leavis ought to be consulted?

Osbert won't let me send him the letter, because he thinks if I continue to tease Dr Leavis he will bring a case against me. I must say, I can't think on what grounds!

Osbert sends his love. Yours affectionately, Edith. And Osbert's and my love to John, please.

159. *To T. S. Eliot*

20 November 1955   Castello di Montegufoni

My dear Tom,
So very many and most grateful thanks to you.

Yes, I understand the reasons about *Sweeney Agonistes*— though I shall miss that very great poem. I am now tearing myself to pieces about which of the *Quartets* I am going to ask for (the moment I choose one, I want the others too, so my life is positively haunted); and I will write to you in a few days.[1]

I may say that I think greed about poetry is the only permissible greed—it is, indeed, unavoidable.

Oh dear! The book will be what I would like the book to be, until we come to Section III of the modern poetry. Until then, it is heavenly. Section II ends with you and with Ezra. Section III not only ends, but also begins, 'Not with a bang but a whimper.' The other day, a reviewer writing about art criticism in general, quoted Dr Johnson as saying 'I prefer to withdraw my attention and think of Tom Thumb.' That is what I would wish to do with Section III. Tom Thumb is a giant in comparison with the denizens of Section III. But I am hoping that the contrast with the rest of the book may startle the readers (and even the reviewers) into some kind of sense.

Please give John my love. Yours affectionately, Edith.

[1] The choice of T. S. Eliot's poems was eventually *The Waste Land* and *Burnt Norton*.

160. *To Benjamin Britten*

18 February 1956   As from The Sesame Club

My dear Ben,

Osbert and I were more than delighted to get your letters. I am writing for both of us. . . .

We were enthralled to think of you and Peter's last months, —the wonders and beauties you must have seen, and also, the very alarming dark side of it. I cannot say that I am attracted by the idea of waiting for Malayan bandits, having no weapons oneself, in the midst of a tropical storm! I don't know, of course what bandits one would be wise to choose, but I think not Malayan!

The idea of constant danger from nature and man that you speak of in your letter is terrible, and great!

How wonderful it must be to have seen the mosaics in St Sophia. Did you know the old American—now dead—who dealt with them? I forget his name now, but we knew him quite well, rather against our will. He was very tiresome in a Bostonian way, but was also a Mahommedan—which made him rather a split personality.

But most of all exciting for you must have been the hearing of this strange music, new to you. Osbert and I were wildly thrilled to hear about this—wondering what it will bring to you (and consequently to us).

I should have written this letter before, but have had rather a trying time. I got influenza twice—or rather it returned to me, this being a habit of the new kind. And then, just as I had recovered, and was walking about with legs made of cotton wool, I crashed on to the stone passage. Why I didn't kill myself, I can't think. But I bruised, strained, and tore every muscle and tendon that could be bruised, strained or torn!

I am beyond anything happy to think that you may be going to set another poem of mine for the Festival. 'Still Falls the Rain' is one of the greatest prides of my life. I suggest, if you think it fitting, 'The Stone-Breakers: A Prison Song' on page 359, *Collected Poems*. But for setting, I have made a few alterations, which I think make it better for the singer, and perhaps more comprehensible at first hearing. But that of course is for you to say. I enclose the version that I have made, for your approval.

It is so very kind of you to say I may look at the proof of 'Still Falls the Rain', to see if I think any additional indications are needed to show where the lines begin. But I am quite sure no more *are* needed. The music holds it together so strongly. How much I long to hear that most wonderful music again. And how happy I am to think of being at Aldeburgh on the 21st of June. I wonder when you return. I do pity you both if it is at this cruel black and white moment. We are *13 degrees below zero* here, and are so cold that not only our bodies but our brains seem frozen.

Apropos of this polar cold, did you know Billy McCann, who is now in Rio de Janeiro? They are in the midst of one of the most terrific heat-waves Brazil has ever known, and one midday, Billy was staring out of his window (which looks over the ocean) when he saw an enormous black and white procession advancing, two by two, for, it seemed miles, in a straight line on the water. As it came nearer, he saw that it consisted of polar bears, polar seals, walruses and/or sea elephants, and penguins. Poor boys and girls, they had been carried straight from the North Pole or the polar opposite number to the Gulf Stream. The authorities from the Zoo gathered them up in air-conditioned ambulances, and they are now sitting on blocks of ice at the Zoo, where they were welcomed with rapture, because the Zoo had no specimens of their kinds.

When will you and Peter be in London? *Please do* suggest a day to come and lunch with me at the Sesame. I shall be there from the 29th February till the middle of May. Lots of love from Osbert and me to you and Peter. We long to see you both. Yours ever, Edith.

It is said that the wolves are out in the mountains. I have suggested that the Priest's step-mother, a very fat woman and a great trial to him and his parishioners, should be exposed, tied to a tree. The suggestion was greeted with enthusiasm.

161. *To Leonard Russell*

10 April 1956   The Sesame Club

Dear Mr Russell,

Here is my review of the Brinnin book on Dylan Thomas.[1] I
hope I haven't made it too long; but I do *beg* of you to print it
in its entirety, because it all needs, and greatly needs, saying. It
is a horribly painful book to review, and I did so with great
difficulty. In the first place, I had to try to defend (A) Dylan,
(B) Caitlin, his wife, and (C) John Brinnin. Nearly all the
conduct portrayed in the book seems to me quite indefensible.
A man said to me the other day, 'The book ought to be called
We Killed Dylan Thomas.' The worst creatures in it are, of
course, the dreadful little women, who pursued him shame-
lessly.

I am quite sure that there is going to be a fearful scandal. My
American publisher, Edward Weeks, and his wife, are about to
appear here, and as soon as they contact me I will write to Mrs
Russell in the hopes that you and she will come to lunch to
meet them. They are *very* nice.

Alas, he published Brinnin's book in America. But then,
publishers will be publishers!

All best wishes to you, and your wife, Yours very sincerely,
Edith Sitwell.

162. *To James Purdy*

20 October 1956   Castello di Montegufoni

Dear Mr Purdy,

I do not know whether it was you, or whether it was your
publishers, who sent me your *Don't Call Me By My Right
Name*. But I owe a debt of gratitude to you and to them.

I think several of the stories—in especial 'Eventide', 'Why

[1] E.S.'s review of *Dylan Thomas in America* by John Brinnin appeared in
the *Sunday Times*, 22 April 1956.

Can't They Tell You Why', and 'Sound of Talking'—as well as many others,—are superb: nothing short of masterpieces. They have a terrible, heart-breaking quality.

I do not know if you have an English publisher already: but I am so deeply impressed by this book that, on the chance that you have not, I wrote to my friend Victor Gollancz, and advised him to get the book.

I hope that we shall soon hear that you have another work ready. Yours sincerely, Edith Sitwell.

163. *To Stephen Spender*

16 November 1956   Castello di Montegufoni

Dearest Stephen,

I only received the tragic telegram about Hungary last night, forwarded *in a letter* from Renishaw. Osbert and I are both horribly distressed. As you know, Osbert has this terrible illness, and it would, of course, be utterly impossible for him to go. The danger is, if we applied for a visa, the Russians *might* let us have it, and then the case would be worsened. And with great distress of mind I am forced to say I cannot apply for one either, because I should only be a liability to the rest of the party if we *did* get visas. I shall be seventy on my next birthday, and am now extremely lame. I have arthritis in both knees, acute rheumatism in both feet, and often am only able to walk —and slowly at that—with the aid of a stick. In addition, I get attacks of sciatica in its most acute form. I had it for over a year, and it returns, so that when I travelled back from Aldeburgh Festival, I could not put my feet to the ground when I reached Liverpool Station, and had to be carried out of the train, wheeled along the platform in a truck, and carried into my club. That doesn't altogether prevent ordinary activities; but what would the rest of the expedition do with me in that terrible city? I could not run, if we had to. I could not go down on the ground quickly if the Russians started firing; and I should only risk, probably, other people's lives. And it would, as I say,

make matters worse if I applied for a visa, got it, and then didn't
go. For Osbert, of course, it is entirely *impossible*.

It would not be possible to exaggerate our wretchedness of
mind in saying this isn't possible. You must, of course, make
every use of my name.

The whole terrible thing is too heart-breaking for words, and
one is haunted by the thought of those people, day and night.

I have been wanting to write to you for ages. (That confounded
book I am writing about Elizabeth I has practically blotted out
my letters for the last year. Thank God it will soon be finished.[1]
How dreadful it is that, now, I should be writing to you on
such a subject.

I think the Russians must be mad. Do they think they will
ever be forgiven?

I do hope Natasha is better. Please give her my best love. I
was so sad not to see you and her before I came here. You, of
course, were abroad; and she was taken ill the day before she
was to have lunched with me.

Osbert's and my best love to you, and to her, and the
children. Yours affectionately, Edith.

164. *To Alberto de Lacerda*

26 November 1956   Castello di Montegufoni

My dear Alberto,

I read, with such sorrow for you, the terrible news contained in
your letter, about your friend. I know well how much you
must have suffered—do suffer. What was the cause of her
despair—I ask myself. But perhaps I should not ask. I hope she
has found peace. I am sure she has. But the thought of that
death is very terrible.

I must tell you—to show that I know what this tragedy
means—that five days after my cousin Irene Carisbrooke's
death, I received a cable from New York, saying that one of

[1] *The Queens and the Hive* was published by Macmillan in 1962.

my greatest friends—Alice Astor was her maiden name,—had died.

She was extremely beautiful—like a Persian miniature; very *racée*, with a look of really tremendous breeding (unusual in Americans) and enormously rich. She had a touching affectionateness.

She sent, *one night*, for her lawyer, and made a fresh will—which he lost in the train, leaving her.—The next morning she was found dead.

I shall always see her now, standing at the corner of a street in New York, blown by the wind. She was very thin.

No, dear Alberto, I have *never* received the French magazines you were so sweet and so kind as to send. I suppose the post, here, has lost them. They are really intolerable. I do thank you, and I am sad that they are lost.

You ask what I meant by saying Yeats was a tragic poet. I meant in his poetry, which is ineffably tragic.—He and his poetry seemed to be completely separate. Of course they could not have been. But his love affairs were silly, and I don't believe he felt them in the slightest. I think he egged himself on to imagine he felt them. But he was a great poet, and the fires there are real.

I have had a fresh accident—a really terrifying one. Ten days ago, a complete stranger (a business acquaintance of Osbert's) was coming to lunch. I was just advancing to meet him on his arrival when—owing to the fact that the housemaid *will* wax the stone floors—I fell with a crash on to my face, and came to to find myself lying in a lake of blood, my dress, three towels, and all the handkerchiefs of everyone present, absolutely swamped in blood, with Miss Andrade holding ice to my head, and the young butler trying to get brandy down my throat. I cannot *think* why I didn't break my nose. But I didn't. However, my face is completely black, blue, green, and yellow.

But how absurd to talk about accidents at this time of horror and heroism and spiritual grandeur.[1]

[1] The Hungarian crisis.

Did I tell you about an American writer called James Purdy
—completely unknown? He is a *much* greater writer than
Faulkner. I can't think of any living prose writer of short
stories and short novels who can come anywhere near him. He
is really *wonderful*. The heart-rending compassion and understanding,—he really turns the knife in the heart. Not a sentence
too much, not a sentence too little.

I am going to America in February (unless our pin-heads
have let us in for a new war!) and I will send you his short
stories and his one short novel from there. I think you would
most probably like to translate them in Portuguese. He is most
truly a *wonder*. I am in correspondence with him.

My head aches, so I will stop; but will write soon. Love from
Osbert and Edith.

165. *To James Purdy*

26 November 1956   Castello di Montegufoni

Dear Mr Purdy,
I am most deeply grateful to you for sending me *63: Dream
Palace*. It arrived, after an astonishingly quick journey, two
days ago, and I have read it twice, already.

What a *wonderful* book! It is a masterpiece from every point
of view. There can't be the slightest doubt that you are a really
great writer, and I can only say that I am quite overcome.

What anguish, what heart-breaking truth! And what utter
simplicity. The knife is turned and turned in one's heart. From
the terrible first pages—(the first sentence is, in itself, a masterpiece) to the heart-rending last pages, there isn't a single false
note, and not a sentence, or a word too much, not a sentence or
a word too little.

Wonderful as the short stories are—and I have read them
many times, and think them—if it were possible to do so—
even more wonderful than when I wrote to you before, this
book is just as great. Indeed, I am not sure if it isn't even

greater. Point after point I go through, and I am inclined to think so.

Have you heard, yet, from Victor Gollancz? Please will you let me know as soon as you do. I will write to him today and tell him of *63: Dream Palace*. Apart from other reasons for this: he *may* (from a publisher's technical point of view—considering the lending libraries' weekend readers, etc.) want a *larger* book. (It could not be a greater). And it strikes me that if you were willing, the two books could be bound together. I am inclined to think that if this suited you, it might be a wise move. Naturally,—I need hardly say—I am not suggesting this to Victor without your permission.

And now I have several other suggestions to make. For the *English* public, I think it would be wise to put 'Don't Call Me By My Right Name'—the *story*, I mean,—later in the book, not at the very beginning. It is a story that English readers who do not know America would not be so quick to grasp as they would with the others.

Then, if I may make the suggestion, I think you ought to have a literary agent in England. Mine (and my brothers') are

Messrs Pearn, Pollinger and Higham
76, Dean Street,
Soho, London W.1.

I will write to *David Higham*, who is in charge of the *book* department, and to *Mrs LeRoy*, who is in charge of the *magazine* department, and will tell them that they may be hearing from you. I strongly advise you to go to them. As the short stories have not appeared, yet, in England, it is possible, (I think, but am not sure) that some might be placed in magazines in England. But Mrs LeRoy would know about that.

Stephen Spender's *Encounter* might be a good place for them. Stephen is at present lecturing in America, so has escaped my grasp, temporarily. But perhaps you know, and will be seeing him? In any case, as soon as he returns, I will get on to him about it.

Lincoln Kirstein tells me he has sent *Don't Call Me By My*

Right Name to Madame Bradley, the Parisian agent. But it is certain you should have an agent in England, as well.

I shall be here until the end of January, or the beginning of February, and in mid-February I sail for New York, arriving, I think, either on the 25th or the 28th—for an immense recital-tour. I do hope so much that we can meet. I do not know if that will be possible for you, but I do hope so.

When I reach New York, I will set about seeing if the two books can be translated into Portuguese. I have a great friend in London, a young Portuguese, a distinguished poet, and one of the most intelligent and subtle people I have ever known, who I hope will do the translation. He is a close friend of all the most important Portuguese reviewers.

If, by any wretched chance, Victor Gollancz can't take the book, we'll try someone else.[1]

My best wishes to you and the books, and my most profound admiration. You are truly a writer of genius. Lincoln Kirstein in his letter to me, said you are 'quite wonderful.' How right he is! Yours very sincerely, Edith Sitwell.

166. *To Jack Lindsay*

January 6, 1957   Castello di Montegufoni

It is so good of you to have sent me these chapters. You know what I feel about *The Starfish Road*—how important I think it. I would like to write about it more fully, but I can't at the moment, because one of my eyes has gone wrong. I have always had very bad eye-trouble—having had the Egyptian ophthalmia when I was a child—and now this accident I have had has brought on acute sinus, so that my left eye pains with tears when I read, and is exceedingly painful.

Unfortunately, like all us poor wretches who are professional writers, I am absolutely *forced* to finish a book for which I have a time-limit, and for which I am nearly four months

[1] Gollancz published *63: Dream Palace* on 1 July 1967.

late—and this entails endless reading, and so I can't, however much I want to, do much else.

I cannot get back to writing poetry, from which I have been separated for *three years*, until I *have* finished the book. (Income Tax!!!! From which you also suffer! Oh dear!)

The chapter on Lautréamont is nothing short of brilliant,—really enthralling. I beg of you to *lengthen* it. It is infinitely the finest exposition of Lautréamont I have read. You will be doing everyone a great service if you lengthen it. The chapter on the romantics and on Baudelaire are full of interest; but, Jack, I am quite certain that the Baudelaire poems *must* be in the *original—not* translations. To my belief—indeed, to my certainty, Baudelaire and de Nerval—possibly, also, Verlaine—are the only French poets who simply *cannot* be translated. Their poems lie entirely within the language. After all, everyone who reads the book will be able to read French. Then—I beg, I absolutely IMPLORE you to *omit entirely any* mention of Ebenezer Jones. He is so unspeakably horrible as a poet that I am left almost speechless! I am sure he had all the civic virtues, and was an estimable person, but he has all the passion of Ella Wheeler Wilcox, the intellect and *Zeitgeist* of the author of

> 'There are girls in the golden city,
> There are women and children too,
> And they cry "Hurry up, for pity",
> So what can a brave man do?'

Seriously, Jack, have you taken your temperature?

You—*you* of all people in the world, compare him to Baudelaire, speak of him in the same breath as Blake!!! Why, the man can't *begin* to write. He is jejune, platitudinous,—the colours of all the words he uses came out in the wash years ago.

As I say, no doubt he had all the civic virtues, but the only thing that makes a man a great poet is—being a great poet.

I get the sort of thing he writes sent me, on an average, three times a month from Nottingham, Leicester, and Birmingham.

The earth, the earth is ours!
(Good God!)
Eternal rocks we stand!

O rich in Gold! Beggars in heart and soul!

I can *hear* the harmonium! I can *see* the people coming *from* the chapel—look you!—and going *to* the chapel—God be with you! I can taste the subsequent cocoa!

You can't, Jack! You *really can't*! I do *loathe* bad poetry, and this is the end!

167. *To Charles Causley*

18 April 1957   Hotel St Regis, New York

Dear Mr Causley,
Or don't you think we could call each other Charles and Edith?—

It was such a great pleasure to me to see Dr Muir's admirable most properly laudatory review in the *New Statesman*.[1] The quotations were lovely, and everything he said was intelligent to a degree.

I have been speaking everywhere of the book, over here. I hope it will have the very great success it deserves. Immediately I return to England I shall send it to everyone here who could be of use.

I have been on a terribly exhausting three weeks' tour, and am not through yet, but sail for England on the 3rd of May, and should arrive on the 7th. I shall be at the Sesame Club, 49 Grosvenor Street. Is there any happy chance of you being in London on Wednesday the 15th? I shall be lecturing to the P.E.N. Club, and shall be speaking of your poetry, and reciting *I don't care*[2] (I have to call it that, as I can't spell the correct name, unless I have it in front of me). If you should be in

[1] Of *Union Street*, Charles Causley's third book of poems, to which E.S. had written a Preface.
[2] 'Ou Phrontis.'

London, we could have a little *very* early supper first (the lecture is at 6.30, and I have to be forcibly fed by the secretary afterwards) and then we could go to the lecture together.

Do forgive the rather vague scrawl, but I only returned here yesterday, and am half dead with exhaustion. However, the recitals were a huge success, and I had 'standing audiences' everywhere. (The Americans don't cheer: they get up and stand, to honour one.) All best wishes, Yours very sincerely, Edith Sitwell.

I leave here for Washington on Monday.

168. *To Jean Cocteau*

[*c.* 1957]   Renishaw Hall

Dear Jean,

May I introduce to you Mr Alberto de Lacerda, a very fine poet (his poems have been translated from the Portuguese by Arthur Waley) and one of my greatest friends.

You could have no more ardent admirer. In his letter to me, asking for this introduction, he said 'Ever since my boyhood it has been my greatest wish to have the honour of meeting Monsieur Cocteau.'[1] And I know how profound that wish is, from the conversations he has with me.

He is a delightful young man, and one of the most intelligent I know. He is also very amusing. When asked by somebody how he got on with me, he replied 'Well, you see, I was born in Portuguese East Africa, and so, as a baby, was lulled to sleep each night by the roar of lions outside the garden gate.'

I have never been sure how to take that. Sometimes I think it a compliment, at other moments I am not so sure.

I do hope you are very well.

We are nearly drowned here—are up to our eyelashes in rainwater. I understand why Groucho Marx says that when he

[1] Mr Lacerda denies ever making this statement.

comes to England he always wears a yachting cap, both out-of-doors and indoors. With great and affectionate admiration, Yours ever, Edith.

169. *To Alberto de Lacerda*

2 May 1957   Hotel St Regis, New York

My dear Alberto,
Thank you so much for your letter—so kind and good. Roy's death has been a great grief and shock to me.[1] I simply *cannot* get over it. I shall never cease to miss him or fail in my devotion to him—nor shall I ever be grateful enough that it was he who introduced you to me.

I was told of his death by an oaf of a reporter at a press conference. He asked me if I knew Roy. I said yes, he is one of my dearest friends, and my godfather. 'Oh, really?' said the oaf. 'Well, he was killed yesterday.' Just like that. And I had to rehearse *Façade* all that afternoon and the next day.

When I think that noble creature and great poet is dead—and what we have left!!

We start for England tomorrow, and should be there on the 7th or 8th. I long to see you. Much love from your friend, Edith.

170. *To Mary Campbell*

23 September 1957   Castello di Montegufoni

My dearest Mary,
My thoughts have been with you *all* this time, in your great grief, desolation, and loneliness.

The reason why I have not written before is because ever since the early summer, griefs and disasters have been heaped on my head—to such a degree that I wondered, sometimes, if it was *possible*. The only thing to do, at such a time, is to be

[1] Roy Campbell (*b.* 1901) had died on 22 April 1957.

silent to those who are suffering more deeply than oneself—not to heap one's sorrows and troubles onto their greater ones, which is the height of selfishness. But now I realise that I must be being taught some lesson.

How are you, my dear Godmother?—I mean, in your health? How much I *long* to see you. And how deeply sad I am just to have missed Anna—to whom my Love—when she came to London.

The *Sunday Times* has promised me that I shall review Roy's poems immediately they come out.

I am furious that what I wrote of him and gave to Alberto (at his request) to translate into Portuguese, was never printed. Neither he nor I know why.

About a fortnight ago, I gave a recital, in London, to raise funds for the restoration of Stonor Chapel (where the Blessed Edmund Campion said Mass just before he was caught). I recited Roy's translation of 'Upon a Gloomy Night' and his wonderful 'Vision of Our Lady over Toledo' to the really *enormous* delight of the audience. He is one of the only really great poets of our time,—such fire, such a holy spirit, such ineffable beauty.

It is just possible—it isn't fully arranged yet—that I may be going to America next spring to give the Inaugural Lecture at all the principal universities. If I do—that lecture will be crammed with expositions of Roy's greatness.

I *still* cannot believe the dreadful thing that has happened, has. Dear Mary, my deep love to you and all my thoughts, Edith.

Osbert sends his love.

171. *To Sir Malcolm Bullock*

27 September 1957   Castello di Montegufoni

My dear Malcolm,
I hear you have great influence with Alan Pryce-Jones. So I am writing to ask you if you will be so kind as to induce him to

allow me to publish a Calendar—*Wit and Wisdom from The Times Literary Supplement: A Great Thought for Every Day in the Year*. I fear he may be reluctant, but am sure that you will be able to persuade him. The paper goes from strength to strength. One interminable paean of praise of a lady versifier says that the wonderful thing about her work is 'that at its best it is *hardly there at all*'. No truer word was ever said.

I want to publish the Calendar as a mark of gratitude to Alan for what he has just done to me.

He urged me to publish my Collected Poems, asked when they were coming out, so that he could give the book the large middle article, didn't review it for nearly two months—and when he did, gave it 655 words. (He wrote the review.) What he said was quite nice, but an old lady like myself does not expect to have her life-work dismissed in 655 words. Perhaps, however, he thought he was spoiling me by giving me five words over the six hundred and fifty.

Osbert and I had a wonderful adventure with an enormous hornet yesterday. It got into the motor as we were driving to Florence. But Osbert forgot the Italian for hornet (*calatrone*) and told the driver that an inhabitant of Calabria, or, alternatively, a species of cabbage had got into the motor.

The driver was bewildered. He saw no inhabitant of Calabria, and no cabbage, and in any case (as he also did not see the hornet) could not understand—even if they *were* in the motor—why I was screaming. Love from Osbert and Edith.

172. *To Elizabeth Salter*[1]

5 November 1957   Castello di Montegufoni

My dear Miss Salter,

Thank you so much for your letter. I was particularly glad to get it, as I really have been *so worried* about you.

That sherry should have reached you already. If it hasn't, by the time you get this, will you please ring up Messrs Matta,

[1] E.S.'s secretary 1957–64.

and ask them if they got my letter, and ask them to send you the sherry at once.

I am nearly driven *mad* by my book. I've gone dead on it.

I can't tell you how much I look forward to *your* new book. And I may tell you that if you go on as you have done already, I am quite sure you are going to get absolutely to the top.

I've had a very cock-a-hoop letter from a lady whose address I enclose. (*Need* I say that her Christian—well, perhaps *not Christian* name is 'Desirée'?) I do not know Desirée. But she writes to say that she has written a book on Blake, is 'looking for someone to write a Preface', and that Graham Greene, whom she knows slightly, says that I 'would be ideal'!!!!

I don't think she ought to spoil me, do you?

She also says she doesn't know if 'Blake is one of the figures who attracts me' (I having written about him at considerable length). Will you please be an angel and write to her, acknowledging the receipt of her letter, and saying that I only write Prefaces under the rarest possible circumstances, and that I regret I cannot find time to do as she asks. Or is that *too* rude? Should one say pressure of work prevents me. But I think she needs a thundering snub, don't you?

My dear, please will you be very kind and have two copies of *this month's Encounter* sent me, under separate cover. (I mean the number that comes out *this* month, as I think Alberto's review of my poems is coming out in this number.)

I send the enclosed chapter, *not* to worry you to type it when you are ill, but simply because I have nowhere, here, to put it.

Take care of yourself. Yours most affectionately, Edith Sitwell.

How tactful of that man to send me that photograph!! Tchelitchew was one of my dearest friends, and only died in August.

173. *To James Purdy*

17 December 1957   Castello di Montegufoni

Dear James,

I do, with all my heart, wish you a very happy Christmas and wonderful new works and glory in the New Year.

Thank you so much for your letter and the cutting. Gosh, what a fool! But always remember that, as this apocryphal poem by Ella Wheeler Wilcox tells us:

> 'It is not the song of the singer
> Though naught could be possibly sweeter
> That touches the spot with a flame that is hot
> But the heart that is back of the metre.
>
> And though I have always loved
> True Art for its own true sake,
> It is not Art, oh no, it is Heart
> That finally takes the cake.'

And as we know, that is an ingredient that is entirely left out of your work. Young Quentin,[1] in a letter to me the other day, said 'I don't know what to say to such a writer. All I can say is "More—more".' And I agree. He is having awful reviews, poor boy.

I forgot if I told you in my last letter that the sweet, interfering, spiteful, bat-witted old —— creature has been by orders of the solicitor of the Society of Authors, tracked down by human bloodhounds. It is now revealed that she is the mother of a clergyman of the Church of England. She *would* be, Christian old pet! The S. of A. is now occupied in making her life one long hell. . . .

Have you read Mr Faulkner's *Requiem for a Nun?* Deeply moving. And have you read, in Mr Thurber's new book, the chapter called *File and Forget?*[2] It is one of the funniest things I have ever read in my life. Especially so to writers, for it is an epitome of what we all go through with our publishers.

[1] Quentin Stevenson.
[2] From *Alarms and Diversions*, 1957.

Has the Vanguard Press sent you my *Eccentrics* yet? They should have *ages* ago. I wrote asking them to before the book appeared. I am annoyed with myself, now, that I didn't include Christopher Smart, but perhaps it would not have been fair. But I do love his phrase: 'The Seal: God's good Englishman.'

Osbert and I, when we were small children, had a much loved friend who was a seal, and we used to ride on his back, which caused us to stink, permanently, of fish.

All affectionate best wishes for the book, Christmas, and everything. Yours ever, Edith.

174. *To Elizabeth Salter*

Monday [1958]   Renishaw Hall

My dear Elizabeth,
I do *hope* you are better, my poor dear. Colds make one feel so rotten. I *do* sympathise.

Thank you so much for your letter. Like an absolute idiot, I have lost the copy book in which I write down people's birthdays, and so *cannot* remember which day yours is. That being so, I enclose a tiny present. (The £2 is for when you and Lorna were my guests at Sheffield, the other £10 is for you to get whatever you would like to have for your birthday.) I forget if I told you that I have had (and still have) the worst attack of sciatica I have ever known, and as a result, when it was coming on (before the pain began) I fell with a crash on to the back stairs, and am bruised from the hip to the toes. I am suffering from bad shock, as a result. And it's awful, because I daren't let Osbert know that I am pretty bad with it.

It is not improved by the fact that I have had a loathsome anonymous letter (I should *think* from that horrible old man). The letter told me I am hated because I am 'vulgar, common' (*çela se voit*, but as I have inherited these characteristics, I should be pitied, not blamed) because I wear 'vulgar rings that the lowest barmaid would disdain to wear' (why should barmaids be called low?) because I am 'a fraud, a fake, a third-rate poetess,' because I 'read good poetry horribly' (he is evidently an authority on the art of poetry) and—*of course*, because I am a Roman Catholic.

I can see that it is worse to be a Roman Catholic than to have a debased heart filled with hatred, and a soul of such creeping, low cowardliness that it dare not sign its name to an abusive letter.

Do you not love the enclosed poem. Osbert says I shall be mad if I do not recite it, as it will bring the house down. Will you please, my dear, make a few copies of it.

And did you ever see anything to *touch* this communication telling me I must put myself over. Please will you keep it, and also make some copies.

And will you please like an angel, answer this letter from an American and that from the photographer, saying I can't.

Can you and Lorna come for a drink in my room at 5.30 next Monday, the 5th.

Please give Gordon my love and deepest sympathy, and say I should have written, but fell downstairs and am suffering from shock.

Best love to you and Lorna, Edith.

175. *To Lady Snow*

31 May 1958   The Sesame Club

Dear Lady Snow,
How much I laughed when I received Sir Charles's letter![1]

I am, at the same time, alarmed, for I am at the moment finishing a book called *The Queens and the Hive*, which is about Queen Elizabeth I and Mary Queen of Scots, and contains a rousing account of Catherine de Medici planning the massacre

---

[1] Sir Charles Snow had written to E.S. because the principal character in Pamela Hansford Johnson's novel *The Unspeakable Skipton* comes into contact, in that novel, with a literary group at the centre of which is an Australian writer of verse-dramas, with seven children, who gives lectures for the British Council. A reader of the MS had suggested that this might be taken for a malicious parody of E.S.!

of St Bartholomew's Eve. I am now terrified that this may be supposed, by any readers I may have, to be a malicious portrait of you. After all, you are not Italian, do not persecute Protestants, and are not the mother-in-law of Mary Queen of Scots, so the likeness springs to the eyes!

What do you suppose I have done with my seven offspring? Eaten them?

Nonsense apart, it is an ill wind that blows nobody any good. I am a very great admirer of you and of Sir Charles, and have longed, for ages, to know you both. And now I shall!

What is more, I shall have the privilege of reading your new book before it comes out. I look forward to it more than I can say. . . . Yours sincerely, Edith Sitwell.

Do you think it would help if I put a note in my book: 'The portrait of Catherine de Medici is *not* meant as a portrait of Miss Pamela Hansford Johnson?'

176. *To James Purdy*

25 July 1958   Renishaw Hall

Dear James,

I dare not imagine what you must think of me for not having written before to thank you for that masterly short story, every sentence of which bears your signature, and for your letter.

The reason I was so slow in writing was *A* that I strained my eyes correcting the proofs of 14th century poems (which are the very devil to do), with the result that I got migraine in its worst form, and *B* that, not allowed to get on with this in peace, I have been dragged ceaselessly from pillar to post. I've had the oddest adventures. In one, Quentin was involved. Two very young men,[1] Americans, and one having a great sweetness of expression, both poets,—you probably have read about them in the *New York Times*,—were introduced to me and came to lunch, accompanied by Quentin, who was looking *terrified!* (I

[1] Gregory Corso and Allen Ginsberg.

may say at this point, that the episode was just as I was beginning the migraine attacks, and was not, as you might say, *curative* in its effects.) They behaved with great courtesy. The poor boy with the sweet expression had, he told me, been sent to prison *at the age of 17 for three years* for organising a bank robbery![1] If ever, in my life, I saw anyone who had obviously been sweetened and in a way re-formed, by such a terrible experience, it was that boy. I am sure he is a kind of haunted saint,—a saint who has lost his way. For he *has* lost it. The other looked like a famished wolf. The trouble is, I understand, that they are both addicted to a habit the result of which is that nobody can *ever* tell *what* they will do next. (But they can be relied on to do it!) In an interview given to the *N.Y.T.* the poor boy who had been in prison said that at a recital he gave of his poems in Paris, he had removed all his clothes, and recited as he was when he was born.

Next day I received a letter from a friend of mine, a Don at Oxford, giving me such really terrifying information, that I took to my bed, and lay there with my mouth open, pondering!

However, the luncheon party went off all right, with no untoward incidents. The young man did not recite, and the old ladies whose only experiences are going to dim churches and dimmer lectures, remained wrapped in their mental cotton wool! The young men returned to Paris, so I haven't seen them again.

How is your play growing? It is so exciting to think of it. I think with joy of your 'Coronation' at the hands of the Academy of Arts and Letters. My, there must have been some sour faces!! Affectionate best wishes, dear James, from Edith.

I wrote these two poems, just before being floored by Fate.

177. *To Leonard Russell*

15 August 1958   Renishaw Hall

Dear Mr Russell,

Thank you so much for your kind telegram and invitation to

[1] Gregory Corso was imprisoned for three years at Clinton, N.Y., 'for stealing'.

review the Ralph Hodgson.[1] How much I wish I could. But alas! Mr Colin Fenton showed me the proofs, which I read carefully. And oh dear! there is *no touch* of the old magic! Nobody would ever know that the dear old man (he is well over 80) is a great poet.

It would be doing him a great disservice if I reviewed him, for I could not possibly praise the poems. It distresses me very much. If you have time to look at them, you will see what I mean. It is very sad.

I am having a terrible time, as I have, like a fool, said I would add to the Everyman *Poems of Our Time* 26 pages of poetry written since 1942, and *ex*clusive of the poets who have appeared there already. There is hardly anything worthy to appear, and I shall be exposed to violent abuse from 'The Movement'.

Mr Alvarez has taken my well-meaning and helpful review of him in *The Sunday Times very* hard. He said on the wireless that poets are a nasty lot, jealous, and detestable. I am terribly jealous of his little poems!!

I hope you and Mrs Russell are very well. We are drowning here.

Please give your wife my love. Warmest best wishes, Yours ever, Edith Sitwell.

178. *To Eva Dworetzki*

4 November 1958   Castello di Montegufoni

My dear Miss Dworetzki,
I was *terribly* distressed to receive your news last night.[2] (How miserable that I wrote that earlier letter to you only yesterday morning, before the news reached me!)

Today is one of those infernal National Holidays, so no post can go out until tomorrow.

---

[1] *The Skylark and Other Poems*, published in a limited edition by Mr Fenton in the autumn of 1958.
[2] Miss Dworetzki had been working as assistant in Bumpus's bookshop, and had lost her job.

Osbert and I had a very long talk last night. His sympathy with you, like mine, is very deep. We thought of several things, several possibilities. In a few days, or a week's time, I *should* be receiving a few extra copies of my giant anthology from America. I am giving this to *no one*, but I will send one to *Miss Christina Foyle*. (Osbert and I think *possibly* there might be an opening there, and I should send the book as a friendly act, as I have not seen her for some time).

Then, a few weeks after that, I would write to her and suggest she should engage you for her Foreign Department, if she has one, or that she should *create* a Foreign Department and put you in charge, if she has not already got one.

Perhaps that is not what you would like, but it would be something to go on with temporarily. And if you *did* go there, I should always be in and out, keeping an eye on things.

And here is another idea. A young man called Anthony Newnham, of Arne House, Arne, Wareham, Dorset, wrote to me recently asking me to let him have a MSS book to sell to the American University which is making that huge collection of English MSS. He came to lunch with me. He is *extremely nice*. He was formerly with Messrs Rota (near the Albany),[1] but when he left, a good many people, such as the Warden of All Souls, for instance, transferred to him, or anyhow, followed him, and he knows the daughter of my great friends Sir Kenneth and Lady Clark very well. He sells for the main part, I *think*, English 18th-century and 19th-century books. How would it be if I wrote to him and suggested he should meet you with a view to you having some sort of partnership with him? I think he sells a great deal to America—he certainly sold all our first editions to Mr William Yeo, the American collector. I think *that* is an idea, although it would mean living out of London. Mr Yeo tells me his wife is delightful, and *that* makes a difference. . . .

Tell me what you think about these suggestions. I will do nothing about any of it until you tell me what you feel. . . . All my sympathy, my dear, and Osbert's, Yours affectionately, Edith Sitwell.

[1] Bertram Rota, the antiquarian booksellers.

179. To Elizabeth Salter

Thursday? [November 1958]   Castello di Montegufoni

Dear Elizabeth,
This is just the shortest of notes, because I have been very ill indeed, though better today. For three days I couldn't keep any food down, and got no sleep at all. The nights were an absolute nightmare of retching, and a kind of mental horror. This was simply brought on by the Income Tax badgering me to send them details I have not got here, and by poor darling Evelyn's plaints. *Entre nous*, she has *all* my Mother's money (which should have been one third of my income) and because I had been left some money (£3,000) by a great aunt, and owing to Evelyn's sister's incessant whining, I gave her £1,000, Evelyn £100 and both fur coats, and this was found out by an aunt from whom I should have inherited another third of my income, I was cut out of that, and so have been left with $\frac{1}{3}$ of what I should have had! Some people might have been rather cross, and I am *beginning* to be a *little* impatient.

She has got nearly all my pictures,[1] and now won't come over to England although I pay for *everything*, because she says she would 'have to get so many things'. She really behaves as if she were Garbo or Monroe. (She had £50 out of my prize last year). That family is a damned nuisance, and of no interest. Oh dear, I had not meant to go in for this long diatribe, but I was so ill yesterday that I thought I was in for a very serious illness, owing, to all that. . . .

There is an appalling scandal here—a sort of Mademoiselle de Maupin one. Savonarola—prepare for a shock—is a *girl*. ~~her cat~~ Not only that. She has killed and eaten nine kittens!!! So *naughty*! She has now been accused of transvestism, incest, child-murder, and cannibalism. But I won't hear a word against her. Best love, Edith.

[1] Towards the end of E.S.'s life Miss Elizabeth Salter went over to Paris and rescued these pictures, all by Tchelitchew, also a large number of notebooks of poems by E.S.

180. *To Father Philip Caraman*

12 December 1958   Castello di Montegufoni

My dear Philip,

All my *most* grateful thanks for the wonderful *Revelations of Divine Love*[1]—a great joy to me. How good it was of you to send it to me.

I was deeply moved by your letter, and especially by what you said of Osbert. He bears that terrible affliction with such bravery, sweetness, and goodness, it is wonderful. How good you are to say you will send him a book. What he would *really* like best would be one of your works. Quite apart from everything else, I think it would be a great help towards furthering our hope, for him to see the unsurpassable bravery, charity of soul, and humility of men who, though they must have realised, fully, their suffering, yet thought they were only doing their duty, and bore it for the love of God and men.

I should have written to you immediately I got your letter, but it arrived just before great happenings here, and the great happenings (a joy to me) ended in my catching a chill, which is still on me.

To commemorate the centenary of the Vision at Lourdes, a shrine has been made in a recently built wall beneath the Castle, and Osbert has presented a Statue of Our Lady for the shrine. On Saturday night, by torchlight, Our Lady was escorted in a procession consisting of one Priest, two neighbouring Priests, 300—yes, three hundred—motor cyclists, and a long procession of villagers from all the villages round, to the Shrine. All the roads were decorated with festoons of vines. Our Lady had a huge halo of lights. She was then escorted back to the Church.

Then, of course, came Sunday.

On the evening of the Feast of the Immaculate Conception, there was another immense procession, all on foot this time, with Our Lady in the centre, and preceded by a wonderful banner—huge, of white and scarlet. And so She went to Her

[1] By Mother Julian of Norwich.

Shrine. I have never in my life seen *anything* more deeply
moving.

I wish the Archbishop of Canterbury had been there. I
think it would have killed him. (I am the sworn foe of Arch-
bishops of Canterbury, because being one is most horribly in
my family!) Archbishop Tate was my father's great-uncle and
guardian,—my grandfather died when my father was 4, and he
was practically brought up at Lambeth. And Edie Tate, the
Archbishop's daughter, married one of his Chaplains, who
afterwards became Archbishop Davidson. The only remarkable
thing I know about the latter is that he once swallowed a locust
in a desert. Why, no one will ever know.

I do, with all my heart, wish you a very happy Christmas,
and so does Osbert.

I write this so long beforehand, as nobody ever knows how
long letters will take from here. And I want to catch you before
you leave London.

I shall think of you so much. All my gratitude, dear Philip.
Yours ever, Edith.

P.S. I have had a review of the *Anthology* in—of all papers—
the *Sunday Dispatch*. It was given *4* lines, and consisted of *one*
remark only: that whereas Burns was only given 3 pages, and
Browning 4, Osbert and Sachie were given 14. 'Who was the
editor? Why, their sister, Dr Edith Sitwell.' (Which doesn't
happen to be my name, anyhow.) Burns is a very bad poet, and
Browning not a very good one. Really, what odious malice!
No mention of all the wonders! I have sent the review to the
solicitor of the Society of Authors, but do not expect he can do
anything.

181. *To Elizabeth Salter*

22 December 1958   Castello di Montegufoni

Dear Elizabeth,

How *very* sweet of you to send me those lovely stockings. They are perfect. I wore them last night (they arrived on Saturday night, together with the Mousies). Thank you ever so much, my dear.

Oh, how I laughed, when I saw the Customs declaration—toy mice.[1] What can they have thought? It reminds me of when my great friend Bryher—I don't think you have met her yet, have you?—asked me to take through some flea-powder to her ex-husband (who still remains a great friend) in Italy for his *cats*. 'And if the Customs people ask you what that grey powder is, Edith say, "Is it my flea-powder".' 'Can't I say it is for Kenneth's cats, Bryher? I hardly like to say "It is *my* flea-powder".' 'No, *don't* say that, Edith. They won't believe you, and will think it is cocaine!'

I have been *ill* with rage over that *New York Times* review. But Osbert—who knows, really, far more than I do about reviews—says it is an excellent *selling* review—wonderful for the publishers to quote from, and all the better because the man, who obviously hates my guts, has *had* to say the book is exciting—not once, but twice. But I cannot *think* why I never get any press cuttings. I suppose it is the post, as usual. . . .

182. *To Lady Snow*

8 January 1959   Castello di Montegufoni

Dear Pamela,

What great pleasure your delightful, charming letter gave me. I got it just before we were incarcerated for the near-week of

---

[1] Miss Salter had sent her stockings for Christmas, with some toy mice for her cat. The customs declaration read: 'For Dame Edith Sitwell, D.B.E. D.Litt. etc. . . . One pair stockings. One dozen toy mice.'

non-stop Sundays inflicted by the Italians at this time of year: religious festas, and national festas, during which no post goes out, and church bells ring from 5.30 a.m. till 6 p.m.

I am so distressed, though, to hear about your poor little boy's bad bronchitis. How very worrying for you. I do *hope* he is better.

To amuse him, I am having my book *Façade* sent him, because children usually like some of the poems—'Madam Mouse Trots', for instance. I will sign it for him when I get back to London. I am so sorry to think how anxious you must have been.

I *long* for *Skipton*. You are an angel to say you will send it to me. I am so grateful. I have been longing for it since I read the manuscript. It is, I think and know, an amazing book. The extraordinary insight into that poor, dreadful, pitiable creature's character is astounding.

I knew one person of more or less the same kind, the late Wyndham Lewis. He would, I think, have been before your time. I knew him very well, because I sat to him every day excepting Sundays, for ten months. It was impossible to like him, and in the end, his attitude became so threatening that I ceased to sit for him, so that the portrait of me by him in the Tate has no hands, and I figured as Lady Harriet in his *The Apes of God*. (And he figured as Mr Henry Debringham in the only novel I have ever written, *I Live Under a Black Sun*. It is out of print, but I will see if I can get a copy for you.)

When one sat to him, in his enormous studio, mice emerged from their holes, and lolled against the furniture, staring in the most insolent manner at the sitter. At last, when Tom Eliot was sitting to him, their behaviour became intolerable. They climbed on to his knee, and would sit staring up at his face. So Lewis bought a large gong which he placed near the mouse-hole, and, when matters reached a certain limit, he would strike this loudly, and the mice would retreat.

My mother—a very rude woman—persecuted him unremittingly, and addressed him by a variety of names, the most usual being 'Mr Wilks'.

I think you have second sight. How on earth did you know

Fuseli's giant women were in my mind when I wrote 'La Bella
Bona Roba'? Also I am founding my recitation of the sleep-
walking scene in *Macbeth* (I am going to recite it in June or
July) on them.

We lunched in Florence on Christmas Day. We are fond of
our hostess and her son, but seemed to find no means of
communication with our fellow-guests. One man asked me if I
liked writing poetry. At last I felt like the Duke of Gloucester,
who was taken, while in Cairo, to a night-club, where a hostess,
blue from her eyelids to her cheek-bones, was presented to
him. He is reported to have stared at her, silently, for ten
minutes, and then to have said: 'I say! Do you know Tid-
worth?' . . .

183. *To Graham Greene*

21 January 1959   Castello di Montegufoni

Dear Graham,
Osbert and I are so sad you will not be able to come to
Montegufoni before you go to the Congo. We do *hope* you
will be able to come on your way back. We shall be here until
about the 12th of March.

All my news consists of travellers' tales. The principal being
the adventure of Billy McCann. I wonder if you know him. He
is a fervent Catholic, and during the war he was the head of the
Iberian section of the Ministry of Information, and led the life
of one of Mr Peter Cheyney's spy-heroes. He was then the
head of Shell-Mex at Rio de Janeiro (if that is how one spells
it). He has a mania for *birds*. On his way through New York to
Janeiro, he paid several visits to a pet-shop, and there a macaw
was seized with such a romantic admiration for Billy that every
time he went into the shop, the bird would faint dead away and
fall off its perch. So Billy thought it would be only kind to buy
it. This he did, then realised he would never be allowed to take
it on the 'plane. He had it drugged, therefore, and made into a
large paper parcel, which he nursed on his knee. Unhappily, the

bird came to, half way through the flight, and the woman sitting next him said '*Must* your parcel wriggle and fidget and poke me in the eye?' There is then a gap in the story, which is only resumed on the arrival of the 'plane, where there was a fearful row at the Customs House, everybody accusing everybody else of this and of that, and the bird staring at Billy and fainting and having to be revived.

It should be a warning to us all—but I don't quite know of what. Bon voyage. Enjoy yourself with the poor lepers. Love from Osbert and Edith.

184. *To Benjamin Britten*

6 March 1959   As from the Sesame Club

My dearest Ben,
I was so excited and happy to get your letter last night.

I should just think I *will* write that poem.[1] I am enthralled at the thought of doing it, and will start on it the moment I recover from the fatigue of my journey to London where I arrive on Friday the 13th. (I am having to be carried in a wheeled chair to and from the boat, as I am very lame from sciatica.) I think the poem should be extremely triumphant and full of pomp, like one of Christopher Smart's paeans—if that is how one spells it: something like this:

> Praise with the purple trumpet
> Praise with the trumpet flower.

I don't mean that those lines would come in like that, but something of that kind. I think the poem had better be called 'In Praise of Great Men'.

I will recite it.

I have taken, I may say, to reciting better lately.

This last year was a *hideous* one for me. When I wasn't

[1] Mr Britten was giving a concert in celebration of the tercentenary of Purcell, and asked E.S. to write a poem for the occasion. He has not yet set the words to music.

worked to death, I was ill. In April I strained my eyes very badly, correcting the proofs of early 15th-century poems for my giant anthology (which you will receive when it appears in England). This gave me persistent and acute migraine. And finally I got an infection in one eye. The anthology is so enormous that the proof reading was enough to kill one.

Then, my American publisher made me sign my name 8,900 times for a special edition! This really threw me out of action altogether. I would come up for air, and then sink back into my forlorn state.

As I say, I shall reach London on the 13th. *Do,* when you and Peter are going to be in London, and have time, say when you can both lunch with me. I shall be there for ages, I think. The only days I am not free are Saturday the 21st, and Saturday the 4th and Sunday the 5th of April, when I have to go to Birmingham to be televised.

I long to see your new house. But isn't moving house hell? Just before being practically consigned to the tomb by my American publisher, I wrote some poems, which I am copying for you and sending under separate cover, as I want this letter to reach you immediately.

Osbert is going to America to see a specialist soon. We both send our love to you and Peter. I do *hope* to see you both very soon. Edith.

I am going to recite the sleep-walking scene from *Macbeth* soon.

185. *To Lady Snow*

6 May 1959   The Sesame Club

My dear Pamela,

Thank you so much for your delightful, and *very* funny letter.

But oh dear! You speak of going away. Does that mean I shall not see you and Charles before I go back to Renishaw on the 16th? I had hoped you would both come for a drink on Thursday the 14th at 5.30. Is that impossible?

I can imagine the condolences you must both have received on figuring in that painfully prominent position in the *T.L.S.* You must both have repined on the utterly *indelicate* publicity! Are not people incredibly envious and spiteful?

When, some years ago, the *Sunday Times* published a very kind Profile, or whatever they call it, of me, John Hayward said to me that 'The whole of London is saying *Osbert* must have written it, because no one else would'.!!! Yet I had never been anything but nice to J.H.!

I am delighted the party went off so well, and that at last you can rest from your labours.

In re labours, I have *just* this morning received a letter, which I am copying for you, verbatim. (I have added nothing, deleted nothing.)[1] You won't believe it, but it is true.

Dear Dame Edith Sitwell, Your recent poems in *The Listener* (query: E.S.—*La Bella Bona Roba? The Yellow Girl?*) brought to my mind Dorothy Perkins, a niece of my brother-in-law the Reverend Alf Perkins of Glasgow whom I met while visiting there. (I was her Scotch Aunt Jessie, at that time Mrs Hobson). I recollect that she had just returned from a visit to you. Now my purpose in writing to you is to find out if you are still in touch with her. If so, let me have her address, and write to her to ask her to communicate with me.

She once met me at Lincoln Station, and took me to stay with her at her home in Lincolnshire.

If you are not in touch with her, kindly trace her.

Yours sincerely,

I have never met, and have never heard of Miss Dorothy Perkins. She has never visited me. I have never heard of the Rev. Alf Perkins either.

In any case, why pester *me?* My temper is very bad at the moment, because I simply am not allowed to get on with my

---

[1] But she disguised the names when she printed the letter in *Taken Care Of*, and we have followed that version.

work. So I have replied that though I notoriously have nothing to do, I regret that tracing people of whom I have never heard does not lie within the scope of my duties. And I enquired why she did not write to her brother-in-law.

Much love and great admiration to you both, Edith.

186. *To Lady Snow*

20 May 1959   Renishaw Hall

My dear Pamela,
Thank you so much for your letter.

I am so distressed to hear you have insomnia. It is horrible, and one really suffers greatly. When I am in London, sometimes I only sleep for two hours a night, if that.

If one could only rid one's mind, completely, of *words* during the night, one would be better.

It hasn't worked lately, because I have been too tired to sleep, anyhow, but at one moment, the following would send me to sleep—and strangely enough, Osbert had the same habit—to imagine oneself in a gondola floating through Venice and regarding, under a full moon—with no sound excepting that of an oar, and nothing near one—only the sleeping palaces, as one floated on and on.

On a more mundane note, a tumbler of *hot* beer in bed can work—or indeed, cold, if it comes to that.

Those tireless nuisances the Income Tax people have written to ask me where I was last employed, and if I gave satisfaction, and when, if at all, I left it.

So I am going to reply that I was last employed, in a menial capacity, by Miss Imregarde A. Potter, of 8 The Grove, Leamington Spa, in 1911; but that I did not give satisfaction: there was some small unpleasantness, and I was dismissed without a character. And that if they want any more details, will they write to Dan Macmillan (whose temper, as you and Charles will know, needs a little sugar adding). Oh, good gracious!

My love and admiration to you both, Yours affectionately, Edith.

And my love to the Poet,[1] too.

187. *To Benjamin Britten*

26 May 1959   Renishaw Hall

Dearest Ben,

Here is your poem, which I *hope* you will allow me to dedicate to you.[2]

I wrote it as a recitation poem—right, I trust, for the voice— as a song without music, not as a poem for the page. I think, and hope, the timing, the length, is right. If I had made it longer, it would have been monotonous, owing to it shouting the one theme.

Would it, or would it not, be a good idea to have it heralded by a Fanfare?

I long to see you and Peter. I imagine we have a rehearsal in the morning of the performance, don't we? (or the day before). (Incidentally, I don't know where the performance will be.) If it won't exhaust and bother you both too much, would you lunch with me? I do hope so.

For the last few months, I have been undergoing an agonis- ing, not a lovely sleepy, hibernation. Unable to work, owing to nervous exhaustion and noise, and almost pestered out of my wits by lunatics and persons with grievances. (I am also afflicted by fibrositis in my right shoulder, which makes my handwriting worse than usual.)

I am involved in a Laocoon correspondence with the step- mother of an English leper (poor man). I was so fascinated by this rather unusual occurrence that the grip tightened round me before I knew what was happening, and she now writes to me *every* day (literally). She is obviously a very saintly woman—so I am in the grip for life. In addition, all my other

---

[1] Their son, Philip Snow.   [2] 'Praise We Great Men.'

unknown correspondents tell me the full histories of their lives—lives that seem to have been longer, and more full of incident, than any other lives of which I have ever heard. . . .

Best love to you and Peter, Edith.

I have, in the poem, drawn on past poems of mine, because, obviously, if one can write *at all*, one can only choose the most suitable medium for what one has to say, and cannot put it into other, weaker words.

188. *To Benjamin Britten*

Tuesday [1959]   The Sesame Club

My dearest Ben,

It was so lovely seeing you again the other day, and I *do* look forward to Tuesday next, and do hope Peter can come too. . . .

Now about Blake. That transcendentally great poet reads aloud *very* badly, alas, because quatrains read badly, and the Prophetic Books, on the contrary, are very loosely constructed. But I'll do the best I can.

I presume you want half an hour recital, half an hour music.[1] Here are some of the poems I'm going to read. I have timed most, but am not sure yet how long they tot up to, *nor* have I arranged them in sequence, as I am interrupted every five minutes by the telephone, and am also having hell with the dentist.

'A Divine Image'	$\frac{1}{2}$ minute
'London' (*Songs of Experience*)	1 minute
'The Chimney Sweeper' 1 & 2 (?) (amongst the most wonderful, but reads the worst)	not timed yet
'Mock on, Mock on, Voltaire, Rousseau'	$\frac{1}{2}$ minute

[1] For the Blake Bicentenary programme at the 1959 Aldeburgh Festival which opened on 25 June.

'Proverbs of Hell' (prose)   to be timed
'Auguries of Innocence'   to be timed
'The Book of Thel' (complete)   11¼ minutes
'The Tyger'
'Vala' or From the Four Zoas (Book
   9) from 'Then all the Slaves from
   every Earth in the Wide Universe'
   down to 'So sang the Human Odors
   round the wine presses of Luvah'.

I'll arrange these properly. That is as far as I've got so far. This is simply to give you *some* idea of the programme. I'll write more fully tomorrow or the day after. Best love to you and Peter. Edith.

189. *To James Purdy*

28 July 1959   The Sesame Club

Dearest James,
It is such *ages* since I have been wanting to write to you, and please believe that it is not my fault that I have not. My life this last three weeks has been undiluted hell, and I feel like a poor worn out electric hare pursued, relentlessly, by mercilessly energetic greyhounds!

I have also had very bad eye trouble again. 'They' (the oculist and the doctor) have been wanting to operate on my eyes for over two years—or rather have been threatening to, and now they have just seen me again, and say they will have to, unless I take it easier. This terrifies me, as it would mean, undoubtedly, having to shelve my *The Queens and the Hive* (and the publishers are already very cross, because I am so late with it). I am having to read up about the Netherlands, Mary Queen of Scots's execution, Leicester in the Netherlands, and the last days of Elizabeth. (All of which, and much [else] is in small print, makes my eyes pain, and my head ache like hell.)

This means, dear James, that I am, *alas!* unable to read to the

end of *Malcolm*. I can't help it, and am nearly *yelling* with frustration. But I am absolutely forced to do this other **
(flavour to taste) reading.

Your publishers sent me the proof, (knowing that I am one of your most fervent admirers) and suggested that I should write something that can be used as advertisement. So what I am saying is this: 'Owing to eye trouble I have been, unfortunately, unable to finish reading *Malcolm* and cannot, therefore, write of it. But it is my strongly held opinion that Mr Purdy's previous work proves him to be a magnificent writer of short stories and of the novella. I am convinced that in the future he will be known as one of the greatest writers produced in America during the last hundred years.'

As far as I have been able to read, I found the chapter 'The Boy on the Beach' extremely moving and extremely funny at the same time. How acute, and terrible, is the phrase 'I suppose if somebody would tell me what to do, I would do it.' That chapter, the midget's terror that he will have to stop pretending to be a small man and be known as a midget—and the part about Estel Blanc—are very strange and fantastic.

As you know, I shall be writing of you, as soon as possible, for *The New York Times*. I know your work so well, I can almost find the passages by touch!

It was such a *very* great pleasure to me to meet your delightful friend (and my co-enthusiast) Mr Andrewski. He came to see me several times, and you can imagine of whom, and of what, we talked!

I am returning to Renishaw on the 30th. Much love, dear James, and great admiration, Edith.

190. *To Sir Malcolm Bullock*

13 October 1959   The Sesame Club

My dear Malcolm,
I daren't imagine what you must think of me for not writing

before to thank you for lending me that really entertaining book.[1] But do please forgive me, for I have had the worst attack of sciatica (and I am the Sciatica Queen—once I had to be lifted out of the train, and wheeled along on the top of my luggage) that I ever remember. I couldn't put my foot to the floor, without screaming. The book *is* extraordinary, and absolutely fascinating.

First of all, we are not in this century at all—but back in the time of Elizabeth I. Don't you agree? Then the portraits of people! Somebody writing about James Purdy's short novel and short stories (I am convinced that in the future he will be regarded as the greatest American prose-writer of our time) said that he has the unblinking eye of a child or a tiger. A wonderful description. And, in a smaller way, I think Prince Obolensky has that. In any case, he has the innocent eye.

I got up for the first time (I arrived here last Monday) the day before yesterday. I had to prevent Osbert from knowing I had this affliction, because he worries. One develops a kind of low cunning which would be useful to those persons who borrow 3 million pounds when they have no assets!

About the 9th of November, I shall be sending you (you will be one of the only six people I shall be sending it to) my gigantic anthology in two volumes, the work of my life.[2] It has the most *heavenly* early religious poems—some quite unknown outside specialist anthologies, wonderful early love poems, Tudor poems, and Elizabethan and 17th-century poems. Also, I claim that I am the first anthologist to represent Clare and Yeats properly. And as for the country ballads and light songs!! . . .

[1] *One Man in his Time* by Serge Obolensky.
[2] *The Atlantic Book of British and American Poetry*, published in Britain by Gollancz on 5 November 1959.

191. *To Lancelot Law Whyte*

December 14, 1960   The Sesame Club

Dear Lance,

I can never express to you the tremendous effect your great
book *The Unconscious Before Freud*[1] has had upon me. It was
like being put in an oxygen tent if one is dying. Everything you
write has this extraordinary revivifying effect, and this book is
magnificent in its greatness. I have known a very few great
men in my time, but I am as sure as I can be of anything in this
world, that you have the greatest mind of them all! This book
will be, as are all the works of yours that I possess, my constant
companion. I never travel without them. I am so grateful to
you.

. . . I do think the Law ought to allow one to commit one
murder, at least.

In the house next door, an electric drill, fastened to my
bedroom wall—(I work in my bedroom) has been active every
day from 8.30 till 5 for two and a half months, alternating with
hammering which sounds as if a fleet of demented giant mice
are superintending the building of a battleship.

I have threatened to enter the house, accompanied by reporters and press photographers, and to use to the workmen all the
words to be found in *Lady Chatterley's Lover*, together with
some others in French and Italian: (I swear like a trooper in
both these languages). . . .

192. *To Lady Snow*

11 September 1961   Flat 10, 53 Rutland Gate, S.W.7

My dear Pamela,

I feel so guilty and ashamed that I never wrote to thank you for

[1] Published with a Foreword by E.S. by Tavistock Publications (1959).

sending me, or causing to be sent, that most interesting collection of essays on Baron Corvo—in itself a most beautiful book, such as one seldom comes across nowadays.[1]

He was a detestable character, wasn't he? but even more fascinating to read about than to read (though I do greatly admire *The Desire and Pursuit of the Whole*). But he must have had a certain charm to make people so ready to lend him money! I don't think that if I had been hard up in Venice I should have found comparative strangers ready to come forward with loans—though needless to say if they *had*, I should have been more grateful to them than Corvo was! I am thankful that he wasn't in Venice in my day.

As I expect you know, Mrs Lonsdale Ragg[2] is still living, in Bath. She must be nearly a hundred. She told me she didn't like to talk about Corvo because she felt she was malicious about him, which showed a truly Christian and forgiving spirit. . . .

193. *To Mrs H. C. Leon*

12 July 1962   Flat 42, Greenhill, N.W.3

My dear Barbara,

What wonderful roses! How very kind and sweet of you and Harry to send them to me. Thank you so much.

They made me recover from a passion of rage I was in yesterday, reading about the poor little fox, who living, was torn to pieces by hounds. And the little pests who allowed this to happen have been acquitted of deliberate cruelty! Sport is sport, and I wish I had a pack of man-eating tigers!

I have been having a wretched time, and have been in bed for *weeks*, having injured my spine. The pain was very bad, and my sense of frustration, owing to not being able to work, made things worse.

The only thing that cheered me at all during that time was

---

[1] *Corvo 1860–1960*, edited by Cecil Woolf and Brocard Sewell, with an Introduction by Pamela Hansford Johnson (1961).

[2] Wife of Canon Lonsdale Ragg who befriended Corvo in Venice—and got small thanks for doing so.

the enchantment of each Tuesday's *Brothers in Law*.[1] Oh dear!
how I laugh.

I must ask Harry, a little later, if he will allow me to quote
the remark in last Tuesday's T.V. about the judge who made
Ghengis Kahn (I can't spell it) look like Godfrey Winn. That
is how the public regards me, and I want to quote it in a book I
am being badgered to write about myself. . . .

194. *To Lancelot Law Whyte*

August 18, 1962   Greenhill

Very dear Lance,
Your wonderful letter moved me more than I can say. I should
have answered it *immediately*, but have been pestered nearly to
death. (Because I wrote a letter to a paper saying that a fresh law
about cruelty should be passed, everybody with a bat in the
belfry has released the bats on to me, told me the stories of
their lives, described the symptoms of their rheumatism, etc. I
don't know *who* they are, or what any of it has to do with me.)

My rule is to deal with everything that maddens me at once,
and then to turn to what interests me, and even, with luck, do a
little work.

I shall always treasure your letter.

It is so sad that you and Eve are going to be in a different
continent until next June. I shall miss you so much. I am very
proud, and very grateful to you for giving me *Everyman
Looks Forward*, which I have begun to read, and for sending
me the list of books, which will be a great help to me.

Oh dear! One ought to have 24 centuries a day, instead of
24 hours, and these ought to be immune from the clothes moths
who fritter one's hours away. At one moment I had the idea of
starting a Society of Blackmailers, who would terrify the clothes
moths out of nibbling one. If I start this, will you join the
Society?

---

[1] A television series based on the book by Judge H. C. Leon under the pen-
name Henry Cecil.

I do hope you had a good crossing. I envy you being in America, which I do love.

The Unconscious Before Freud is my constant companion. It would be, of course. How wonderful this passage in your letter is: 'Perhaps I am the John the Baptist of One who will speak clearly of a great truth that will startle the race and provide a fresh start.' But you *have* spoken of great truths that should provide a fresh start. If I were among the first to, in a small way, hail that—if I thought I were, how proud I should be. My homage, and love to you and Eve, Edith.

195. *To John Gore* [Postcard]

[10 September 1962]   Greenhill

Don't be silly![1]
                    Edith Sitwell.

196. *To John Gore* [Postcard]

15 September 1962

Dear Mr Gore,
All is forgiven! I liked your card. I was feeling irritable because of arthritis, writer's cramp, and the incessant attacks on my time by thousands of Persons from Porlock. Edith Sitwell.

197. *To Noël Coward* [Telegram]

LONDON 21–9–62 NOEL COWARD LES AVANTS SUR MONTREUX SWITZERLAND DELIGHTED STOP FRIEND-SHIP NEVER TOO LATE INVITE YOU BIRTHDAY CONCERT

[1] Mr Gore had reviewed *The Queens and the Hive* in *The Sphere*. His reply to this postcard suggested that E.S. had been thin-skinned.

AND SUPPER FESTIVAL HALL OCTOBER 9TH 8 P.M.—
EDITH SITWELL

198. *To Noël Coward*

26 September 1962   Greenhill

Dear Mr Coward,
Thank you so much for your letter in answer to my telegram,
and above all let me thank you for your charming previous
letter, which pleased and touched me more than I can say.

I had to answer by telegram, as I had acute writer's cramp;
(indeed I have only just emerged from bandages and a sling).
How I wish that *un*professional writers would suffer, sometimes, from this disease!

I am very greatly disappointed that you will not be able to
come on the 9th, and am *very* sorry for the cause. I do hope the
operation won't be very painful, and that you will soon be able
to escape from hospital. (Oh, those smiling Christmasy faces!
Oh, those cups of tea!)

The 9th should be a day for all present to remember. Never
before, I think, has anyone attended their own Memorial
Service. (The Press is madly excited at my being 75, and is
looking forward avidly to my funeral.)

I do hope you *will* find time to come and have sherry or a
cocktail with me when you come to London. Do please ring
me up. . . . All good wishes, Yours ever, Edith Sitwell.

199. *To Sir John Gielgud*

3 October 1962   Greenhill

Dear John,
In spite of your letter, which I only received last night, I
refuse to have you call me Dame Edith, or to call you Sir John,
and I shall still bow to you if we should happen to come across
each other at a railway station, say.

I don't know what you mean by talking about our slight acquaintanceship; I thought we were friends.

My long silence was due to the fact that I have been really very ill indeed, for ages. At one time I had to have three nurses taking it in turns. And I have been so despondent and wretched that I never contacted anyone unless they contacted me first.

I had to go all round the United States in a wheeled chair on a recital tour (having slipped two discs). Half dead from fatigue, what with the tour and the immense work involved in this huge book of mine, I have been ill ever since, had two months in hospital in Sheffield, was given disease of the middle ear as soon as I reached London, by the incessant hammering and the noise of an electric drill fastened to the wall of my room; I am still in a wheeled chair, and cannot stand at all without help. (I have to go in this, and in an ambulance to the Festival Hall.)

I hate all this with such violence that, as I say, I haven't contacted anyone unless they contacted me first, as I loathe for them to see me like this. (They will have to, at the concert, as my energetic young nephew, Francis, is digging me out of my retreat for the occasion, also the television people kidnapped me, to my fury, and got me into a kind of Laocoon-like entanglement. My doctor has now charged them like a mad bull.)

I do hope you can come to the supper party *after the concert*, I have just telegraphed to you on the subject. I nearly did so as soon as the concert was arranged, then didn't, because I thought the concert might bore you, and that it might add to the non-stop intrusions on your time that must be your fate.

My affectionate and deep homage to you, Yours ever, Edith.

What the reporters are like! They are mad with excitement at the thought of my approaching demise. Kind Sister Farquhar, my nurse, spends much of her time in throwing them downstairs. But one got in the other day, and asked me if I mind the fact that I must die.

200. *To Noël Coward*

13 October 1962   Greenhill

Dear Mr Coward,
How very charming of you to send me that telegram. I
appreciated it very much.

Osbert and I were so very sorry you couldn't come, so was
Sachie. And we were so sorry for the cause. I do hope the
wretched thing is over and done with, and that you weren't in
great pain.

The concert and supper party were fun, in a way. But it was
all rather like something macabre out of Proust.

The papers excelled themselves,—the *Sketch* particularly.
I had never met the nice well-meaning reporter who 'covered'
the event, but according to him he sat beside me as my weary
head sank into my pillow, and just as I was dropping asleep, I
uttered these

Famous Last Words
'Be *kind* to me! Not many people are!'

Very moving, I think, don't you?

All my best wishes for your quick recovery. And please don't
forget that if you can spare the time, you are coming to see me
when you are in London. Yours very sincerely, Edith Sitwell.

Osbert sends his love.

201. *To Benjamin Britten*

25 December 1962   Greenhill

My dearest Ben,
I am more proud than I can say to have received from you, the
greatest work that has emerged from the grief, the horror, and
yet the pride and faith, of our time.[1] What a wonderful work it

---
[1] The *War Requiem*.

is! Not in an age has such a work been engendered or born. I am most *deeply* grateful to you for sending it to me. It is now in my book-case between the 2nd Folio Shakespeare and the 3rd Folio Shakespeare, that was lent me by Bryher, the late Sir John Ellerman's daughter.

To my rage, I missed the performance at Coventry, because I was having migraine, and so didn't see it announced. *No fog* would have kept me from the performance here. Consideration for you, Peter, and the audience did. For many weeks—indeed months—I have been so crippled that I am clamped to a wheel-chair and have to be taken everywhere in an ambulance, and it would have disturbed the whole solemn atmosphere if, before the performance began, I had had to be wheeled in. (At my birthday celebration, this had to happen; but it was not a solemn occasion, and if I have not the right to disturb myself, who has, I should like to know!)

I therefore could only listen on the wireless. I am not a person who ever really *cries*. Tears remain at the back of my eyes. On this occasion, the tears were blood.

I am so distressed and worried to hear of your high fever. I don't wonder you have this after that great masterpiece. Doctors and other well-meaning persons say 'You mustn't *work* so hard.' But not to work is a torture invented by the devil; at the same time I *do* think that you treat your physique in too contemptuous a manner.

On the physical level, there was an odd illness going about this spring. One of the sweet, unnecessary aged pests who infest my club came, uninvited, and breathed on me. I got a temperature of 105 which lasted for a week. She brought off this coup just as I had finished a long spell of very arduous work. No doctor could find out what the germ was. I write this only in case it may comfort you a little. I emerged from it, eventually, feeling less ghastly than I would have thought possible. But I did rather avoid heavy breathers. I think it may be that one of these scourges got at you. I do hope that by now, your temperature has gone down.

Poor Peter! How dreadfully ill he must have felt, getting out of bed for the concert. Such courage! I hope he is better.

I have just had rather a depressing letter from a gentleman called R. Riley, who says he respects me because of my great age, but that I am 'suffering from senile decay' *and* (as an afterthought) 'softening of the brain'.

Some time I must tell you of my adventures in re Wilfred Owen. They are most extraordinary, and would have horrified that great poet had he not been dead, and unable to show me justice.

Best love to you and Peter for the New Year. I do *hope* to see you when you can come. My homage and deep gratitude, Edith.

202. *To Graham Greene*

12 March 1963   S.S. *Arcadia*

Dearest Graham,

Thank you and Jeanne and Sherman *so* much for that very lovely pink and blue basket, which is still alive and reviving me after a free fight between Sister Farquhar and two old gentlemen who were bringing me on board, and who were intent on breaking my right ankle.

I was more than disappointed not to see you before I left, and look forward so much to seeing you in mid-May when I return.[1]

There is a new terror in Hampstead. A Club for the purpose of reciting. They helped themselves (without permission) to my poem 'Still Falls the Rain' (which *is* copyright), and a quantity of them recited this, first doing a Twist, and then staring out of the window, so that the poem is evidently not, as I had thought, a very tragic poem about the bombing of England, but an advertisement for mackintoshes!—Some people might be rather cross.

Much love and so very many thanks, Edith.

[1] E.S. left for her disastrous trip to Australia in early 1963, and returned seriously ill.

203. *To Benjamin Britten*

23 August 1963   Greenhill

My dearest Ben,

Thank you so much for your letter, which I was so happy to get.

How much I have missed seeing you and Peter all the long time. *Do* both come and see me when you are not too busy. (I know how people will pester one when one is both ill and busy —so I swear to you I won't add to the number.) I do hope you are better than you were at this time last year.

I am so furious at having missed your public performances all this long age, as I couldn't put my feet the the ground, *and* had to be lifted in and out of a wheeled chair. If I *do* try to put my feet to the ground, I shriek in a most pitiable manner, and have to be carried back to bed!

What a wonder the *Requiem* must be. By the way, it was I who prepared the Owen poems for publication—the first edition, before Blunden produced his.

It does excite and enthral me the idea of doing this work for Aldeburgh with Mr Williamson.[1] You and Peter haven't got the latest edition of *English Eccentrics*, and I shall send you both copies. The Carlyle *ménage* ought to give us a lot of fun. Nothing ever seemed to go right!

The book you *have* got contains a chapter about the Carlyles, but the new chapter about them, and that about George Eliot, are much more amusing, I think. I sympathise with Carlyle, who was much bothered by Harriet Martineau, and who said 'I wish this dear good Harriet would go and be happy somewhere else.'

I do hope you are not too terribly exhausted. I do look forward to seeing you both in the late Autumn.

How right it is that St Cecilia's Day should be your birthday.

With love, my dear Ben, to you and Peter. Yours affectionately, Edith.

[1] Malcolm Williamson's opera, *English Eccentrics*, based on E.S.'s book of that title.

204. *To Judge and Mrs H. C. Leon*

25 June 1964   Branksome Tower Hotel, Bournemouth

My dear Harry and Barbara,

Thank you both a hundred times for the lovely roses that have brought back my youth to me—the most romantic episode of my youth. I was 17. I was staying in my grandmother Sitwell's house in Bournemouth, and at 6 o'clock in the morning, I ran away to visit Swinburne's grave in the Isle of Wight, taking with me a bunch of red roses, a laurel wreath, and a jug of milk; also my extremely disagreeable lady's maid.

I had a really frightful row with the sexton . . . but poured the libation onto the grave, over which bloomed a huge red fuchsia.

When I returned to my grandmother's house there was, of course, a terrible row, and I found that (in my absence) a man called Losey and his wife had induced her to burn my volume of the 1st Swinburne *Poems and Ballads*, because these would corrupt my mind! (I hadn't the slightest idea of anything wrong in them). . . .

205. *To Sir Maurice Bowra*

[Fragment, undated, unaddressed]

I should have written to say how disappointed I was to miss you, but I had a ridiculous, very frightening, and painful accident in the train.

The straps of my bed had not been hooked properly. The bed suddenly shot me out, and then crashed on top of me, burying me completely excepting for my head. Every time the train jerked, the bed lifted itself up and then banged me on the floor, I was in the dark, and could get no help. At last, after, I should think, a couple of hours, the train stopped to let in, or out, some passengers, and I yelled piercingly, and was rescued. But I was very badly bruised and shaken.

I have got a very nice new lunatic—a lady in Dublin. She has written to tell me that all R.C. priests have lots of illegitimate children—usually by their 15-year-old nieces. I am replying that I know they have. My own dear confessor often brings round his happy little brood of ten to have tea with me. Four are by his own niece, but he is sadly forgetful about who are the mothers of the rest. There *were* eleven, but unfortunately he ate one, in a fit of absent-mindedness, one Friday.

Osbert says I must not write this, as it will be published, and people will say (A) that I have no moral sense, (B) that I am flippant; but I reply that it will not be the first, second, or third time that these charges have been brought against me.

INDEX